# Re-enchanting the World

**KAIROS**

In ancient Greek philosophy, *kairos* signifies the right time or the "moment of transition." We believe that we live in such a transitional period. The most important task of social science in time of transformation is to transform itself into a force of liberation. Kairos, an editorial imprint of the Anthropology and Social Change department housed in the California Institute of Integral Studies, publishes groundbreaking works in critical social sciences, including anthropology, sociology, geography, theory of education, political ecology, political theory, and history.

Series editor: Andrej Grubačić

**Kairos books:**

*Practical Utopia: Strategies for a Desirable Society* by Michael Albert

*In, Against, and Beyond Capitalism: The San Francisco Lectures* by John Holloway

*Anthropocene or Capitalocene? Nature, History, and the Crisis of Capitalism* edited by Jason W. Moore

*Birth Work as Care Work: Stories from Activist Birth Communities* by Alana Apfel

*We Are the Crisis of Capital: A John Holloway Reader* by John Holloway

*Archive That, Comrade! Left Legacies and the Counter Culture of Remembrance* by Phil Cohen

*Beyond Crisis: After the Collapse of Institutional Hope in Greece, What?* edited by John Holloway, Katerina Nasioka, and Panagiotis Doulos

*Re-enchanting the World: Feminism and the Politics of the Commons* by Silvia Federici

*Occult Features of Anarchism: With Attention to the Conspiracy of Kings and the Conspiracy of the Peoples* by Erica Lagalisse

*Autonomy Is in Our Hearts: Zapatista Autonomous Government through the Lens of the Tsotsil Language* by Dylan Eldredge Fitzwater

# Re-enchanting the World

## Feminism and the Politics of the Commons

### Silvia Federici

KAIROS

BTL

*Re-enchanting the World: Feminism and the Politics of the Commons*
Silvia Federici
© 2019 PM Press.

ISBN: 978-1-62963-569-9
Library of Congress Control Number: 2018931520

Cover by John Yates / www.stealworks.com
Interior design by briandesign
Cover painting by Elizabeth Downer
Frontispiece art by Erik Ruin

10 9 8 7 6 5 4 3

PM Press
PO Box 23912
Oakland, CA 94623
www.pmpress.org

Autonomedia
PO Box 568 Williamsburg Station
Brooklyn, NY 11211-0568 USA
info@autonomedia.org
www.autonomedia.org

This edition first published in Canada in 2018 by Between the Lines
401 Richmond Street West, Studio 281, Toronto, Ontario, M5V 3A8, Canada
1-800-718-7201
www.btlbooks.com

Canadian cataloguing information is available from Library and Archives Canada.

ISBN 978-1-77113-377-7 Between the Lines paperback
ISBN 978-1-77113-378-4 Between the Lines epub
ISBN 978-1-77113-379-1 Between the Lines pdf

Printed in the USA by the Employee Owners of Thomson-Shore in Dexter, Michigan.
www.thomsonshore.com

# Contents

# Acknowledgments

This book is thoroughly indebted to discussions I have had with dozens of compañer@s in different parts of the world. Here I will only mention some of the women and men who, over the years, have inspired me with their research, their activism, and their vision of a different world, translated into a practice of mutual support and friendship. My deepest gratitude goes to George Caffentzis, with whom I have collaborated for many years, rethinking the history of the commons and reflecting on the political principles involved, including as part of the Midnight Notes Collective; Hans Widmer (alias P.M.), who was one of the first to introduce me to the politics of the commons, with his writings, his imaginative paintings documenting the enclosure of urban space in New York, and his collective housing experiments in Zurich, from Carthago to Kraftwerk; Nick Faraclas, whose study of the African and Papua New Guinean pidgins brought to light for me the commoning dimension of language; Chris Carlsson, who, in the face of a triumphant neoliberalism, dared to say that the commons are not a utopia and put that into practice retaking the streets through Critical Mass; Kevin Van Meter, Craig, and the Team Colors Collective, with whom, in New York at ABC No Rio, we began a long discussion on commoning and self-reproducing movements; Maria Mies who taught us that at the heart of the commons is a profound sense of responsibility toward other people and the land, and that commoning is reuniting those parts of our social life that capitalism has divided; Peter Linebaugh, lifetime brother and comrade, who has made 'commoning' and the lives of those who have struggled to build communitarian worlds the main theme of his historical work—to him I owe my understanding of history as a common; Massimo De

Angelis, who has not only written classic texts on the commons but has put commoning into practice in a village on the Italian Appenine Mountains (Massimo lives a daily life that is 'outside of capitalism,' something which in his view is recreated through our daily acts of individual and collective refusal); the Unitierra Center in Oaxaca and its founder and promoter Gustavo Esteva, who even in the darkest moment of our recent history has never tired of asserting that the commons are already all around us; Raquel Gutiérrez Aguilar, whose powerful account of the rhythms of Pachakuti in the water wars in Bolivia has brought to life the insurgent power of communitarian forms of reproduction; Mina Lorena Navarro, who has shown us that the preservation and recreation of collective memory is a key condition for the defense of the commons; Gladys Tzul Tzul, who has given us an insightful description of how in communal regimes politics emanates from the reproduction of daily life and made it possible for me to better understand the meaning of communitarian relations. I also owe to Gladys the possibility of meetings recently in Guatemala with women from different indigenous organizations. My gratitude also to Beatriz Garcia and Ana Méndez de Andés, who have introduced me to the Quinzeme and organized my journey through the Spanish villages that had seen the infamous war on the commons that was the witch hunt; Joen Vedel, who has introduced me to Christiania and other commons in Copenhagen. My gratitude also to Lucia Linsalata, Verónica Gago, Natalia Quiroga, Betty Ruth Lozano, Marina Sitrin, Richard Pithouse, Caitlin Manning, Iain Boal, Mercedes Oliveras Bustamante, Rosaluz Perez Espinosa, Raúl Zibechi, Mariana Menendez, Noel Sosa, Yvonne Yanez, Jules Falquet, Mariarosa Dalla Costa, Ariel Salleh, and, not least, Elizabeth Downer, whose powerful paintings provide a visual text of the ongoing reclamation of communal spaces and activities on the American continent. Thanks to Josh MacPhee and to Erik Ruin of Justseeds for his painting of the Maypole dance *Reclaiming the Commons*. I also want to remember the late Rodolfo Morales, one of the most important twentieth-century Mexican artists, who dedicated his life to celebrate women's community building capacity, representing their bodies and activities as the elements that hold the community together.

Thanks also to the many who over the years have shown me or sent me their work on the commons or directed me to important sources. Thanks to Kasia Paprocki for sharing with me her research on microcredit in Bangladesh and to Ousseina Alidou for her notes on the management of microcredit in Niger, to Betsy Taylor for sending me her coauthored

*Recovering the Commons,* to Giovanna Ricoveri for giving me her book *Beni Comuni, Fra Tradizione e Futuro,* and Órla Donovan for organizing a conference on the commons in Cork, Ireland, in 2015.

And I wish to express my gratitude and solidarity with the activists that I have met in different parts of the world and whose struggles have been directed to the defense of communal forms of life and the construction of new forms of solidarity. My solidarity above all to the activists of the NO TAV Movement in Val di Susa, Italy, the Clandestina network in Greece, Acción Ecológica and the Colectivo Miradas Críticas in Ecuador, the Frente Popular Darío Santillán and the women of the Movimiento por la Dignidad and the Corriente Villera Independiente of Villa Retiro Bis in Buenos Aires, the CIDECI-Unitierra Center in San Cristobal de Las Casas, and especially its founder and coordinator Raymundo Sánchez Barraza, the Abahali movement in Durban, South Africa, the compañeras of the Colectivo Minerva and the journal *Contrapunto* in Uruguay, the compañeras of Mujeres Creando in La Paz, especially María Galindo, the Bristol Radical History Group, Bob Stone and Betsy Bowman and the Center for Global Justice in San Miguel de Allende, Mexico, the CUTE movement in Québec, which is struggling to deprivatize education. Thanks also to Monserrat Fernandez Aren and the other organizers of the Semana Galega de Filosofía, a unique event involving the entire population of Pontevedra, Galicia, which in 2018 was dedicated to the theme of the commons.

Special thanks to the people who have helped me to produce the book. First of all, Camille Barbagallo, with whom I have shared so many projects and political spaces that I can say the collaboration for this book is truly a product of the commons. Thanks again to Elizabeth Downer for generously allowing me to use her inspiring painting on the cover and to Erik Ruin, who also let me use one of his paintings for this book.

Thanks to Arlen Austin for patiently transferring my PDFs into Word documents. Thanks to the many journal and book editors who have allowed me to reprint the articles included in this book. Not least, thanks to Ramsey Kanaan of PM Press for his support, patience, and consistent vigorous encouragement.

"Introduction to the New Enclosures" is an edited version of the original, published in *The New Enclosures, Midnight Notes* no. 10 (1990): 1–9.

"The Debt Crisis, Africa, and the New Enclosure" is an edited version of the original, published in *The New Enclosures,* 10–17.

"China: Breaking the Iron Rice Bowl" was originally published as "Inscrutable China: Reading Struggles through the Media," *The New Enclosures*, 30–34.

"On Primitive Accumulation, Globalization, and Reproduction" was originally published in German as "Ursprunglishe Akkumuation, Globalisierung und Reproduktion," in *Die globale Einhegung-Krise, Ursprüngliche Akkumulation und Landnahmen im Kapitalismus*, eds. Maria Backhouse, Olaf Gerlach, Stefan Kalmring, and Andreas Nowak (Münster: Westfälisches Dampfboot, 2013), 40–52.

"From Commoning to Debt: Financialization, Microcredit, and the Changing Architecture of Capitalist Accumulation" first appeared in the *South Atlantic Quarterly* 113, no. 2 (May 2014): 231–44.

"Feminism and the Politics of the Commons in an Era of Primitive Accumulation" was originally published in Team Colors Collective, eds., *Uses of a Whirlwind: Movement, Movements, and Contemporary Radical Currents in the United States* (Oakland: AK Press, 2010), 283–94.

"Beneath the United States, the Commons" was first published in *the Journal of Labor and Society* 14, no. 1 (March 2011): 41–46.

"Commons against and beyond Capitalism" was first published in *Upping the Anti: A Journal of Theory and Action* 15 (September 2013): 83–98.

"Women's Struggles for Land and the Common Good in Latin America" was originally published as "In Struggle to Change the World: Women, Reproduction, and Resistance in Latin America" in *Documenta 14 Reader* (Munich: Prestel Verlag: 2017), 603–30.

"Marxism, Feminism, and the Commons" was originally published in *Communism in the 21st Century*, Vol. 1, ed. Shannon K. Brincat (Santa Barbara, CA: Praeger, 2014), 171–94.

"From Crisis to Commons: Reproductive Work, Affective Labor and Technology, and the Transformation of Everyday Life" was first published in *Psychology and the Conduct of Everyday Life*, eds. Ernst Schraube and Charlotte Højolt (London: Routledge, 2015), 192–204.

"Re-enchanting the World: Technology, the Body, and the Construction of the Commons" was first published in *The Anomie of the Earth: Philosophy, Politics, and Autonomy in Europe and the Americas*, eds. Federico Luisetti, John Pickles, and Wilson Kaiser (Durham: Duke University Press, 2015), 202–15.

# Foreword

In February 1493, on shipboard on his way home from his first voyage to America, Christopher Columbus reported to the king of Spain about the people he had just met. "Of anything they have, if it be asked for, they never say no, but do rather invite the person to accept it, and show as much lovingness as though their hearts went with it."[1]

Columbus had come across a commons.

Silvia Federici writes in the spirit of those people, that is, those living and commoning there, only we must say those living and commoning now, here in our world, because Federici does not romanticize the primitive. She's interested in a new world, re-enchanted.

Instead of writing on shipboard and reporting to the king, Federici takes flight across the oceans, sits on bumpy buses, joins crowds in subways, or rides her bicycle and talks to common people, especially women, in Africa, in Latin America, in Europe, and in North America. With pen, pencil, typewriter, or laptop, Federici records not the 'planet of slums' but our planet of the commons. As a woman and a feminist, she observes the production of the commons in the everyday labors of reproduction—the washing, cuddling, cooking, consoling, sweeping, pleasing, cleaning, exciting, mopping, reassuring, dusting, dressing, feeding children, *having* children, and caring for the sick and the elderly.

Federici is a teacher, a social theorist, an activist, a historian, who will separate neither politics from economics nor ideas from life. She writes from those sites where history is made, the sidewalk with the street vendors, the group kitchen, the storefront collective, the park, the women's shelter, and there she listens while she talks. Her feminist

Marxism is an analytical tool sharpened with Brechtian attitude. To her, Marxism is no longer an *ism* or an ideological option of the individual intellectual consumer; it is an achievement of collective subjectivities, an essential part of our common intelligence. She helps to turn the grumblings of the aggrieved into common sense. The center of gravity in her analytic thinking is no longer wage labor but the hierarchies of labor and unequal power relations that tear the commons apart.[2]

Federici is a scholar who generously recognizes her debt to other scholars in Latin America, Africa, Europe, and North America. She acknowledges the work of Mariarosa Dalla Costa, Nawal El Saadawi, Maria Mies, and Raquel Gutiérrez. She gives shoutouts to *Midnight Notes*. The Zapatista women are one of her reference points, as is their Women's Revolutionary Law of 1993.[3] Her bibliographies will please the ardent researcher, beginner and advanced.

She is a people's intellectual, and as such she is an antidote to the heaviness of Hannah Arendt. There is something of Virginia Woolf's *Three Guineas* in the power of her reasoning, something of Meridel Le Seuer in her class loyalty to the common life of proletarians, and something of the strength of Simone Weil in the ethical intensity of her spirit. Her passion is accompanied by what I call revolutionary decorum. To Federici, revolutionary decorum does not have to do with false courtesy and still less with propriety. However blasting may be her condemnation of 'things as they are,' she retains a modesty of expression that has everything to do with the mutual obligation inherent to commons.

As a scholar and social theorist, she both criticizes and pays homage to her tradition, as is clear from her title, *Re-enchanting the World*, which alludes to the German sociologist Max Weber's 1917 lecture. Amid the bloody slaughter of World War I and on the eve of revolution, Weber spoke of the *disenchantment* of the world.

As a Marxist feminist scholar she peers beneath the surface. Take the asphalt of the university campus for instance. Hearkening to the great slogan of Paris in 1968, she finds beneath the stones not the beach but the pasture. The life of the common is not a thing of the past; she saw it at the University of Calabar, Nigeria—cattle grazing on the campus. She peers beneath the surface in another sense. Technology requires diamonds, coltan, lithium, and petroleum. To extract them capitalism must privatize communal lands. Weber said technological rationalization was inevitable and an essential requirement to progress. Federici denounces the so-called progressive nature of the capitalist mode of production and sees the universalization of knowledge and technology as a colonial legacy. Mechanization of the world was preceded by mechanization of the body; the latter is slavery and the former the effect of the labor of slaves.

For those who have been reading her over the years, we find that rather than mellowing with time, she has become more effective, persuasive, and efficient. She is not one to waste her breath. She is as fierce, as uncompromising, and as concentrated as ever. The flames of youthful passion, far from diminishing into dying embers, have only conflagrated a new generation of women and men internationally.

Rejecting the idea of a universalizing political culture, she envisions the commons as constructed out of different histories of oppression and struggle, differences, however, that do not create political divisions. At the heart of the commons is the refusal of privilege, a theme always present in Federici's work. "We need to resignify what the very concept of communism means to us," she says, "and free ourselves from the interiorization of capitalist relations and values so that commoning defines not only our property relations but our relations to ourselves and others. In other words, commons are not a given but a product of struggle." In a rotten society no one can expect to be without bruises.

*Re-enchanting the World* resignifies Marxist categories, reinterpreting them from a feminist perspective. 'Accumulation' is one such concept. 'Reproduction' is a second. 'Class struggle' is a third and is inseparable from the fourth, 'capital.' For Federici the 'labor theory of value' is still a key to understanding capitalism, though her feminist reading of it redefines what work is and how value is produced. She shows, for instance, that debt too is productive for capital; it is a powerful lever of primitive accumulation—student loan, mortgage, credit cards, and microfinance—and an engine of social divisions. Reproduction (education, health care, pensions) has been financialized. Accompanying it is a deliberate and calculated ethnography of shame, epitomized by the Grameen Bank, which will deprive innocent, impoverished 'entrepreneurs' of even their cooking pot if they fall behind in their payments. John Milton, the author of *Paradise Lost*, the epic poem of the English Revolution, condemned this practice of "seizing of pots and pans from the poor."[4] He saw too the shame and the cunning: first enclose the land, then take the cooking pot. (Or is it the other way around?)

Federici has a position to take, and she takes it distinctly from others. There is the school of 'common pool resources,' the commons without class struggle. There is the school that emphasizes information and cognitive capitalism but overlooks women's labor in the material basis of the cyber economy. There is the school of 'the critique of everyday life,' which hides the unpaid, endless work of women. Not only is the reproduction of a human being a collective project, it is the most labor intensive of all work. We learn that "women are the subsistence farmers of the world. In Africa they produced 80 percent of the food people consume." Women are the custodians of land and communal wealth. They are also the 'weavers of memory.' She looks at the body on a continuum with the land, as both possess historical memory and both are implicated in liberation.

Since 1973, the large-scale reorganization of the accumulation process—of the land, the house, the wage—has been underway. The whole earth has been seen as an *oikos* to be managed rather than a terrain of class struggle. A neoliberal feminism has emerged that accepts market 'rationalities' and sees the ceiling, rather than the hearth, as the symbolic center of its architecture and the ladder rather than the roundtable as its furniture.

In recuperation of revolutionary feminism and rejection of the neoliberal celebration of the private and the individual which gives us *Homo idioticus* (from the Greek word for "private") Federici offers us *Femina communia*. In her political vision there is no commons without community, and there is no community without women.

What are the commons? While Federici eschews an essentialist answer, her essays dance around on two points, collective reappropriation and collective struggle against the ways we have been divided. Examples are manifold. Sometimes she offers four characteristics: 1) all wealth should be shared, 2) commons requires obligation as well as entitlement, 3) commons of care are also communities of resistance that oppose all social hierarchies, and 4) commons are the 'other' of the state form. Indeed, the discourse of the commons is rooted in the crisis of the state, which now perverts the term to its own ends.

Capitalism postures as the environmental guardian of the earth, 'the planetary commons,' just like the gated community postures as 'the commons,' while making other people homeless, or the shopping mall as the 'commodity commons.' In light of the capitalist perversion of the commons, we can understand Federici's stubborn insistence on our bodies and on our land as the commons' touchstone.

Federici is at her most persuasive, most passionate, most committed, and most clear when she demands that we challenge the social conditions that require that life for some be attained only by production of death for others. This is not division of labor, it is government by death, thanatocracy!

What is enchantment? It is to fall under a rapturous spell of magical influences. By 1917, however, the meanings of the term had changed, losing its connections to the sublime or the sacred, and, like similar changes to the meanings of spell, magic, and glamour, its meaning found a limited discursive home in high fashion, the decorative arts, and Hollywood. No longer expressing powers of the cosmos and the body, these terms became limited to superficialities and superfluities.

To Federici, enchantment refers not to the past but to the future. It is part, perhaps the leading part, of the revolutionary project and inseparable from the commons. The only thing sacred about the earth is that we can help make and care for it . . . well, we with worms withal.

The word 'enchantment' comes from a French word, 'chanter,' to sing. For sure 'chanting' the world into existence may be meditative—sometimes the movement must stop and sit on its hands. But if we understand 'song' to include poetry, then the call for enchanting the world, for singing creation into being, is both rhapsodic and prophetic. It is a choral accomplishment. In the olden days, when Columbus sailed, the people in America sang while the corn grew; it was believed that they even sang it into growth. The first European historian of the Americas, Peter Martyr, collected the stories of the conquerors as they came in. He summarized the knowledge of the people already living there in America, "Myne and Thyne (the seedes of all myscheefe) have no place."

Nothing is gained by yearning and tarrying. Read, study, think, listen, talk, and with others act, by which I mean *fight*. As Federici tells us the new world is around us, it is about us, and only our struggle can bring it into existence and re-enchant it.

**Peter Linebaugh**
**Michigan, 2017**

**Notes**

1   William Brandon, *New Worlds for Old: Reports from the New World and Their Effect on the Development of Social Thought in Europe, 1500–1800* (Athens: Ohio University Press, 1986), 7–8.

2   See Federici, *Revolution at Point Zero: Housework, Reproduction, and Feminist Struggle* (Oakland: PM Press, 2012).

3   Hilary Klein, *Compañeras: Zapatista Women's Stories* (New York: Seven Stories Press, 2015).

4   John Milton, *Means to Remove Hirelings* (1659), accessed June 2, 2018, https://archive.org/details/miltonsconsideroomiltgoog.

# Introduction

To publish a book dedicated to the politics of the commons may seem a sign of naivety, surrounded as we are by wars, economic and ecological crises that devastate entire regions, and the rise of white supremacist, neo-Nazi, and paramilitary organizations now operating with almost complete impunity in every part of the world. Yet the very sense that we are living at the edge of a volcano makes it even more crucial to recognize that, in the midst of much destruction, another world is growing, like the grass in the cracks of the urban pavement, challenging the hegemony of capital and the state and affirming our interdependence and capacity for cooperation. Though differently articulated—*commoning, el común, comunalidad*—the language and the politics of the *commons are today the expression of this alternative world*. For what the commons in essence stands for is the recognition that life in a Hobbesian world, where one competes against all and prosperity is gained at the expense of others, is not worth living and is a sure recipe for defeat. This is the meaning and the strength of the many struggles that people are waging across the planet to oppose the expansion of capitalist relations, defend the existing commons, and rebuild the fabric of communities destroyed by years of neoliberal assault on the most basic means of our reproduction.

On this subject, a vast body of literature has grown over the years to which I am deeply indebted. But the main inspiration for my work on the commons comes from my experience while teaching in the early 1980s in Nigeria, and later from learning about social movements and meeting with women's organizations in South America.

During months of teaching at the University of Port Harcourt over the course of three years, I came to realize that much of the land I crossed with my bicycle to go to school or to the market was still communally held, and I also learned to recognize the signs that communalism has left in the culture, manners, and habits of the people I met. I ceased to be surprised, for instance, when entering a 'mama-put'[1] a student would pick food from the plate of a friend, when bicycling to my classes I would see women farming on the side of the road, reappropriating land from which they had been expropriated for the construction of the campus, or when colleagues would shake their heads upon learning that my sole security was a wage and that I had no village to return to, no community to support me in case of hard times. What I learned in Nigeria had a profound effect on my thinking and my politics. As a result, for years, in the United States, I devoted most of my political work to fighting together with colleagues from Africa against the termination of free education on most of the continent, as demanded by the International Monetary Fund as part of its 'structural adjustment program,' and to campaigning in the antiglobalization movement.[2] It was in this process that I came into contact with the literature on the commons produced by feminists like Vandana Shiva and Maria Mies. Read at the time of the Zapatista uprising, while I was writing about women's struggle against enclosure in sixteenth-century Europe, the encounter with Shiva's and Mies's work opened new political horizons. In the 1970s, I had campaigned for wages for housework, as the feminist strategy most apt to end women's 'gift' of unpaid labor to capital and to begin of a process of reappropriation of the wealth that women have produced through their work. Reading Shiva's account of the Chikpo movement and her description of the Indian forest as a full reproductive system—providing food, medicine, shelter, and spiritual nourishment—expanded my view of what a feminist struggle over reproduction could be.[3] The encounter in recent years with the struggle of women in South America—indigenous, *campesina, villera*—has further convinced me that the reappropriation of common wealth and disaccumulation of capital—the two main goals of wages for housework—could equally and more powerfully be achieved through the deprivatization of land, water, and urban spaces and the creation of forms of reproduction built on self-management, collective labor, and collective decision-making.

This vision, which is articulated in the work of some of the most important feminist scholars in Latin America, inspires many of the essays included in this volume. The first part, however, is dedicated to an analysis of the new forms of enclosure that are the backbone of the globalization of capital in our time and the motivation, in part, for the emergence of the politics of the commons. The literature on this subject is now immense and growing. I include in Part One three essays published in the 1990s in *Midnight Notes*—a radical journal on which I collaborated from 1980 to 2000—to remind us of the beginning of a process that now has a global reach and risks being normalized.[4] Particularly important in this context is the article titled "Introduction to the New Enclosures," which was collectively written and was one of the first documents in the United States to read the globalization process as a process of 'primitive accumulation.' In it, I reflected on my experience traveling back and forth between Nigeria and the U.S., seeing in the streets of Brooklyn the effects of the displacement in that country in the form of students working in car washes or getting by selling goods in the streets, in a new diaspora adding millions to the world labor market. The theoretical perspective proposed in "Introduction to the New Enclosures" is further extended in the articles on the 'debt crisis' in Africa and the transition to capitalism in China, which demonstrate that, despite the differences in social context, the destruction of communal land regimes remains the backbone of the present phase of capitalist development and the cause of the surge of the violence that is affecting so many regions across the world, although dispossession today is also imposed through the generalization of debt.

What these articles also document, however, are the intense struggles that people in Africa and China have been waging against the multiple forms of dispossession (of lands, territories, means of subsistence, knowledges, and decisional power) to which they are subjected. In leftist literature such struggles are often dismissed as purely defensive. But this view is deeply mistaken. It is impossible, in fact, to defend existing communal rights without creating a new reality, in the sense of new strategies, new alliances, and new forms of social organization. A mine is opened threatening the air that people breathe and the water that everyone drinks; coastal waters are drilled to extract petroleum poisoning the sea, the beaches, and the cropland; an old neighborhood is razed to the ground to make space for a stadium—immediately new lines are drawn. Not only communities but families are restructured, often along opposing lines, for the danger faced has a consciousness-raising effect and calls for everyone to take a stand and define one's principles of social and ethical behavior.

While Part One reconstructs the social context in which the politics of the commons has matured, Part Two looks at the commons both as an already present reality, especially in the form of existing communitarian forms of social organization, and a perspective anticipating in an embryonic way a world beyond capitalism and placing at the center of social change the question of social reproduction. From a feminist viewpoint, one of the attractions exercised by the idea of the commons is the possibility of overcoming the isolation in which reproductive activities are performed and the separation between the private and the public spheres that has contributed so much to hiding and rationalizing women's exploitation in the family and the home.

This is not an entirely new endeavor. In the U.S., in the second part of the nineteenth century, as Dolores Hayden has documented, a variety of 'materialist feminists'—utopian socialists (Fourierists, Owenites, Saint-Simonians), as well as reformist feminists—set out to deprivatize the home and domestic work, proposing the construction of buildings with collective kitchens and urban plans centered on cooperative housing.[5] While in the nineteenth century these were relatively limited experiments, carried out mostly by white, middle-class women who often did not hesitate to employ female servants for their execution, today the drive to socialize the reproduction of life comes from the poorest strata of the world's female proletariat, motivated not by ideology but by necessity, and it has as its objective not only the reorganization of reproductive activities on a collective basis but also the reappropriation of the material resources necessary for their realization.

As already anticipated, the most substantive parts of my analysis in this work are inspired by the women's movements that are organizing under the heading of 'popular feminism' in South America. But in North America, too, examples of a communalization of reproduction motivated by the need for economic survival and resistance to capitalist exploitation are not lacking. Exemplary is the great common that was formed at Standing Rock in 2016, organized mostly by initiative of indigenous women who called themselves the 'water protectors'—running kitchens, starting schools, organizing supplies, and supporting, at the peak of the mobilization, more than seven thousand people in some of the most difficult environmental conditions and under the constant threat of violence.[6]

Like Standing Rock and the Occupy movement's encampments, some of the commoning activities reported in the book are no longer in place.

Once the state of economic emergency that had brought them into existence ceased, some of the reproductive commons that had been built were
abandoned. This has raised questions of the sustainability of these efforts
and the extent to which such initiatives can provide the base for a broader
change in the mode of (re)production. These are valid concerns. But the
fact that capitalist development today is promising only more hardships,
forcing millions of people to act collectively and to collectively organize
their reproduction, is of great significance. Appropriations of urban and
rural spaces are being constantly reenacted, resulting in an increasing
number of settlements where space and resources are shared, decisions
about daily reproduction are collectively taken, and family relations are
redefined. Moreover, the commoning activities that are created under
emergency conditions do not disappear without leaving some traces,
although not always visible to the naked eye. The great camp at Standing
Rock, where thousands went in a sort of political pilgrimage, to help, learn,
and witness with their own eyes this historic event, has produced a new
awareness in the U.S. social justice movements and a connection with the
struggle of indigenous people that so far had only been achieved at local
levels at best. Similarly, the commoning reproductive activities organized
in more than six hundred U.S. cities in the fall of 2011, at the height of the
Occupy movement, has begun to change how politics is done in ways that
were once only typical of feminist organizations. The need for a politics
that refuses to separate the time of political organizing from that of reproduction is a lesson that many Occupiers have not forgotten and is one of
the main themes of this volume.[7]

Reproduction does not only concern our material needs—such as
housing, food preparation, the organization of space, childrearing, sex,
and procreation. An important aspect of it is the reproduction of our collective memory and the cultural symbols that give meaning to our life
and nourish our struggles. With this in mind, Part Two begins with an
essay that acknowledges the legacy of the Native American peoples, the
first commoners on this land. This is important because we cannot think
of turning, or even hope to turn, North America into a land of commons
unless we join the struggle of indigenous peoples to cease being prisoners on the reservations and to reclaim the land that once was their
own. Other commons have existed beneath the United States that we also
need to remember and learn from. In a still-unpublished article, George
Caffentzis has traced the outlines of a research on the maroon/African

5

commons that fugitive slaves constructed in the heart of the plantation economies.[8] We also need to revisit the radical experiments with communalism that socialists, and even religious groups like the Shakers, have created in different parts of the country,[9] and not least the communes built in the 1960s in northern California.[10] As Native activist Paula Gunn Allen reminds us, "We as feminists must be aware of the history of this continent," for "the root of oppression is loss of memory."[11] This is a fact that the U.S. government has never forgotten, and it has devoted many resources and much energy to the destruction of everything, at home and abroad, that might strengthen the sense of pride and identity of the peoples it has intended to conquer and exploit. Hence the policy of constant demolition, through 'urban renewal' or (as now in the Middle East) carpet-bombings, turning cities into piles of rubble, destroying homes, infrastructures, historic buildings, anything that might constitute a tie with the land and the history of past struggles and cultures.

Revisiting the history of the commons warns us, however, that though guaranteeing the reproduction of their members, commons have not always been egalitarian forms of social organization. Even today, in several indigenous communities of Africa and South America, women do not have the right to participate in assemblies where decisions are made, and they risk seeing their children excluded from access to the land because membership in the commons is established through male lines. In this volume, I examine this problem and show how it has been exploited by the World Bank to promote its land privatization drive and how women in indigenous communities are responding to this threat. At the same time, I argue for the need to distinguish communal/communitarian social formations that work within a noncapitalist horizon from forms of commoning that are compatible with the logic of capitalist accumulation and may function as the safety valve with which a capitalist system in crisis tries to diffuse the tensions its policies inevitably generate. This, however, is a distinction that already has its critics.

In *Omnia Sunt Communia*, Massimo De Angelis warns us, for instance, against the attempt to constrain the necessarily fluid, experimental character of every form of communalism within the mold of aprioristically defined ideological models.[12] Equally, it is impossible to anticipate the evolution of a time bank, a communal garden, or an urban squat. It is important, however, without falling into a dogmatic posture, to identify the distinctive elements of commoning, insofar as we conceive it as a principle of social organization, surrounded as we are by commons that unite in ways that protect privilege and are exclusionary on the basis of ethnicity, class, religious identities, or income levels. Thus, in "Commons against and beyond Capitalism," written with George Caffentzis, we draw some broad distinctions that have immediate implications for social justice movements, like the distinction between the common and the public or between commons that operate outside of the market—as is the case of most of the activities that are taking place in the Zapatista territories—and commons that are producing for the market. These distinctions are fluid and subject to change, and we should not presume that in a world governed by capitalist relations commons can escape all contamination. But they remind us that commons exist in a field of antagonistic social relations and can easily become means of accommodation to the status quo.

In this spirit, in Part Two I also examine the relation between commonism and communism in the works of Marx and Engels, at least those that Marx decided to publish and that directly influenced the socialist movement internationally.[13] My scope, in this regard, is rather limited. Absent from my account is a questioning of the process by which the 'communion of goods,' identified primarily as the communal use of land—until the eighteenth century the main ideal of revolutionaries in Europe from Winstanley[14] to Babeuf[15]—was in the nineteenth century replaced by 'communism,' identified with the abolition of private property and the management of communal wealth by the proletarian state. What, for instance, induced Frederick Engels to declare in *The Housing Question* that industrial workers in his time were absolutely uninterested in possessing land?[16] This is an important question. But my primary concern in this volume is a different one. It is to demonstrate that the principle of the commons, as upheld today by feminists, anarchists, ecologists, and non-orthodox Marxists, contrasts with the assumption shared by Marxist developmentalists, accelerationists, and Marx himself concerning the necessity of land privatization as a path to large-scale production and of globalization as the instrument for the unification of the world proletariat.

Commoners today repudiate the progressive role of capital, demand control over the decisions that most affect their lives, assert their capacity for self-government, and reject the imposition of a unitary model of social and cultural life, in the spirit of the Zapatistas' "One No, and Many Yeses," that is, many roads to the common, corresponding to our different historic and cultural trajectories and environmental conditions. Furthermore, 150 years after the publication of *Capital*, we can verify that the technological development to which Marx consigned the task of constructing the material bases of communism is destroying not only the remaining communitarian regimes but also the possibility of life and reproduction on this earth for a growing number of species.

Furthermore, we must ask: Is the mechanization and even robotization of our daily life the best that thousands of years of human labor can produce? Can we imagine reconstructing our lives around a commoning of our relations with others, including animals, waters, plants, and mountains—which the large-scale construction of robots will certainly destroy? This is the horizon that the discourse and the politics of the commons opens for us today, not the promise of an impossible return to the past but the possibility of recovering the power of collectively deciding our fate on this earth. This is what I call re-enchanting the world.

**Notes**

1    'Mama-put' is the name students gave to the places near the university where they would usually eat, generally run by women.

2    In 1990, with colleagues from Africa and the U.S., we founded the Committee for Academic Freedom in Africa, whose purpose was to analyze and mobilize against the destruction of the educational systems in Africa, especially at the tertiary level, planned by the IMF and World Bank, as part of the austerity measures adopted under the rubric of structural adjustment. For thirteen years CAFA produced newsletters and campaigned against the World Bank, including its participation in African studies conferences, scandalous in our view considering the role the bank had played in the defunding of African universities and research programs. Most important, we documented the struggles students and teachers were waging across the continent, aiming to raise support for them in North American universities. See Silvia Federici, George Caffentzis, and Ousseina Alidou, eds., *A Thousand Flowers: Social Struggles against Structural Adjustment in African Universities* (Trenton, NJ: Africa World Press, 2000).

3    As described in Vandana Shiva, *Staying Alive: Women, Ecology and Development* (London: Zed Books, 1989), 57–77, the Chikpo movement started in the mountain regions of the Himalayas "to protect the forest from commercial exploitation," and then spread to other regions north and south of the Central Indian highland: "It expressed the philosophy and politics of peasant women who rejected the commercial use and destruction of the forests, and even challenged the men of their communities who supported it." Shiva has also written extensively on the principle of the commons in *Earth Democracy: Justice, Sustainability, and Peace* (Cambridge, MA: South End Press, 2005).

4    The essays in this volume taken from *Midnight Notes* appeared in the issue titled *The New Enclosures*, published in the fall of 1990.

5    See Dolores Hayden, *The Grand Domestic Revolution: A History of Feminist Designs for American Homes, Neighborhoods, and Cities* (Cambridge, MA: MIT Press, 1985 [1981]).

6    Standing Rock is the site of the Sioux reservation that hosted the camp for the resistance against the construction of the Dakota Access Pipeline, which threatened to contaminate both the Missouri River on which the reservation depends for its water and its sacred grounds.

7    On the Occupy movement, see, among others, Sarah van Gelder and the staff of *Yes! Magazine*, eds., *This Changes Everything: Occupy Wall Street and the 99% Movement* (Oakland: Berrett-Koehler Publishers, 2011) and Todd Gitlin, *Occupy Nation: The Roots, the Spirit, and the Promise of Occupy Wall Street* (New York: HarperCollins, 2012).

8    George Caffentzis, "African American Commons," unpublished manuscript, 2015.

9    On socialist and Shakers commons in the U.S., see Charles Nordhoff, *The Communistic Societies of the United States* (New York: Dover Publications, 1966).

10   See Iain Boal, Janferie Stone, Michael Watts, and Cal Winslow, *West of Eden: Communes and Utopia in Northern California* (Oakland: PM Press, 2012).

11   Paula Gunn Allen, "Who Is Your Mother? Red Roots of White Feminism," in *Multicultural Literacy*, eds. Rick Simonson and Scott Walker (Saint Paul, MN: Graywolf Press,1988), 18–19.

12   Massimo De Angelis, *Omnia Sunt Communia: On the Commons and the Transformation to Postcapitalism* (London: Zed Books, 2017).

13   It appears that after the end of the Paris Commune Marx changed his view of the potential of the commons as the foundation for the development of communism. After reading the work of Lewis Henry Morgan, in his correspondence with a Russian revolutionary he hinted at the possibility of a transition to communism not requiring a process of primitive accumulation, built instead, in Russia at least, on the peasant commune. See Teodor Shanin, *Late Marx and the Russian Road: Marx and the Peripheries of Capitalism* (New York: Monthly Review Press, 1983).

14   Gerrard Winstanley (October 19, 1609–September 10, 1676) "was an English Protestant religious reformer and political activist during the Protectorate of Oliver Cromwell. He was one of the founders of the group known as the True Levellers or Diggers. The group occupied public lands that had been enclosed, pulling down hedges to plant crops. True Levellers was the name the group used to describe itself, whereas the term Diggers was coined by contemporaries"; "Diggers," *Wikipedia*, accessed June 5, 2018, https://en.wikipedia.org/wiki/Diggers. In a tract called *The True Levellers Standard Advanced; or, The State of Community Opened, and Presented to the Sons of Man*, Winstanley spoke of making the Earth a Common Treasure for all, rich and poor alike, accessed June 2, 2018, https://www.marxists.org/reference/archive/winstanley/1649/levellers-standard.htm.

15  "Gracchus" Babeuf (November 23, 1760–May 27, 1797) was a journalist who edited his own paper, *Le tribun du peuple*, in which he denounced the failure of the French Revolution to bring about a truly egalitarian society. Condemned in 1796 as instigator of a conspiracy to overthrow the republic, he was executed in 1797. In his defense speech at his trial he spoke against the privatization of land and for the "Community of Goods." "We declare ourselves unable to tolerate any longer a situation—he said—in which the great majority of men toil and sweat in the service of the pleasure of a tiny minority. . . . Let it come to an end . . . this great scandal that our posterity will never believe! Disappear at last, revolting distinctions between rich and poor, great and small, masters and servants, governors and governed"; Albert Fried and Ronald Sanders ed., *Socialist Thought: A Documentary History* (Garden City, NY: Doubleday Anchor Books, 1964), 51–55.

16  Frederick Engels, "The Housing Question" (1872), accessed June 2, 2018, https://www.marxists.org/archive/marx/works/1872/housing-question/.

# PART ONE
## On the New Enclosures

# Introduction to Part One

The articles included in this section focus on a set of programs that, starting in the late 1970s, opened a new process of 'primitive' (originary) accumulation. The purpose is to show the continuity between the World Bank and IMF 'structural adjustment programs,' which by the mid-1980s had been imposed on most of the former colonial world, and the transition of communist China to capitalism, as well as the development of a debt economy, by which individual debt has amplified the consequences of national debt. To these structural developments I have given the name of 'new enclosures,' taken from a 1990 issue of *Midnight Notes* dedicated to this topic, because their effects have been as devastating as the effects of colonization and the expulsion of the peasantry from communal land, the processes that, as we know, set the conditions for capitalist development in sixteenth-century Europe and the so-called New World.

The decision to begin my discussion of the commons with a set of articles on the new enclosures stems from the need to contextualize the new interest in communitarian relations in different radical movements—feminist, ecological, anarchist, and even Marxist—and because I realized that these developments, which only three decades ago were epoch-making, have faded in the memory of many among the new generations, at least in Europe and the United States. Yet we cannot understand the depth of the emergency that we are living unless we reckon with the cumulative impact of these policies, which have resulted in the displacement of millions of people from their ancestral homes, often condemning them to a life of misery and death. As such, I have included in Part One the three articles published in *Midnight Notes* under the title of *The New Enclosures*, heavily edited to bring out those aspects of the analyses that are more relevant to present concerns. This section also discusses the formation of a 'debt economy,' and in particular the global spread of microcredit and microfinance, which I describe as an egregious attack not only on people's means of subsistence but on mutual aid and solidarity relations among women.

As an overview on the war on the commons this section is far from complete. Absent is an account of the demise of the commons caused by the worsening ecological crisis. Also, the consequences of 'extractivism' on communal economies and cultures are only discussed in general terms, as is the violence, especially against women, which is their necessary condition. For a discussion of these aspects of the new enclosures I refer the reader to the growing body of literature on these topics. My goal in Part One is primarily to identify the social developments to which the new interest in the commons and the new forms of resistance being organized worldwide in rural and urban sites are responding. By highlighting the structural/systemic character of the new enclosures and their continuity with past trends in capitalist development, I also wish to demonstrate that the growing interest in the commons is not a passing political fad. Even to the many of us who have grown up in a world where most of the wealth that we need for our sustenance has been enclosed, the principle of the commons today appears as a guarantee of not only economic survival but social agency and social solidarity—in sum that harmony with ourselves, others, and the natural world that in the South of the American continent is expressed by the concept of the *buen vivir*.

# On Primitive Accumulation, Globalization, and Reproduction

## Rethinking Primitive Accumulation

Starting with the 1990 issue of *Midnight Notes* on the "new enclosures,"[1] followed by David Harvey's theory of "accumulation by dispossession"[2] and by the many essays on primitive accumulation that have been published in the *Commoner*,[3] an extensive body of literature has explored the political meaning of this concept and applied it to an analysis of 'globalization.' Artists have contributed to this process. An outstanding example is the 2010 Potosí Principle exhibit presented by German, Bolivian, and Spanish artists and curators,[4] who worked to demonstrate the continuity between the imagery found in several sixteenth-century colonial paintings produced in the Andean region at the peak of primitive accumulation in the 'New World' and the imagery coming from the 'new enclosures' that have been central to the globalization program. The work of feminist writers like Maria Mies, Mariarosa Dalla Costa, and Claudia von Werlhof, who recognized "the extent to which [the] modern political economy, up to the present, builds upon the producers', men's, and even more so women's, permanent worldwide expropriation and deprivation of power" has also been very important in this context.[5]

Thanks to these studies and artistic contributions we now recognize that primitive accumulation is not a one-time historical event confined to the origins of capitalism, as the point of departure of 'accumulation proper.' It is a phenomenon constitutive of capitalist relations at all times, eternally recurrent, "part of the continuous process of capitalist accumulation"[6] and "always contemporaneous with its expansion."[7] This does not mean that primitive accumulation can be 'normalized' or that we should

15

underplay the importance of those moments in history—the times of clearances, wars, imperial drives "when great masses of men are suddenly and forcibly torn from their means of subsistence and hurled onto the labor market as free, unprotected and right-less proletarians."[8]

It means, however, that we should conceive the 'separation of the producer from the means of production'—for Marx the essence of primitive accumulation—as something that has to be continuously reenacted, especially in times of capitalist crisis, when class relations are challenged and have to be given new foundations. Contrary to Marx's view that with the development of capitalism a working class comes into existence that views capitalist relations as "self-evident natural laws,"[9] violence—the secret of primitive accumulation in Marx[10]—is always necessary to establish and maintain the capitalist work discipline. Not surprisingly, in response to the culmination of an unprecedented cycle of struggle—anticolonial, blue-collar, feminist—in the 1960s and 1970s, primitive accumulation became a global and seemingly permanent process,[11] with economic crises, wars, and massive expropriations now appearing in every part of the planet as the preconditions for the organization of production and accumulation on a world scale. It is a merit of the political debates that I have mentioned that we can now better understand the "nature of the enclosing force that we are facing,"[12] the logic by which it is driven, and its consequences for us. For to think of the world political economy through the prism of primitive accumulation is to place ourselves immediately on a battlefield.

But to fully comprehend the political implications of this development we must expand the concept of primitive accumulation beyond Marx's description in more than one way. We must first acknowledge that the history of primitive accumulation cannot be understood from the viewpoint of an abstract universal subject. For an essential aspect of the capitalist project has been the disarticulation of the social body, through the imposition of different disciplinary regimes producing an accumulation of 'differences' and hierarchies that profoundly affect how capitalist relations are experienced. We, therefore, have different histories of primitive accumulation, each providing a particular perspective on capitalist relations necessary to reconstruct their totality and unmask the mechanisms by which capitalism has maintained its power. This means that the history of primitive accumulation past and present cannot be fully comprehended until it is written not only from the viewpoint of the future or former waged workers, but from the viewpoint of the enslaved, the colonized, the indigenous people whose lands continue to be the main target of the enclosures, and the many social subjects whose place in the history of capitalist society cannot be assimilated into the history of the waged.

This was the methodology that I used in *Caliban and the Witch* to analyze primitive accumulation from the viewpoint of its effects on 'women,' the 'body,' and the production of labor power, arguing that this approach gives us a much broader understanding of the historical processes that have shaped the rise of capitalism than we gain from Marx's work, where the discussion of primitive accumulation centers on preconditions for the formation of waged labor.[13]

Two processes in particular have been most essential from a historical and methodological viewpoint: (a) the constitution of reproduction work—that is the work of reproducing individuals and labor power—as 'women's labor' and as a separate social sphere, seemingly located outside the sphere of economic relations and, as such, devalued from a capitalist viewpoint, a development coeval with the separation of the peasantry from the land and the formation of a commodity market; (b) the institutionalization of the state's control over women's sexuality and reproductive capacity, through the criminalization of abortion and the introduction of a system of surveillance and punishment that literally expropriates women's bodies.

Both these developments, which have been characteristic of the extension of capitalist relations in every historical period, have had crucial social consequences. The expulsion of reproductive work from the spheres of economic relations and its deceptive relegation to the sphere of the 'private,' the 'personal,' 'outside' of capital accumulation, and, above all, 'feminine' has made it invisible as work and has naturalized its exploitation.[14] It has also been the basis for the institution of a new sexual division of labor and a new family organization, subordinating women to men and further socially and psychologically differentiating women and men. At the same time, the state's appropriation of women's bodies and their reproductive capacity was the beginning of its regulation of 'human resources,' its first 'biopolitical' intervention, in the Foucauldian sense of the word,[15] and its contribution to the accumulation of capital insofar as this is essentially the multiplication of the proletariat.[16]

As I have shown, the witch hunts that took place in many countries of Europe and the Andean regions in the sixteenth and seventeenth centuries, leading to the execution of hundreds of thousands of women, were fundamental to this process. None of the historic changes in the organization of reproductive work that I have outlined would have been possible or would be possible today without a major attack on the social power of women, in the same way as capitalist development could not have succeeded without the slave trade or the conquest of the Americas without a relentless imperial drive continuing to this day and the construction of a web of racial hierarchies that have effectively divided the world proletariat.

## Primitive Accumulation and the Restructuring of Social Reproduction in the Global Economy

It is with these assumptions and this theoretical framework in mind that, in this essay, I analyze 'globalization' as a process of primitive accumulation, this time imposed on a global scale. This view undoubtedly is at odds with the neoliberal theory that celebrates the expansion of capitalist relations as evidence of a 'democratization' of social life. But it is also in contrast to the Marxist autonomists' view of the restructuring of the global economy, which, focusing on the computer and information revolution and the rise of cognitive capitalism, describes this phase of capitalist development as a step toward the autonomation of labor.[17] I propose, instead, that the pillar of this restructuring has been a concerted attack on our most basic means of reproduction, the land, the house, and the wage, aiming to expand the global workforce and drastically reduce the cost of labor.[18] Structural adjustment, the dismantling of the welfare state, the financialization of reproduction, leading to the debt and mortgage crisis, and war: different policies have been required to activate the new accumulation drive. But in each case it has entailed the destruction of our 'common wealth,' and it has made no difference that over the years its architects have multiplied with the arrival of China and other emerging capitalist powers, joining the World Bank, the International Monetary Fund, the World Trade Organization, and the governments that support these institutions as competitors at the feast. Behind the nationalist appearances and particularities, there is only one logic driving the new forms of primitive accumulation: to form a labor force reduced to abstract labor, pure labor power, with no guarantees, no protections, ready to be moved from place to place and job to job, employed mostly through short-term contracts and at the lowest possible wage.

What is the political meaning of this development? Even if we accept that primitive accumulation is an endemic part of life and work in capitalism (as Massimo De Angelis, among others, has insisted),[19] how can we account for the fact that after five hundred years of relentless exploitation of workers across the planet, the capitalist class in its different embodiments still needs to pauperize multitudes of people worldwide?

There is no obvious answer to this question. But if we consider how 'globalization' is changing the organization of social reproduction we can reach some preliminary conclusions. We can see that capitalism can only provide pockets of prosperity to limited populations of workers for limited amounts of time, ready to destroy them (as it has done during the last several decades through the globalization process) as soon as their needs and desires exceed the limits which the quest for profitability imposes. We can see, in particular, that the limited prosperity that waged workers in industrial countries were able to achieve in the post–World War II period was never intended to be generalized. As revolt spread from the colonial plantations of Africa and Asia to the ghettos, the factories, the schools, the kitchens, and even the war front, undermining both the Fordist exchange between higher wages and higher productivity and the use of the colonies (external and internal) as reservoirs of cheap and unpaid labor, the capitalist class resorted to the strategy it has always used to confront its crises: violence, expropriation, and the expansion of the world labor market.

A Marx would be needed to describe the destructive social forces that have been mobilized for this task. Never have so many people been attacked and on so many fronts at once. We must return to the slave trade to find forms of exploitation as brutal as those that globalization has generated in many parts of the world. Not only is slavery reappearing in many forms, but famines have returned, and cannibalistic forms of exploitation unimaginable in the 1960s and 1970s have emerged, including human organ trafficking. In some countries, even the sale of hair, reminiscent of nineteenth-century novels, has been revived. More commonly, in the more than eighty countries affected, globalization has been a story of untreated illnesses, malnourished children, lost lives, and desperation. Impoverishment in much of the world has reached a magnitude never seen before, now affecting up to 70 percent of the population. Just in sub-Saharan Africa the number of those living in poverty and chronic hunger and malnutrition by 2010 had reached 239 million,[20] while across the continent immense amounts of money were obscenely siphoned off to the banks of London, Paris, and New York.

As in the first phase of capitalist development, those most directly affected by these policies have been women, especially low-income women and women of color who in communities across the world today lack the means to reproduce themselves and their families or can do so only by selling their labor on the world labor market and reproducing other families and other children than their own in conditions that separate them from their communities and make their reproductive work more abstract and subject to multiple forms of restriction and surveillance. As an alternative, many give up their children for adoption, work as surrogate mothers, or (in a more recent development) sell their eggs to medical labs for stem cell research. They are also having fewer children, as the need to secure some income has a sterilizing effect. But everywhere their capacity to control their own reproduction is under attack. Paradoxically—and again recapitulating the very conditions that shaped women's entrance in capitalist society and instigated two centuries of witch hunts—the same political class that makes it almost impossible for women to provide for themselves and their families criminalizes them for trying to obtain an abortion. In the U.S. just being pregnant places poor women, particularly black women, in constant danger of arrest.[21]

Women are also targeted because of their subsistence activities, especially their involvement—in Africa, above all—in subsistence farming, which stands in the way of the World Bank's attempt to create land markets and place all natural resources in the hands of commercial enterprises. As I have written elsewhere,[22] the World Bank has adopted the creed that only money is productive, while land is sterile and a cause of poverty if 'only' used for subsistence. Thus, not only has the bank campaigned against subsistence farming, through land law reform, individual titling, and the abolition of customary land tenure, it has also spared no effort to bring women under the control of monetary relations, for example, through the promotion of microfinance, a policy that has already turned millions into indentured servants to the banks and the NGOs that manage the loans.[23] Thus, after years promoting population control through massive sales of contraceptives, the bank now obtains the same result by preventing women from eking out a living by subsistence farming, which (contrary to its claims) is for millions the difference between life and death.[24] It is important to add that the institutional violence against women and the devaluation of the activities around which their lives have been constructed have as their counterpart a documented increase of violence against them by the men in their communities. For, in the face of diminishing wages and diminishing access to land many see women's labor and bodies, and in many cases women's lives and labors, as their bridge to the world market, as is the case with trafficking and dowry murders. Witch-hunting too has returned with globalization, and in many regions of the world—Africa and India, in particular—is generally carried out by young, unemployed men eager to acquire the land of the women they accuse of being witches.[25]

Examples could be multiplied of the ways in which globalization process recapitulates older forms of primitive accumulation. My immediate concern, however, is not to describe the specific forms this return of primitive accumulation has taken but to understand what it reveals about the nature of the capitalist system and what it projects for the future.

The first certainty delivered by this approach is that capitalist accumulation continues to be the accumulation of labor, and as such it continues to require the production of misery and scarcity on a world scale. It continues to require the degradation of human life and the reconstruction of social hierarchies and divisions on the basis of gender, race, and age. Most important, by persisting after five hundred years of capitalist development, these 'original sins' prove to be structural aspects of the capitalist system, precluding any possibility of reform. Indeed, the economic and social programs that international capital has put into place to defeat the liberation movements of the 1960s and 1970s by themselves guarantee that dispossession (from lands and all acquired rights), precarity of access to monetary income and employment, a life under the sign of uncertainty and insecurity, and the deepening of racial and sexual hierarchies will be the conditions of production for generations to come. It is evident, for instance, that by undermining the self-sufficiency of every region and creating a total economic interdependence, even among distant countries, globalization generates not only recurrent food crises but a need for an unlimited exploitation of labor and the natural environment.

As in the past, the foundation of this process is the enclosure of land. This is currently so extensive that even areas of agricultural life that in the past had remained untouched, enabling peasant communities to reproduce themselves, are now privatized, taken over by governments and companies for mineral extraction and other commercial schemes. As 'extractivism'[26] triumphs in many regions, compounded by land grabbing for biofuel, communal landownership is legally terminated, and dispossession is so massive that we are fast approaching the stage described by Marx where "One section of society here demands a tribute from the other for the very right to live on the earth, just as landed property in general involves the right of the proprietors to exploit the earth's surface, the bowels of the earth, the air and thereby the maintenance and development of life."[27]

In Africa, in particular, it is calculated that if the present trends continue, by the middle of the century 50 percent of the population of the continent will live outside of it. This, however, may not be an exceptional situation. Everywhere, because of the impoverishment and displacement globalization has produced, the figure of the worker has become that of the migrant, the itinerant,[28] the refugee. The speed at which capital can travel, destroying in its wake local economies and struggles, and the relentless drive to squeeze out every drop of oil and every mineral that the earth holds in its bowels accelerates this process.

It is not surprising, then, that under these circumstances life expectancy for the working class is diminishing even in 'rich countries' like Germany and the U.S., with the 'poor' expected to live several years less than their parents for the first time since World War II.[29] Meanwhile, some 'Third World' countries are approximating a situation similar to that which prevailed between the sixteenth and eighteenth century, that of a working class hardly capable of reproducing itself. Indeed, Marx's argument in *The Communist Manifesto* that capitalist development produces the absolute impoverishment of the working class is now empirically verified. Witness the incessant migration from the 'South' to the 'North' since the late 1980s, mostly motivated by economic need and the many wars that the corporate lust for mineral resources is generating. We are told that there is no remedy to this immiseration. Plausibly assured by virtue of its military arsenals that, like it or not, the '99%' have no alternatives to life under capitalism and confident that its global reach will provide large markets and ample supplies of labor, the capitalist class now makes little pretense of progress, declaring crises and catastrophes inevitable aspects of economic life, while rushing to remove the guarantees that more than a century of workers' struggles had obtained.

I would argue, however, that this confidence is misplaced. Without indulging in any optimism, which would be irresponsible given the unspeakable devastation unfolding under our eyes, I would affirm that worldwide a consciousness is taking shape—more and more translated into action—that capitalism is 'unsustainable' and creating a different social economic system is the most urgent task for most of the world population. For any system that is unable to reproduce its workforce and has nothing to offer to it except more crises is doomed. If after exploiting every part of the planet for centuries capitalism cannot provide even the minimal conditions of reproduction to all and must continue to plunge millions into miserable living conditions, then this system is bankrupt and has to be replaced. No political system, moreover, can sustain itself in the long term purely by force. Yet it is clear that force is all that the capitalist system has left at its disposal and can now prevail only because of the violence it mobilizes against its opponents.

## Notes

1   Midnight Notes Collective, *The New Enclosures, Midnight Notes* no. 10 (1990).
2   David Harvey, *The New Imperialism* (Oxford: Oxford University Press, 2003).
3   See *The Commoner* no. 2 (September 2001), accessed June 2, 2018, http://www.commoner.org.uk/?p=5.
4   Alice Creischer, Max Jorge Hinderer, and Andreas Siekmann, ed., *The Potosí Principle: Colonial Image Production in the Global Economy* (Cologne: Verlag der Buchhandlung Walther König, 2010).
5   See Mariarosa Dalla Costa, "Capitalism and Reproduction," in *Open Marxism, Vol. 3: Emancipating Marx*, ed. Werner Bonefeld, John Holloway, and Kosmas Psychopedis (London: Pluto Press, 1995), 7–16; Maria Mies, *Patriarchy and Accumulation on a World Scale* (London: Zed Books, 1986); Claudia von Werlhof, "Globalization and the 'Permanent' Process of 'Primitive Accumulation': The Example of the MAI, the Multilateral Agreement on Investment," *Journal of World-Systems Research* 6, no. 3 (2000): 731, accessed June 11, 2018, http://jwsr.pitt.edu/ojs/index.php/jwsr/article/view/199/211.
6   von Werlhof, "Globalization and the 'Permanent' Process of 'Primitive Accumulation,'" 142.
7   Maurizio Lazzarato, *The Making of the Indebted Man: An Essay on the Neoliberal Condition*, Semiotext(e) Intervention Series no. 13 (Cambridge, MA: MIT Press, 2012), 44.
8   Karl Marx, *Capital: A Critique of Political Economy*, Vol. 1, ed. Frederick Engels, trans. Ben Fowkes (London: Penguin, 1990, 876.
9   Marx, *Capital*, Vol. 1, 899.
10  I am quoting von Werlhof, "Globalization and the 'Permanent' Process of 'Primitive Accumulation,'" 733.
11  See von Werlhof, "Globalization and the 'Permanent' Process," 728–47.
12  Massimo De Angelis, *The Beginning of History: Value Struggles and Global Capitalism* (London: Pluto Press, 2007), 134.

13   Federici, *Caliban and the Witch: Women, the Body and Primitive Accumulation* (Brooklyn: Autonomedia, 2004).

14   See *Caliban and the Witch*, especially Chapter 2; Leopoldina Fortunati, *The Arcane of Reproduction: Housework, Prostitution, Labor and Capital*, ed. Jim Fleming, trans. Hillary Creek (Brooklyn: Autonomedia, 1995).

15   Foucault used the concept of 'biopolitics' to describe a new form of power that emerged in Europe in the eighteenth century and was exercised through the regulation of life processes, such as health, disease, and procreation.

16   Marx, *Capital*, Vol.1, 764.

17   I refer here to the argument developed by Hardt and Negri in several works, from *Empire* (Cambridge, MA: Harvard University Press, 2000) to *Commonwealth* (Cambridge, MA: Harvard University Press, 2009) that in the present phase of capitalist development, presumably characterized by the tendential dominance of immaterial labor, the capitalists withdraw from the organization of the labor process, so that workers achieve a higher degree of autonomy and control over the conditions of their work. This theory follows Marx in accentuating the progressive character of capitalist development, seen as the (forced) actualization of the objectives expressed by workers' struggles, which capitalism, against its own interest, must incorporate to reactivate the accumulation process. For a critique of this theory and in particular of the concept of cognitive capitalism, see George Caffentzis and Silvia Federici, "Notes on Edu-factory and Cognitive Capitalism," in *Toward a Global Autonomous University: Cognitive Labor, the Production of Knowledge, and Exodus from the Education Factory*, eds. the Edu-factory Collective (Brooklyn: Autonomedia, 2009), 119–24; Federici, "On Affective Labor," in *Cognitive Capitalism, Education and Digital Labor*, eds. Michael A. Peters and Ergin Bulut (New York: Peter Lang, 2011), 57–74.

18   Federici, "The Reproduction of Labor-Power in the Global Economy," in *Revolution at Point Zero: Housework, Reproduction, and Feminist Struggle* (Oakland: PM Press, 2012).

19   De Angelis, *The Beginning of History*, 136–41.

20   According to statistics issued by the FAO (UN Food and Agriculture Organization), which also calculates that almost a billion people today suffer poverty and hunger worldwide; see "Africa Hunger Facts," *Hunger Notes*, accessed June 2, 2018, https://www.worldhunger.org/africa-hunger-poverty-facts/.

21   See Lynn M. Paltrow and Jeanne Flavin, "Arrests of and Forced Interventions on Pregnant Women in the United States, 1973–2005: Implications for Women's Legal Status and Public Health," *Journal of Health Politics, Policy and Law* 38, no. 2 (April 2013); Lynn M. Paltrow and Jeanne Flavin, "New Study Shows Anti-Choice Policies Leading to Widespread Arrests of and Forced Interventions on Pregnant Women," *Rewire News*, January 14, 2013, accessed June 2, 2018, https://rewire.news/article/2013/01/14/new-study-reveals-impact-post-roe-v-wade-anti-abortion-measures-on-women/.

22   Federici, "Witch-Hunting, Globalization and Feminist Solidarity in Africa Today," *Journal of International Women's Studies* 10, no. 1 (2008): 21–35;

reprinted in Federici, *Witches, Witch-Hunting, and Women* (Oakland: PM Press, 2018), 60–86.

23   See Lamia Karim, *Microfinance and Its Discontents: Women in Debt in Bangladesh* (Minneapolis: University of Minnesota Press, 2011).

24   Sharon Hostetler et al., 'Extractivism': A Heavy Price to Pay (Washington, DC: Witness for Peace, 1995), 3.

25   Hostetler et al., 'Extractivism,' 3.

26   Extractivism is the policy by which governments finance their economic and political programs by exporting their countries' mineral resources, a practice that, according to critics, produces poverty and a process of internal colonization. This term has been especially used by social theorists in Latin America (e.g., Alberto Acosta, Louis Tapia, Raúl Zibechi, Maristella Svampa) to describe and criticize the economic policies of the presumably progressive governments of Bolivia, Ecuador, and Brazil.

27   Karl Marx, *Capital, A Critique of Political Economy*, Vol. 3, ed. Frederick Engels, trans. Ben Fowkes (London: Penguin, 1993), 908–9.

28   This is the term Randy Martin used to describe this process, in *Financialization of Daily Life* (Philadelphia: Temple University Press, 2002).

29   As reported by Maurizio Lazzarato, in Germany life expectancy for low-income earners has dropped from 77.5 years old in 2001 to 75.6 in 2011, while in East Germany it has gone from 77.9 to 74.1. Lazzarato comments that at this pace, with twenty more years of cuts and "efforts to 'save' Social Security," the retirement age will finally coincide with the death age; *The Making of the Indebted Man*, 177. In the U.S., as well, the 'poor' are living shorter lives. According to the August issue of the *Journal of Health Affairs*, from 1990 to 2008 there was an actual decline in life expectancy among blacks and among white women and men who did not complete high school. The study found that white men with 16 years or more of education live 14 years longer than black men with less than 12 years of education, and the disparities are widening. In 1990, the most educated men and women lived 13.4 years and 7.7 years longer, respectively, than the least educated. The most shocking finding of this study is the speed at which this gap has widened. For example, "In 1990 the gap in life expectancy between the most and least educated white females was 1.9 years; now it's 10.4 years." Deirdre Griswold, "Racism, Schooling Gap Cuts Years from Life," *Workers World*, September 27, 2012, accessed June 2, 2018, https://www.workers.org/2012/09/27/racism-schooling-gap-cut-years-from-life/. On the decline of life expectancy among whites in the U.S., see Linda Tavernese, *New York Times*, September 20, 2012. Tavernese writes that among the least educated whites life expectancy has fallen by four years between 1990 and 2012. The decline of life expectancy in the U.S. has accelerated in recent years also due to the opioid epidemic. See Olga Kazan, "A Shocking Decline in American Life Expectancy," *Atlantic*, December 21, 2017, accessed June 21, 2018, https://www.theatlantic.com/health/archive/2017/12/life-expectancy/548981/.

# Introduction to the New Enclosures
## (Midnight Notes Collective)

The historical movement which changes the producers into wage-workers, appears on the one hand as their emancipation from serfdom and from the fetters of the guilds, and this side alone exists for our bourgeois historians. But on the other hand these new freedmen became sellers of themselves only after they had been robbed of all their own means of production and all the guarantees of existence afforded by the old feudal arrangements. And the history of this, their expropriation, is written in the annals of mankind in letters of blood and fire.

—Karl Marx, *Capital*, Vol. 1

The docile Sambo could and did become the revolutionary Nat Turner overnight. The slaves, under the leadership of those from the more complex African societies, fought and ran away, stole and feigned innocence, malingered on the job while seeming to work as hard as possible. And they lived to fight another day.

—George Rawick, *From Sundown to Sunup:
The Making of the Black Community* (1973)

Glasnost; End of the Cold War; United Europe; We Are the World; Save the Amazon Rain Forest.

These are typical slogans of the day. They suggest an age of historic openness, globalism, and the breakdown of political and economic barriers. Yet the last decade has seen the largest enclosure of the worldly commons in history. This introduction explains the meaning

26

and importance of the enclosures, old and new, in the planetary class struggle.

The old enclosures were a counterrevolutionary process whereby, after a century of high wages and breakdown of feudal authority, beginning in the late 1400s, farmers in England had their land and commons expropriated by state officials and landlords. They were turned into paupers, vagabonds, and beggars, and later waged workers, while the land was put to work to feed the incipient international market for agricultural commodities.

According to the Marxist tradition, the enclosures were the starting point of capitalist society,"[1] They were the basic device of 'original accumulation,' which created a population of workers 'free' from any means of reproduction and thus compelled (in time) to work for a wage. The enclosures, however, are not a one-time process exhausted at the dawn of capitalism. They are a regular reoccurrence on the path of capitalist accumulation and a structural component of class struggle.

**The End of All Deals**

Today, once again, the enclosures are a common denominator of proletarian experience across the globe. In the biggest diaspora of the century, on every continent millions are uprooted from their land, their jobs, their homes through wars, famines, plagues, and IMF-ordered devaluations (the four knights of the modern apocalypse) and are scattered to the four corners of the globe.

In Nigeria people are thrown off communally owned land by the military, to make way for plantations owned and managed by the World Bank. The government justifies these measures in the name of the 'debt crisis' and the 'structural adjustment program' allegedly devised to solve it. The SAP for Nigeria is similar to those implemented in Asia, Africa, and Latin America. It includes the commercialization of agriculture and the demonetization of the economy by means of massive devaluations, reducing money wages to their paper value. The result is the destruction of village communities and emigration.

In the United States too, millions are homeless and on the move. The immediate causes are highly publicized: the farm crisis, the steep rise of rental and mortgage payments relative to wages, the warehousing of apartments and the gentrification process, the collapse of the social safety net, and union busting. Behind these factors, however, there is a common reality. The post–World War II interclass deal that guaranteed real wage increases—in exchange for increases in productivity—is over, and even those who have escaped its collapse suffer the loss of the natural commons, due to the vanishing ozone layer and the burning of forests. In China too we have new enclosures. The transition to a 'free market economy' has led to the displacement of one hundred million people from their communally operated lands. Meanwhile, their urban counterparts face the loss of guaranteed jobs in factories and offices and must migrate from one city to another to look for a wage. The 'iron rice bowl' is to be smashed, and a similar scenario is developing in the Soviet Union and Eastern Europe.

The 'debt crisis,' 'homelessness,' and 'the collapse of socialism' are frequently treated as different phenomena by the media and the left. But they are aspects of a single unified process that operates across the planet in different but totally interdependent ways. Under the logic of capitalist accumulation in this period, for every factory in a free-trade zone in China privatized and sold to a New York commercial bank or for every acre of land enclosed by a World Bank development project in Africa or Asia as part of a 'debt for equity' swap, a corresponding enclosure must occur in the U.S. and Western Europe. With each contraction of 'communal rights' in the Third World or of 'socialist rights' in the Soviet Union and China comes a subtraction of our seemingly sacred 'social rights' in the U.S. This subtraction is so thorough that even the definition of what it means to be a human is being revised.

The new enclosures stand for a large-scale reorganization of the accumulation process that has been underway since the mid-1970s, and whose main objective is to uproot workers from the terrain on which their organizational power has been built, so that, like the African slaves transplanted to the Americas, they are forced to work and fight in a strange environment where the forms of resistance possible at home are no longer available. *Thus, once again, as at the dawn of capitalism, the physiognomy of the world proletariat is that of the pauper, the vagabond, the criminal, the panhandler, the street peddler, the refugee sweatshop worker, the mercenary, the rioter.*

**Methods and Consequences of the New Enclosures**

How do the new enclosures work? As in the case of the old enclosures, it is by ending the communal control over the means of subsistence. There are very few populations today who can still directly provide for their needs with their land and work. The last 'aboriginal' populations from

Indonesia to the Amazonas are being violently enclosed in governmental reservations. More commonly, 'peasants' in the Third World today are persons who survive thanks to remittances from brothers or sisters who have emigrated to New York or by working under the most dangerous conditions, growing poppies or coca leaves for export, prostituting to the carriers of hard currency (the greatest and perhaps only aphrodisiac of the age), or migrating to nearby cities or abroad, to join the swelling ranks of day laborers, street peddlers, or 'free enterprise zone' workers, whose conditions are often more dangerous than in the poppy fields back at home.

As in the past, a common method for carrying out the new enclosures is the seizure of land as payment for debt. Just as the Tudor court sold off huge tracts of communal land to its creditors, today's African and Asian governments capitalize and 'rationalize' agricultural land to satisfy the IMF's auditors, who only 'forgive' foreign loans under these conditions. Just as the heads of clans in the Scottish Highlands of the eighteenth century connived with local merchants and bankers, to whom they were indebted, to 'clear the land' of their own clansmen and clanswomen, local chiefs in Africa and Asia exchange communal land rights for unredeemed loans. The result, now as then, is the destruction of customary rights and forms of subsistence. This is the secret of the 'debt crisis.'

The new enclosures make mobile and migrant labor the dominant form of labor. We are now the most geographically mobile labor force since the advent of capitalism. Capital keeps us constantly on the move, separating us from our countries, farms, gardens, homes, and workplaces, because this guarantees cheap wages, communal disorganization, and a maximum vulnerability in front of the law, the courts, and the police. Another consequence of the new enclosures is a dramatic increase in the international competition among workers and an enormous expansion of the world labor market. Socialist workers—one third of the world labor force—will now be forced to compete with the rest of the world proletariat, in exchange for a long forbidden access to the world commodity market.

Another aspect of the new enclosures is the attack on our reproduction that makes us mutants as well as migrants. The disappearance of the rain forest, the hole in the ozone layer, the pollution of the air, the seas, and the beaches, along with the obvious shrinking of our living spaces, all combine to destroy our earthly commons. Even the high seas were enclosed in the 1980s with the dramatic extension of the traditional territorial limits. It is not science fiction to imagine that we are guinea pigs in a capitalist experiment in nonevolutionary species change. We are not alone in this process. Animals, from protozoa to cows, are being engineered and patented to eat oil spills, produce more eggs per hour, secrete more hormones. Increasingly, the land is no longer valued for how much food it can grow or what kind of buildings it can support but for how much radioactive waste it can 'safely' store. *Thus tired earthly commons, the gift of billions of years of laborless transformation, meet tired human bodies.*

Capital has long dreamed of sending us to work in space, where nothing would be left to us except our work machines and rarified and repressive work relations. But the fact is that the earth is becoming a space station where millions are already living in space colony conditions: no oxygen to breathe, limited social and physical contact, a desexualized life, difficulty of communication, lack of sun and green . . . even the voices of migrating birds are missing. Our own bodies are being enclosed. Appearance and attitude are now closely monitored in jobs in the 'service industries,' from restaurants to hospitals. Those who 'work with the public' have their bodies—from their urine to their sweat glands to their brains—constantly checked. Capital treats us today as did the inquisitors of old, looking for the devil's marks of the class struggle on our bodies and demanding that we open them up for inspection. The duty to look pleasant and acceptable explains workers' increasing recourse to reconstructive surgery. The much-publicized silicone breasts of the recent Miss America are an example of this trend. Not only must beauty queens and male leads buy and rebuild their bodies piece by piece, reconstructive surgery is now a must for many jobs in the service economy, further revealing the commodity nature of capitalist relations.

### The Spiral of Struggle

The new enclosures are being fiercely fought, however. The planet is reverberating with anti-IMF demonstrations, riots, and rebellions. In 1989 alone, the streets and campuses of Venezuela, Burma, Zaire, Nigeria, and Argentina saw confrontations between armed troops and students and workers chanting "Death to the IMF," looting foreign commodities markets, decarcerating prisoners, and burning banks. Not only is the money form resisted. From the Andes to Central America and Mexico there is now a war over control of the land. In West Africa there are farmers' struggles against land seizures by the state and the development banks, misrepresented in the United States as 'tribal wars.' In southern Africa, the battle over land, both in town and country, is part of the struggle against apartheid. The struggle for the land is the core of the 'Palestinian issue.' And in Afghanistan, India, Sri Lanka, the Philippines, and Indonesia, proletarians are in up arms against the new enclosures. This is not only a Third World phenomenon. From West Berlin to Zurich, Amsterdam, London, and New York, squatters and homeless people have battled the police, the arsonists in the pay of real estate developers, and other agents of 'spatial deconcentration,' demanding not only 'housing' but land with all that it means.

The new enclosures have also had unintended consequences. They have led to an enormous increase of proletarian knowledge. West African proletarians in the 1980s know what deals can be made in Brooklyn, London, or Venice. Never have proletarians been so compelled to overcome regionalism and nationalism. The very intensity of the debt crisis has forced workers to develop new forms of autonomy and organize reproduction outside the money relation and the standard operating procedures of capitalist society.

**The Marxist Ghost at Midnight**
It is ironic that at the very time when socialism is collapsing, Marx's predictions concerning the development of capitalism are being verified. Though 'postist' intellectuals are now dancing on Marx's grave and 'Marxists' are desperately trying to revise their curriculum vitae, Marx's theory has never seemed so true. What are we seeing now but the famous "immiseration of the working class," "the expansion of the world market," the "universal competition among workers,"[2] and "rising organic composition of capital"? How can we understand anything about this world without using the axioms of Marx's theory of work, money, and profit?

Theoretically, then, Marx's ghost still speaks to us at midnight. Strategically, however, Marx and Engels fail at this moment of the new enclosures. The Marx of *Capital* would understand the new enclosures as he did the old, as a stage in the 'progressive nature' of capitalist development preparing the material conditions for a communist society. The two decisive achievements in this development according to Marx are: the breaking down of local barriers and the unification of the international working class, producing a truly universal human being capable of benefitting from the worldwide production of cultural and material wealth and recognizing a common interest. Indeed, for all the 'blood and fire' they caused, the enclosures were for Marx a historically positive event, for they brought about "the dissolution of private property based on the labor of its owner."

According to Marx, by destroying a mode of production "in which the laborer is the private owner of his means of labor set in action by himself: the peasant of the land which he cultivates, the artisan of the tool which he handles as a virtuoso,"[3] the enclosures have set the stage for the creation of capitalist private property resting on socialized production. The enclosures, therefore, are for Marx the "protracted, violent, and difficult" transformation that makes possible the easier "expropriation of a few usurpers by the mass of people" in the communist revolution.[4]

The problem with this analysis is simple: the new enclosures (and many of the old) are not aimed at petty private producers and their property. They aim to destroy communal lands and spaces that are the basis of proletarian power. A Quiche Indian village in the Guatemalan hills, a tract of communally cultivated land in the Niger Delta, an urban neighborhood like Tepito in Mexico City, or a town surrounding a paper mill controlled by striking paper workers like Jay, Maine, do not fit into Marx's concept of the target of the enclosures. It would be absurd in fact to view the demise of such villages, tracts of land, and neighborhoods as necessary, ultimately positive sacrifices to the development of a truly 'universal' proletariat. Living proletarians must put their feet some place, must strike from some place, must rest some place, must retreat to some place. Class war does not happen on an abstract board toting up profits and losses, it needs a terrain.

In 1867, Marx did not see the power emerging from the communal organization of life of millions in Africa, Asia, Oceania, and the Americas. This failure remains a key element of Marxist thought to this day. "Third World" Marxists still speak of the progressive character of original accumulation. Thus, though they officially fight against capital's new enclosures, they envision a time when their party and state will carry out enclosures of their own, even more efficiently than the capitalists. They too believe that communal ownership of land and local markets has no place in a revolutionary society. Their aim is to nationalize land and wipe out local markets, as well as to expel the IMF and the 'compradora' bourgeoisie from their countries. Consequently, they clash with many of the people who fight against the new enclosures. The confusion escalates at victory time, when there is a tendency to create state plantations (as in Mozambique) and capitalist farms (as in Zimbabwe) at the expense of communal possibilities and actualities. Inevitably, the conditions for counterrevolution ripen, while carrying out autarkic economic measures becomes impossible, as the structures that might have sustained self-sufficiency and denied land to 'contras' are destroyed by the revolutionary forces themselves. Hence the crisis of the Third Worldist left is rooted not only in the maneuvers of the CIA but in the failure of the Marxist view of the enclosures. In contrast, capital's reading of the new enclosures in the face of the collapse of the socialist model and the crisis of the "Third World" revolution is "the End of History"—that is, the triumph of the world market as the mark of a planetary commodification glorified as "Westernization" and "democratization."

How seriously we should take this product of State Department postmodernism is moot, but the scenario it suggests is simple. It brings back the class struggle to its pre–World War I situation, offering two choices to OECD workers: 'liberalism' or 'imperialism.' The liberal option accepts the 'market mechanism,' where we meet as functions of the work process in a triage-like environment, such that upgrading our 'survival skills' becomes the only goal in life. The imperialist one promotes the internationalization of conquest and plunder whereby we become accomplices of our bosses in the exploitation of other proletarians, so that victory means a South African deal: better wages and a home protected by martial law, torture cells at home and abroad, and a gun in the handbag. More probably we'll get a pernicious mix of the two!

## Notes

1   For Marx's analysis of the enclosure process in the development of capitalism, see *Capital: A Critique of Political Economy*, Vol. 1, ed. Frederick Engels, trans. Ben Fowkes (London: Penguin, 1990), Part 8, Chap. 26: "The Secret of Primitive Accumulation."

2   The 'immiseration of the working class,' the 'expansion of the world market,' and the 'universal competition among workers' are the tendencies in capitalist development anticipated by Karl Marx and Frederick Engels in *The Communist Manifesto*, trans. Samuel More (New York: Penguin, 1967 [1848]) and *The German Ideology*, Part 1, ed. C.J. Arthur (New York: International Publishers, 1970 [1847]).

3   Marx, *Capital*, Vol. 1, Part 8, Chap. 32, "The Historical Tendency of Capitalist Accumulation."

4   The reference is to Marx, *Capital*, Vol. 1, Part 8, Chap. 32, "The Historical Tendency of Capitalist Accumulation," p. 930, where Marx writes that while capitalist development was based upon "the expropriation of the mass of people by a few usurpers," in the case of the communist revolution "we have the expropriation of a few usurpers by the mass of the people."

# The Debt Crisis, Africa, and the New Enclosures

> In that brief moment the world seemed to stand still, waiting. There
> was utter silence. The men of Umuofia were merged into the mute
> backcloth of trees and giant creepers, waiting.
>
> The spell was broken by the head messenger. "Let me pass!" he
> ordered.
>
> "What do you want here?"
>
> "The white man whose power you know too well has ordered this
> meeting to stop."
>
> —Chinua Achebe, *Things Fall Apart* (1959).

The international debt crisis can be described as the existence of more
than a trillion dollars of loans, given at quite steep interest rates to Third
World countries, which cannot possibly pay the interest and much less the
principal on these loans due to the collapse of primary commodity prices
and the intense competition in international trade for light manufactured
goods. There have been two major perspectives in the interpretation of
the meaning and consequences of this crisis.

On the one hand, the right sees the crisis as a potential threat to the
international banking system, given the possible default of major Third
World debtor countries. The left, on the other hand, condemns the crisis
as the main obstacle to Third World development. In both cases the proposed solutions stem from the understanding of the 'problems' the crisis
presumably poses. The right sees in the debt crisis an almost ontological
threat to the money form internationally, a justification for the harsh policies the IMF has imposed to force Third World countries to 'pay up.' By

34

contrast, left economists have not only decried the human costs of these policies but have argued that since they block the development of Third World economies, they will necessarily prolong the debt crisis. In brief, for the right the debt crisis threatens the 'stable growth' of the creditor economies, while for the left the debt crisis is the main obstacle to the economic development of the debtor nations. These two contrasting views share one common assumption: the debt crisis is a threat or an obstacle to capitalist development in the 1990s. We disagree with this assumption and argue that the debt crisis has been a productive crisis for the capitalist classes of both the debtor and the creditor nations. For the debt crisis has been a key instrument that capital has used to shift the balance of class forces on both poles of the debt relation, thereby resolving its productivity crisis.

That the debt crisis is a productive crisis for capital is nowhere as visible as in Africa. Here we can see that the policies which the debt crisis has generated aim to 'rationalize' class relations, beginning with the most vexed question of capitalist development: Who owns the land? It is an axiom of development theory that no capitalist industry can be created without a 'rationalized' agriculture. Rationalization is not only a matter of using tractors and fertilizers; privatizing land property relations is infinitely more important. The debt crisis has been a crucial instrument of this 'rationalization' of land property in Africa.

### Settling the Land Question

Why is the 'land question' so central in Africa? The answer is simple. On most of the African continent communal claims to the land are still strong, for colonial domination failed to destroy (to a degree unmatched in any other part of the world) preexisting communal relations, beginning with people's relation to the land. This is a factor bemoaned by leftist and rightist developers alike as the main reason for Africa's economic 'backwardness.' The London *Economist* spelled it out in a May 1986 "Nigeria Survey," stressing how crucial "the land question" still is in the region. In a section titled "The Capitalist Flaw," we read that "with two exceptions, Kenya and Zimbabwe (which) were both subjected to farming by white men under European laws of ownership and inheritance, practically everywhere in the African continent, customary land-use laws prevail, which recognize ancient, communal rights to the land."

This means that a prospective investor must negotiate with and pay the community "for each tree, for firewood rights, for the grazing of women's goats, for grandfather's grave." This is true even in countries like Nigeria, where the state nationalized all the land in 1978. To illustrate this scandal, the survey shows the picture of a herd of cows circulating undisturbed, side by side with a car, in the midst of a Nigerian city, cowherd et al.

Predictably, the *Economist* concludes that Africa's land "must be enclosed, and traditional rights of use, access and grazing must be extinguished," for everywhere "it is private ownership of land that has made capital work."[1] Land expropriation therefore, is the precondition both for a commercialized agriculture and for a wage-dependent and disciplined proletariat.

The survey overlooks the fact that land expropriation has by no means been limited to settlers' economies, and that the privatization of land has proceeded at an accelerated pace, including in the 1970s and 1980s, due to World Bank Agricultural Development Projects, which under the guise of 'modernization' have introduced not only tractors but new class ownership relations in Africa's rural areas. New property relations have also been spurred by government dictated expropriation drives (for infrastructural development, oil exploration, etc.), as well as by the massive urbanization process, and not least the growing refusal of the new generations to spend their life 'in the bush' following their parents footsteps.

Yet to this day at least 65 percent of the sub-Saharan African population lives by subsistence farming, carried out mostly by women.[2] Even when urbanized, many Africans expect to draw some support from the village, as the place where one may get food when on strike, where one thinks of returning in old age, where, if one has nothing to live on, one may get some unused land to cultivate from a local chief or a plate of soup from neighbors and kin. The village is the symbol of a communal organization of life that, though under attack, has not completely disintegrated. Witness the responsibility that those who move to the cities still have toward the community at home, a responsibility that easily becomes a burden but serves to support many who otherwise would remain behind. In Nigeria, for instance, villages often pull together to pay the fees to send some children to school, with the expectation that once in possession of a diploma they, in turn, will help people at home.

'The village' to this day forms the reproductive basis of many African countries, particularly for the proletariat, who, once urbanized, can rarely afford the nuclear-family 'lifestyle' that is typical among the middle class. Yet even among the middle class the nuclear family still competes with the village, which (thanks mostly to its women) refuses to be treated like an obsolescent factory. This conflict between city and village is the subject of many tales picturing overdemanding kin driving their urbanized children into corruption by their unreasonable expectations. But in reality, these 'unreasonable' demands have kept the pressure on the urban wage, ensuring a higher level of consumption both in village and in the urban centers, such that the consciousness of the cultural and material wealth produced worldwide exists in every bush.

The survival of communal ties and the lack of a tradition of wage dependence have had many consequences in Africa's political economy. First, they have fostered a sense of entitlement with respect to the distribution of wealth in the community and by the state. Second, they have been responsible for the fact that most African proletarians fail to experience capital's laws as natural laws, even though the struggle to gain access to what industrial development can provide is now a general factor of social change.

This must be emphasized, given the tendency in the United States to see Africans as either helpless victims (of government corruption or natural disasters) or protagonists of backward struggles revolving around tribal allegiances (a myth perpetrated by the Western media to encourage a standoff policy with respect to people's struggles in the continent). In reality, from the fields to the factories, the markets, and the schools, struggles are being carried out that not only are often unmatched for their combativeness but are very 'modern' in their content. Their objective is not the preservation of a mythical past but the redefinition of what development means for the proletariat: access to the wealth produced internationally but not at the price that capital puts on it.

Examples of the combativeness and modernity of proletarian struggle in Africa could be multiplied, ranging from the resistance to being counted (in Nigeria the idea of a census is still a government 'utopia') through the resistance to tax collection (an occupation which often calls for bodyguards) to the resistance to land expropriation (which often turns into an open warfare). Even though the land has been nationalized in Nigeria, negotiations with local chiefs are still necessary before any tract of land can be appropriated by the government and, until recently, compensation for trees and crops had to be paid. Finally, resistance to waged work far exceeds what could be expected from a workforce that is at most 20 percent of the population.

The African proletariat's resistance to capital's laws has escalated among the new generations who have grown up in a period of intense liberation struggles (Guinea-Bissau in 1975, Angola and Mozambique in 1976, Zimbabwe in 1980) and now see 'the West' through the eyes of Soweto. Over the last decades, this youth has made international capital despair of the possibility of increasing Africans' discipline and productivity.

Thus, throughout the 1970s and 1980s, prior to the debt crisis, a consensus grew within international capital that Africa was a basket case, and the only hope for its future lay in a drastic reduction of its population. On trial has been 'Africa's resistance to development.' The *Wall Street Journal* tells us that Africa is the only region in the world that has experienced no growth in the post–World War II period. Further, the Africans' attachment to 'their traditional ways'—code for anticapitalist behavior—and their demand for a higher standard of living, particularly in countries like Nigeria or Zambia, which in the 1970s (due to oil and copper prices) experienced a leap in the national wealth, must be combated, if any form of capitalist development is to take place in the region. In response to these structural and political problems, international capital has put into place a policy of planned underdevelopment, with the denial of communal land claims at its core. Not only have companies fled from Africa in search of safer havens in American or Swiss banks, but foreign investors have dwindled to a handful. Africa in the 1970s and 1980s was the region that attracted the lowest rate of capital investment. Foreign aid and African exports have also collapsed. Meanwhile the dangers of 'population explosion' as a harbinger of revolution have become the gospel of international agencies and African politicians alike. As a result, in the words of Alden W. Clausen, the president of the World Bank, "Africa today is experiencing the worst depression of any world region since World War II." This means that from capital's viewpoint, Africa is the bottom of the barrel, the area where the most resistance to development is met.

The extent to which capital despairs of the profitability of African economies is made clear by the gloomy tones in which Africa is usually discussed and the disregard international capital displays with respect to the preservation of African labor. Africa is now the place for medical testing of anti-AIDS vaccines.[3] It is the chemical/nuclear dustbin of the world, the region where expired pharmaceutical products or products banned in Europe or the United States, from medicines to pesticides, are dumped.[4]

It is within this scenario that we must understand the development of the debt crisis, which by the early 1980s affected more than twenty-five African countries.

## The Debt Crisis as Productive Crisis for Capital

It is difficult to measure to what extent the escalation of the debt has been caused by the pressure exercised by proletarian demands, which in the 1970s forced African governments to borrow money from foreign banks or was engineered by international capital to force African governments to implement drastic policy reforms. What is certain is that the debt crisis has provided national and international capital with a golden opportunity to implement a wide-ranging restructuring of class relations aimed to cheapen the cost of labor, raise social productivity, reverse 'social expectations,' and open the continent to a full penetration of capitalist relations, having the capitalist use of the land as its basis.

As in other Third World areas, the crisis in Africa has unfolded through two different phases, each differentiated by a more or less direct intervention of foreign governments and by the role played by international agencies. There has been, in fact, a division of labor between the International Monetary Fund (IMF) and the World Bank, corresponding not so much to the need to integrate 'soft cop/hard cop' policies, as to the need to deal with different levels of proletarian resistance, the key factor in the dialectic of development and repression. Phase I, roughly lasting from 1980 to 1984, was dominated by IMF 'monetarist policies.' This was the phase when, as country after country defaulted on interest payments, arrangements were made with the IMF for standby loans in exchange for the infamous IMF conditionalities: cuts in subsidies to products and programs, wage freeze, retrenchment in the public sector, and massive devaluations, which in many cases virtually demonetarized the affected economies. But by 1984, such was the resistance to further austerity measures and the hatred for the IMF that a new strategy had to be devised, accompanied by a change of the guard in the form of a World Bank takeover. Thus Phase II, which began in 1984, took the form of a World Bank promoted 'economic recovery' and 'development' plan.

The World Bank is an old acquaintance of the African continent, where in the post-independence period it rushed to replace the departing colonial administrators. In the 1980s, it has played the role of capital's éminence grise in Africa. Hardly a plan or a deal has been made

39

without its intervention, in its capacity as lender, advisor, or controller, and in its latest self-representation as 'knowledge bank.' In 1984, the bank announced it would raise $1 billion to provide fifty 'soft loans' to sub-Saharan nations prepared to accept its recipe for 'economic recovery' and embark on the path of economic reforms. This 'special facility for Africa,' which under the name of 'structural adjustment program' (SAP) was the model for the Baker Plan launched at Seoul in October 1985 at an international meeting of the IMF and World Bank,[5] emerged as the vehicle for the much hailed conversion to a free-market economy undergone by many African countries since 1985.

The SAP, in fact, is Reaganite laissez-faire applied to the Third World. Its essential model is Milton Friedman's formula for post-Allende Chile, which demands the removal of all measures protecting the standard of living of the working class and forces workers to survive only to the extent that they work in conditions competitive with those of other proletarians worldwide. Hence, wage levels are decided by an assessment of the international labor market combined with state repression, to ensure that wages never rise to 'international levels.'

SAPs require much repression. In Chile, its implementation cost the lives of thirty thousand workers, butchered in homage to the new market freedom. An SAP also means that in exchange for 'growth-oriented' loans, a country accepts the liberalization of imports, the privatization of state industries, the abolition of all restrictions on currency exchange and commodity prices, the demise of any subsidy program, and further devaluations, with the loans financing these programs and setting up export-oriented agricultural and industrial sectors. In the rhetoric of business and the World Bank, once the prices of commodities, services, and labor are allowed to 'adjust to their market value' and imported commodities are once again available in the markets, everyone will be incentivized to produce more, foreign investment will flow, exports will grow, earning solid hard currency, and recovery will finally be at hand. But in reality, the SAP means that millions of Africans, whose monthly wages average at best thirty dollars, are asked to pay American-type prices for the commodities and services they need. Even the local food prices reach prohibitive levels as the land is increasingly cultivated with crops that are not destined for local consumption.

The SAP, in fact, is the vehicle for the integration of the African proletariat into the world market along lines not dissimilar to those of colonial times, as they are now expected to produce crops they will not consume and pay for what they buy at the international price levels, at the very time when their wages not only have vanished because of retrenchment but have become meaningless in the face of astronomical devaluations. The integration of the African proletariat into the world market via the SAP is visible also at the level of the new bosses. With the new productivity campaign, all attempts at 'indigenization' have been dropped and expatriate managers and technicians are flocking back, as in the old colonial days. The hope is that white masters will be more effective in making people work than their African counterparts have been.

As key managers of this new turn have been foreign agencies (IMF, World Bank, the Paris Club, and the London Club, in addition to the commercial banks), the measures adopted have written another chapter in neocolonial relations, with Western banks and agencies replacing the colonial powers in their imperial role. The comparison with colonial times is not unfounded. Once in the grip of IMF and Co., a country loses any shred economic and political independence. IMF representatives sit on the board of the central bank, no major economic project can be carried out without their approval, storms of foreign officers periodically descend on it to check account books, and no government can steer a politically independent path, even if it wanted to, since every few months it must plead with foreign agencies for debt rescheduling or new loans.

The case of Liberia, which a few years ago asked Washington to send a team of managers to run its economy,[6] is but an extreme example of what is happening in most of Africa today. Equally telling are the overtures African governments (e.g., Cameroon, Ivory Coast, Nigeria) are making to Israel and South Africa, with whom, for a long time, caution advised secret relations. Thus, it is possible to speak of the recolonization of Africa under the hegemony of Western powers, who are using the crisis to recuperate what was lost in the wake of the anticolonial struggles.

All this should not hide the fact that both the crisis and the help from abroad have been welcomed by the dominant sectors of the African ruling class. For they have used the external debt to free themselves from the concessions they were forced to make to workers in the aftermath of independence and to stem the militancy of the new generations. Undoubtedly African leaders have had to swallow a few bitter pills. For the African ruling class today, integration with international capital is a different deal from the one that it was able to strike in the post-independence period.

African nations were then confronting a less unified capitalist front (with the U.S. competing with the old colonial powers and the Soviet Union for a political role in the continent). Today the main branches of international capital are integrated. Thus, the nationalist games that African leaders were able to play—publicly boasting nonalignment and pan-Africanism while dealing behind closed doors with South Africa (e.g., Nigeria) and taking money from 'East' and 'West'—are no longer possible. Nor is it possible for them to continue to oscillate between the Scylla of a demagogic socialism and the Charybdis of a waste of capital funds for visibly unproductive purposes.

The African leaders have also been put on trial. The golden mouthpieces of international capital have accused them of a personalistic attachment to capital (the famous 'corruption' charge) and lack of managerial skills. But the chastisement has been acknowledged as useful in most African quarters. The debt crisis has been a 'consciousness-raising' process for African leaders, who have learned that they cannot rule without the help of Washington, London, and Paris, and who, in face of the 'crisis,' have shown the fundamental similarities of their political stands, regardless of how much socialist rhetoric some may flaunt. This is why they have so easily bent to foreign capital's demands. It was not because of their helplessness in the face of Washington and London but because of their helplessness in the face of the African people. Not accidentally, with the brief exception of Tanzania under Nyerere, nowhere has an African government attempted to mobilize the population that would have eagerly responded to the call for default. On the contrary, they have 'passed along' the most murderous austerity policies, diverting substantial amounts of presumably scarce foreign currency to buttress their armies and police forces with the latest anti-riot equipment, while playing helpless before the IMF. The debt crisis has, thus, unambiguously shown that in order to maintain their rule African governments must depend on the support of Washington, London, and Paris.

One of the main results of the debt crisis has been the reorganization of the mechanism of capitalist command, beginning with the unification of 'metropolitan' and 'peripheral' capital. Such has been the willingness of African leaders to comply with international capital—often implementing austerity measures stiffer than those required by World Bank and the IMF—that a number of African countries (e.g., Morocco, Ghana, and Nigeria) are becoming showpieces for multinational agencies.

The turning point came in the spring of 1986, when the Organization of African Unity (OAU) decided to bring Africa's debt problem to the United Nations, asking Western countries to help solve it. By this time almost every country in the continent was defaulting on its interest payments and many countries were devoting 30 to 40 percent of their budgets to debt servicing—a percentage that leftist economists consider a recipe for economic disaster.

This unprecedented move was a decisive ideological victory for the Western Powers who, after decades of anti-imperialist rhetoric, felt vindicated in their pre-independence misgivings. ("We told you that you were not ready!") By defeating a resolution pointing to their responsibility in the African crisis at this special UN session, they made it clear they would no longer hear about how colonialism has pauperized Africa. Indeed, it is now accepted wisdom in the U.S. media that colonialism bears no responsibility for what's happening today in Africa.

The 1986 UN session was the Canossa of African governments. They publicly recognized that by themselves they cannot rule the continent. The meeting served as the occasion for the old and new colonial powers (like Japan) to jump into the saddle. Shultz's triumphal trip through Africa in June 1986 and the murder, one year later, of the president of Burkina Faso, Thomas Sankara, at the time the living symbol of pan-Africanism and anti-imperialism, sealed the deal.[7]

Since then, the 'debt crisis' has unfolded in Africa in all its mathematical logic, showing how misleading it is to view it as a quantitative crisis, as it is usually presented. The fallacy of the numerical approach is to believe that from capital's viewpoint 'economic recovery' is equal to 'debt reduction.' But if this were the case, much of what is happening around the debt would be incomprehensible. For in most countries, the debt has escalated dramatically since the acceptance of the IMF–World Bank's economic recovery measures. The Nigerian debt rose, for instance, from $20 to $30 billion after structural adjustment measures were introduced. The reason for this apparently paradoxical result is that the debt crisis is not determined by the amount of debt due or paid up but by the processes activated through it: wage freezes, the collapse of any local industry not connected to foreign capital (which provides the hard currency needed for technology and capital investment), the banning of unions, the end of free education even at the primary level, the imposition of draconian laws making strikes and other social struggles an act of economic sabotage, the banning of militant student organizations, and above all the privatization of land. The function of the debt crisis is best seen perhaps in the well-financed escalation of repressive measures in the debtor countries. The latest technological tools of repression (cars, walkie-talkies, Israeli security guards) have arrived in Africa in the wake of the debt crisis. 'Defense' spending is the only type of spending that international agencies have not begrudged African governments, although they count every penny when it comes to health or education. For capital, 'crisis' is a misnomer—but it is a crisis for the working class.

What this has meant for people can be seen by looking at Ghana, an IMF 'success story,' from the viewpoint of the extensiveness of the trade liberalization allowed and the present growth rate. Since 1983, when Ghana decided to comply with the IMF, the national currency, the cedi, has collapsed nearly 100 percent in value. As a result, the banknotes that people are paid with are worthless, which means that the majority of Ghanaians have been demonetized. Unions, however, have been sufficiently intimidated (thanks also to Jerry Rawlings's past reputation as 'man of the people') as to subscribe to the plan and keep workers from striking. Thus, international capital's initiative has forced Ghanaians to leap beyond the money relation. Today the monthly salary of midlevel civil servants hardly pays for one-third of their families' monthly food bill. This means that their lives must be a constant wheeling and dealing, which today consumes all their energies. (In the long run, though, the experience of having to constantly invent new means of reproduction may produce some unexpected results.)

Currently in Ghana, many hold on to a waged job only in the hope of 'chopping for the work side,' which means using the facilities and utilities of the workplace for their reproduction. Wage or no wage, eking out a living is an endless struggle, with prostitution, touting to tourists, subsistence farming, and remittances from abroad being (for most) the only alternatives to starving or thieving. Meanwhile, over the last four years two million Ghanaians, almost 20 percent of the Ghanaian population, have emigrated to Italy, Iceland, and Australia, and many others are on the way out. They are called 'road people,' planetary transients, often thrown overboard from ships they illegally boarded, going from port to port in search of a country that will let them in, ready to work under any conditions, since a few dollars earned selling watches or bags in New York can support a family in Accra or Dakar. The flight from all parts of Africa is so massive that it has turned into a job of its own, with people specializing in how to circumvent the restrictions foreign embassies place on visas.

Everywhere, from Nigeria to Tanzania, a new diaspora is at work, sending millions to work in Europe and the U.S. This diaspora is a gold mine for European and American capital, which still relishes the basic principle of the old slave trade: people are more productive once uprooted from their homes. Meanwhile, the number and status of the migrants are monitored by World Bank demographers, who, with Nazi-like scientific precision, periodically record what countries fall below the caloric requirements for work, or 'just' survival. Hunger is reappearing in surprising places like Nigeria, traditionally the yam basket of Africa, even in times of bumper crops. Not only is meat disappearing, gari (cassava flour), traditionally the cheapest and most basic staple, is becoming unaffordable, at least in the urban centers, where it must be transported by trucks and vans fueled with gasoline costing now what whisky cost in the past. At the heart of the debt crisis agenda there is the annihilation of the old African system of reproduction of life and labor power, the village and communal land tenure, as the aim of the IMF and the World Bank is to make both land and people available for more intense exploitation.

The first phase of the debt crisis—the demonetization of African economies—told Africans that from a capitalist point of view they were dead, and the time when they could live in the interstices between the village and the international market was over. The famines of 1984–1985 made this point with brutal force throughout Africa. The second phase of the debt crisis, the SAP phase, was (and continues to be) the time of land enclosures. Its message has been that either farmers and miners employ the land for production for the national and international market or the land will be appropriated by those who will. If this 'structural adjustment' succeeds, 'Mother Africa' will be finished.

### New Social Struggles

The debt crisis is almost a textbook case of the old-time truth that economic liberalism not only is compatible with but, at crucial times, requires social fascism. The Chilean road to economic recovery is today applied to most of the liberalized, structurally adjusted countries of Africa. The Chilean recipe has been learned almost by rote: student organizations must be banned and driven underground, unions must be intimidated, security forces must be remodeled (usually with the help of shadowy

U.S.-British-French-Israeli advisors). New anti-crime legislations are also now standard. In Nigeria we have Decree 20 against 'economic sabotage'— this includes strikes at oil sites (establishing a death penalty for such saboteurs)—and Decree 2 establishing preventive detention for up to six months. Increasingly, capital punishment is used as a weapon in the 'war against armed robbery,' the Nigerian equivalent of 'the War on Drugs.' As for the spaces left to 'freedom of speech,' let us just mention the case of Nigeria, where even seminars on the SAP attended by Nobel Prize winners like Wole Soyinka are nowadays met with armed policemen at the doors.

But none of these measures have put an end to the resistance against the 'economic recovery measures.' The first major failure of IMF policies appeared in Zambia in December of 1986, a few months after the UN conference on Africa. The Zambian government, amid Kenneth Kaunda's tears, had to turn its back on the IMF following massive anti-IMF, anti-austerity riots in the north of the country—the heart of the copper fields. After another round of price increases and a further devaluation of the kwacha, people engaged in the most violent protests since independence. The government had to call in army combat units and seal off the borders. The riot was sparked by the announcement that the government was going to double the price of maize meal as demanded by the IMF. Upon hearing of this plan, housewives, youth, and the unemployed took to the streets, attacking warehouses where the maize was stored, and soon every other store became a target. The crowd appropriated TVs, stereos, and even cars, stoned policemen, attacked government offices, and burned down the presidential headquarters in Kalulushi (hence Kaunda's tears). Ten people were reportedly killed in the many days of rioting, but in the end the government had to reduce the price of maize and tell the IMF that it could no longer comply.

The resistance in Nigeria has been equally violent and persistent. From the earliest phase of the government's negotiations with the IMF, students, market women, and workers have gone in to the street protesting against the end of free education, against the requirement of tax certificates for school children enrolled in primary schools, against wage freezes and the removal of subsidies for domestically sold petroleum.

The involvement of students in the riots in both Zambia and Nigeria is not surprising. All over Africa students have been at the forefront of the anti-SAP protest.[8] Despite the fact that they are a privileged minority, often ready after graduation to compromise their political convictions for a government job, students in many African countries are now forced by the objective conditions of the IMF plans for education in Africa to take a more radical stand, as the IMF prescribes a drastic reduction in the number of high school and college graduates in order to contain wages and reduce expectations. Structural adjustment is the death pill of the post-independence 'social contract' that promised a secure future to those with a high school or university degree. Following its introduction unemployment has become rampant among graduate students. Currently many graduates, even university-trained engineers, are lucky if they manage to drive a cab. It is no accident, then, that the imposition of the IMF austerity measures has been accompanied by an attack on students and students' organizations.

A good example of this violent repression has occurred on May 26, 1986. In the wake of a peaceful demonstration held at Ahmadu Bello University in Zaria (northern Nigeria) and one week prior to the arrival of IMF–World Bank officers in Lagos, who were to check Nigeria's books and economic plans, truckloads of mobile policemen invaded the campus, shooting students and visitors on sight. Machine-gun-firing police chased the students into the dorms, where scores were later found wounded or dead, and into surrounding village houses where they had tried to take refuge. More than forty people were killed and many more were wounded. The massacre did not stop the protests, however. In the following days, riots exploded all over the country. Students in Lagos, Ibadan, and other campuses blocked the streets, attacked government buildings and prisons (decarcerating hundreds of prisoners, including some from death row), and vandalized the premises of those newspapers that had ignored the protest.

Since then, anti-SAP riots have become endemic in Nigeria, culminating in May and June of 1989, with new uprisings in the main southern cities of Lagos, Bendel, and Port Harcourt. Once again, crowds of students, women, and the unemployed jointly confronted the police and burned many government buildings to the ground. In Bendel, the prison was ransacked, hundreds of prisoners were set free, and food was confiscated in the prison pantry and later distributed to the hospitals, where patients notoriously starve unless they can provide their own food. More than four hundred people reportedly were killed in Nigeria in the same days as Tiananmen Square, although barely a word about the riots and these massacres could be found in the U.S. media.

Anti-IMF protests have also occurred in Zaire, where in December 1988 a crowd of women were machine-gunned by government troops. Then in February 1989, scores of students were killed or wounded in Kinshasa and at the University of Lumumbashi following protests against the rise of bus fares, which had led some students to take over a government bus. In Ghana too student-government confrontation has been the order of the day since the implementation of the IMF deal.

Massive uprisings are but one part of resistance against austerity and structural adjustment. Daily warfare is fought at the motor parks against the hike of transport prices, at the *'bukas'* where people insist on having a piece of meat in their soup without having to pay the extra price, and at the markets where people defy government attempts to ban 'illegal' (i.e., non-taxpaying) vendors. Along with this micro-struggle against the IMF policies, armed robbery, smuggling, and land wars have also exploded. These struggles have not been in vain. The recent decision at the Paris summit of the OECD (held during the bicentennial of the storming of the Bastille) to cancel a part of the African debt for those countries that implemented SAPs (up to 50 percent for the 'poorest') is a recognition of their power.

### Jubilees, Moratoriums, and the End of the Debt Crisis

In conclusion, I have shown that both the left and right analyses of the debt crisis are inadequate to the task: charting its dynamics and determining its end. The debt crisis constitutes a problem of accumulation for both right and left. But neither can explain why the crisis appeared at this time, and why it has developed into a chronic aspect of contemporary capitalist development. Most fundamentally, neither can suggest what may put an end to the crisis. The reason for the failure of both right and left analyses is that they do not see that the target of the debt crisis is not the official debtors (the Third World nations, banks, and corporations) but those who fall outside of the credit system in the first place: the African workers. This failure is most easily recognized in Africa where the idea—for instance—that a wage worker in Lagos or a farmer in the rural Kano province of Nigeria may be in debt to the IMF appears immediately absurd. Once we view the debt crisis as directed at the non-debtors it becomes clear why the crisis has become chronic, despite the manipulation of a Brady or a Baker. No one in the capitalist class, inside or outside of Africa, wants to end the debt crisis in Africa. Rather, the idea is to manage it. For debt is doing its job as part of the credit system, that is supposed to "accelerate the material development of the productive forces and the establishment of the world market."

This being said, we must recognize that the debt crisis is a rather dangerous instrument, as its internationalization opens a worldwide circuit of struggle that increasingly includes Eastern Europe, the USSR, and even China. Thus, it may produce new forms of solidarity within the international proletariat. Indeed, the swindle of the debt crisis can be turned into the "dissolution of the old mode of production,"[9] as was once predicted by an old Moorish debtor.

## Notes

1    "Nigeria Survey," *Economist*, May 3, 1986.
2    Stephanie Hanson, "Backgrounder: African Agriculture," *New York Times*, May 28, 2008, accessed June 21, 2018, https://archive.nytimes.com/www. nytimes.com/cfr/world/slot2_20080528.html?pagewanted=print.
3    In the 1980s, both French and U.S. medical centers conducted tests in the Congo and other parts of Africa, often using live vaccines. One reason given for the choice of Africa as the testing ground according to Dr. Robert W. Ryder, the director of the American AIDS research program: "What we can do here [Zaire]...that we cannot do in the United States is to follow thousands and thousands of AIDS victims because wages are low enough to permit it"; *New York Times*, August 2, 1988. Even more explicit was Dr. Jeffrey C. Laurence, an AIDS researcher at the Cornell Medical Center, who argued that "until researchers devise new techniques . . . it is almost inevitable that science will get a little quick and dirty." Lawrence K. Altman, "Test on Humans Near in AIDS Vaccine Hunt," *New York Times*, March 18, 1987, accessed July 13, 2018, https://www. nytimes.com/1987/03/18/us/test-on-humans-near-in-aids-vaccine-hunt.html. Today, as well, Africa is the land of experimentation for vaccines for AIDS. A large-scale testing was slated to begin in November 2016, as announced by Anthony S. Fauci, the director of the U.S. Centers for Disease Control: see National Institutes of Health, "Large-Scale HIV Vaccine Trial to Launch in South Africa," May 18, 2016, accessed May 20, 2018, https://www.nih.gov/news-events/news-releases/large-scale-hiv-vaccine-trial-launch-south-africa.
4    At the time of the writing the U.S. was exporting hazardous waste to Africa. The U.S. was also among a small number of countries who, years later, in 1998, refused to sign on to a decision by the European Union to ban the export of toxic waste to countries of the Third World. See "International—Western firms dump toxic waste in Africa," October 19, 2006, accessed May 20, 2018, www.anphoblacht.com/contents/15909. A 1998 article reported that international waters were filled with ships waiting to unload their toxic cargo.
5    The plan James Baker, at the time U.S. Secretary of the Treasury, launched in Seoul was advertised as the solution for combating the international debt crisis.

6   In 1987, the United States agreed to send seventeen financial experts to Liberia "with authority to manage that country's debt-ridden economy"; see "U.S. Experts to Manage Ailing Liberian Economy," *New York Times*, March 5, 1987, accessed May 20, 2018, https://www.nytimes.com/1987/03/05/business/ us-experts-to-manage-ailing-liberia-economy.html.

7   At the time of his assassination, clearly motivated by the desire to silence one of Africa's most inspiring rebel voices, Thomas Sankara was the symbol of anti-imperialism in Africa. His government eschewed all foreign aid, planned to nationalize all land and mineral wealth, rejected reliance on the IMF and World Bank. His domestic policies focused on agrarian self-sufficiency and land reform, prioritized education, and promoted public health. "Other components of his national agenda included planting trees to halt the desertification of the Sahel, redistributing land from feudal lords to peasants, ending rural poll taxes and establishing a road and railway construction programme to 'tie the nation together'"; "Thomas Sankara," *Wikipedia*, accessed May 20, 2018, https://en.wikipedia.org/wiki/Thomas_Sankara.

8   For an analysis and account of student struggles against the IMF and the SAP, see Silvia Federici, George Caffentzis, and Ousseina Alidou, *A Thousand Flowers: Social Struggles against Structural Adjustment in African Universities* (Trenton, NJ: Africa World Press, 2000).

9   The reference is to Karl Marx, *Capital: A Critique of Political Economy*, Vol. 3, ed. Frederick Engels, trans. Ben Fowkes (London: Penguin, 1991), Part IV, Chapter 27, 572. Marx writes, "The credit system accelerates the material development of the productive forces and the creation of the world market.... At the same time, credit accelerates the violent outbreaks of this contradiction, crises, and with these the elements of dissolution of the old mode of production."

# China: Breaking the Iron Rice Bowl

The bourgeoisie, by the rapid improvement of all instruments of production, by the immensely facilitated means of communication, draws all, even the most barbarian, nations into civilization. The cheap prices of its commodities are the heavy artillery with which it batters down all Chinese walls, with which it forces the barbarians' intensely obstinate hatred of foreigners to capitulate.
—Karl Marx, *The Communist Manifesto*

Why are the people starving?
Because the rulers eat up the money in taxes.
Therefore the people are starving.
Why are the people rebellious?
Because the rulers interfere too much.
Therefore they are rebellious.
Why do the people think so little of death?
Because the rulers demand too much of life.
Therefore the people take death lightly.
Having little to live on, one knows better than to value life too much.
—Lao Tzu, *Tao Te Ching*

The repression of the worker and student protest in China is presented by the media and the U.S. government as one more example of the pitfalls of realized socialism, as well as an unambiguous sign of the commitment by the Chinese proletariat to a free-market economy. Thus, we are told that the students and workers on Tiananmen Square fought for Freedom and

Democracy and for the acceleration of the process that, over the last fifteen years, has put China on the road to a liberalized economy.

That this is the portrait of the events in China we are presented is no surprise. Both the Chinese and U.S. governments have much to gain by such an account. From the U.S. viewpoint, presenting the student-worker struggle as one exclusively aiming at political liberalization serves to hide its economic dimension. Reporters have not asked students about their living conditions or the demands of the Workers Autonomous Association, the new independent workers' union that has a tent in Tiananmen Square together with the students. This account also serves to bolster the claim that what is at stake is a choice between freedom (i.e., capitalism) and total-itarianism, and thus to refuel the Cold War ideology currently in danger of being debunked by Gorbachev's love affair with the 'free market' and the rush of Eastern Europe to 'Westernize.' The too-rapid collapse of Cold War tensions worries the U.S. government, because it risks undermining its right to maintain a nuclear arsenal in Europe, which—as Kissinger recently reminded us—is a must for U.S. hegemony. (Hence, the current Kissinger-Bush policy efforts to simultaneously bolster the Deng govern-ment, while continuing to make of it an ideological enemy). From this perspective, to maintain the specter of a totalitarian, bloodthirsty com-munism is a must, particularly when dealing with allies like the Germans, who are calling for an immediate reduction of U.S. short-range missiles in Europe, while simultaneously profiting from the labor of the 'communist' workers of Eastern Europe.

As for the Chinese government, it is in their interest to present the worker-student movement as a foreign, 'counterrevolutionary' plot. As in other Third World countries, they know that appealing to anti-imperialist feelings is a good card. They capitalize on the hostility that is growing in China against the economic liberalization process, though they are com-mitted to continue on the liberalization path, the more so now that resist-ance to it has been, if not crushed, powerfully subdued.

Was the spring 1989 movement in China pro-capitalist, as the U.S. and Chinese media claim? Have the Chinese government's massacres, exe-cutions, and incarceration of students and workers since June 4 been a defense of socialism? We do not think so. The agreement between the U.S. and Chinese media is based on an elaborate lie, as demonstrated by the articles that the *New York Times* itself published in the months prior to the events of the spring of 1989.

How little the crackdown on students and workers was the expression of a new commitment to 'socialist goals' is indicated by the indefatigable efforts that the communist leaders made, as soon as the bloody streets of Beijing were washed, to lure back foreign investors who, we are told, were prudently parked not too far away in Hong Kong. Their call was not unanswered, according to this piece. Investors are flocking back at such a pace that the Japanese government had to warn its businessmen to be a bit more discreet.

Several other articles further indicate that months prior to the student demonstrations a debate had gone on in China reflecting the extent of workers' dissatisfaction with the liberalization process and the dilemma facing the Chinese leadership caught between the desire to further liberalize and the fear of social uprising. Under pressure by foreign investors, who complained that "China is still paternal towards its companies," throughout March, the Chinese leaders debated the feasibility of new bankruptcy laws, whereby unprofitable companies would no longer be rescued but would have to go bankrupt and therefore lay off their workers. That the bankruptcy issue had to do with workers' discipline was clearly stated by *another* article entitled "Socialism Grabs a Stick; Bankruptcy in China." According to this article, "Chinese officials say the bankruptcy laws are important more for the message they send to the workers: that profitability matters, even in socialist society." The article adds that among the problems plaguing Chinese companies there is the fact that they "share an enormous burden of pension expenses, sometimes supporting four times as many retired workers as those on the job." Moreover, experiments made in some towns (e.g., in Shenyang) with layoffs have not produced 'satisfactory results.' The companies had to pay collectively into a welfare fund to provide insurance to the laid off workers, thus eliminating the very risks that bankruptcy was intended to create. "Indeed, workers have been allowed to collect substantial wage benefits even when they leave their jobs voluntarily." The article concludes: "While some economists think bankruptcy should become a more common sanction, they acknowledge that if the government did close down money losing companies it could face serious labor problems. A Western diplomat in China, who has followed the Shenyang experiments, noted that workers, already disgruntled by inflation, might cause serious labor disturbances if they lost their jobs."[1]

The 'labor problem' has been one of the thorniest issues for the Chinese government in recent years. Reports from China repeatedly have pointed to a coming showdown with workers. A January 10, 1989, *New York Times* article entitled "Three Chinese Economists Urge an End to State Owned Industry" stated, "Companies try to maximize benefits for employees rather than profits and productivity." Right before the beginning of the demonstrations in Tiananmen Square, on April 6, 1989, the *New York Times* ran an article entitled, "Second Thoughts on Laissez Faire or Plain Unfair?" It stated: "Inflation and corruption, along with fear of unemployment and resentment of the newly wealthy, seem to be fostering a reassessment among Chinese farmers and workers about the benefits of sweeping economic change. Some Chinese officials and foreign diplomats are growing concerned that the Chinese people, instead of helping the market economy, will become an obstacle to it."

The article, written by Nicholas Kristof, mentions a factory that had been attacked by sixty "jealous" people, who smashed the windows and cut the power supply. A hundred residents of the town in which the factory was located sued the factory owner to force him to share his profits. The article speaks of a new phenomenon, "the red eye disease," that according to the Chinese authorities affects those who are jealous of the wealthy. It says that in Inner Mongolia the government has established a special team of bodyguards to protect entrepreneurs from neighbors with the "red eye disease," and in the northern city of Shenyang, a seat of the new experiments in modernization and liberalization, a worker killed his boss last year. He was executed but became a folk hero because the boss was regarded as a tyrant. Summing up, the article states that the Chinese had previously regarded the market as a "cozy place of prosperity, not a source of pain . . . [but] everybody in China seems to be grumbling these days, and even the government acknowledges the depth of the discontent." The article also cites a *People's Daily* forecast of not only economic but also political crisis, noting that urban residents with a fixed income are hurt by the 27 percent inflation rate.

Many people in China are worried hearing the government's talk of "smashing the iron rice bowl," which is "the system of lifetime employment usually associated with laziness in the Chinese factories." Factory managers want the right to dismiss inefficient workers or lay them off when times are bad. Though the government is "gingerly moving in this direction, so far there have been no massive layoffs, even in Shenyang where the plan has gone the furthest." A Western diplomat worries that if the liberalization of the workplace results in many layoffs there could be severe wildcat strikes and social unrest. "Many people want to retain the 'iron rice bowl,'" an Asian diplomat said. "It's a good system for those who do not want to work too hard."[2]

The 'iron rice bowl' is not the only guarantee the workers are slated to lose. Housing is another one. In a March 1, 1989, *New York Times* article, "Chinese Face Epochal Wait for Housing," we are told that Zhao Ziyang had decided to make housing reform "one of the mainstays of the national economy." The article adds, "The decision to privatize home ownership was not taken lightly, for it challenges the underpinning of society as it has been interpreted here. For the last forty years, virtually free housing supplied by one's 'workers unit,' or employer, has been as much a staple of urban Chinese life as rice or noodles. Housing used to be a kind of welfare system, says a company head, 'We used to rent out very cheaply, but there was a terrible shortage. Now we're encouraging workers to buy houses.'" Concluding, the article notes: "The consensus is growing that rents are too low. Rents for a family of four averages the equivalent of sixty cents a month." Now, with the reform, houses being put on the market cost anywhere from $13,000 to $41,000, "momentous sums in a country where the monthly wage averages about $25 a month."[3]

All the above goes a long way to explaining the general silence by both the Chinese and U.S. media about the 'new union movement' that was present in Tiananmen Square with the students. It also explains why, though the demonstrations were largely pictured as student dominated, the wrath of the Communist government has been directed primarily against the workers. The bulk of those executed for the 'crimes' committed during the spring events were young workers and unemployed men. But labor troubles were only one part of the problem the state faced trying to convince the Chinese masses about the virtues of laissez-faire.

One of the most deep-seated causes of the present rebellion are the changes that have taken place in the rural areas, following a decade-long process of privatization of land tenure and the commercialization of agriculture. This, coupled with the expansion of China's export capacity, has had profound structural effects on living conditions in the rural and urban areas. Among its main consequences is the fact that people are being thrown off the land. This means that China is experiencing a massive enclosure process, possibly on a scale unmatched by any other country.

It is thought that the surplus 100 million will grow to 200 million by the end of the century. Meanwhile, the government reckons that China has a floating population of 50 million transients, uprooted peasants who drift in and out of cities without any legal right to be there. It is guessed that on an average day in Shanghai, in 1987, there were 1.3 million such people, in Canton 1 million, and in Beijing 1.1 million, half of whom stayed in the capital for at least three months. Even the city officials concede that the transients have their good points, filling casual jobs that might otherwise go begging. But the transients are said to be responsible for a third of urban crime and help eat up the subsidized food that is meant for permanent residents: 400,000 kilos of vegetables and 130,000 kilos of meat a day in Canton. The problem then is 'the strain on services.' Some Chinese economists believe that the only solution is to phase out subsidies and have an 'as you go' system based on the 'law of value.' "Give those free reign, though," the *Economist* continues, "and the likely short-term result will be greater income inequalities, higher inflation and urban unrest."

A further consequence of the commercialization of agriculture has been rising prices, such that for the first time since the 'Great Leap Forward' the Chinese face starvation. An October 28, 1988, *New York Times* article reported that in May of that year the government lifted the controls from many agricultural prices and "permitted the market to determine the cost of many goods and services," and the result had been surging prices and panic buying. Inflation was as high as 50 percent in some cities.[4] Indicating the consequences of the continuously rising inflation for living conditions, the *Wall Street Journal* stated that in 1987 the standard of living declined by 21 percent for city wage earners, causing panic buying, bank runs, and even strikes in some state factories.[5] There was rising anger among urban residents against the government. All this indicates that the protests of spring 1989 were the latest, most explosive expression of a long process of resistance against laissez-faire economics, continuous with the uprisings against 'structural adjustment' that have taken place across the Third World, including the riots and mass demonstrations in Venezuela, Argentina, Burma, and Nigeria that protested against the price hikes, the removal of subsidies, and the liberalization of the economy in the spring of 1989.

That it was the students who took the initiative is not surprising. There is evidence that students too have suffered from the inflationary spiral of the last years. There are veiled references in the media to governmental promises to raise the budget for education. Given the worldwide experience with laissez-faire and liberalization, one can easily imagine how the cutting of subsidies have affected students. It is interesting to note that a May 25, 1989, *New York Times* article, "Aspiring Party Leaders at the Forefront of Revolt," reported that the leaders of the revolt were not the students of the University of Beijing but the more proletarian, less Westernized students of the People's University, who were more likely to feel the consequences of the cuts in subsidies.[6] Another reference to the hardships that students faced is found in another *New York Times* article of the same date, in which a student says that, unlike in Beijing, in Canton students can always find ways of moonlighting to make ends meet. "People can always find an extra job in a hotel or driving a taxi."[7]

Undoubtedly there are among the students some who correspond to the dominant media image of pro-Western, anticommunist intellectuals who suffer most from restrictions on freedom of expression. But by and large, the media also shows that the student movement in China moves along the same lines as student movements in other parts of the Third World, beginning with the student movements immediately adjacent to China, those of South Korea and Burma.

For example, the Burmese students have used their social position and organizational possibilities to lay the basis of a mass protest against the government and its corruption. For more than a year, they have protested alongside workers and the unemployed in the face of massacres and torture. Similarly, the most common demand of the Chinese students has been that voiced by those with the 'red eye disease': "End Corruption!"—which refers to the capitalization of the Chinese Communist Party, that is, the Communist Party officials becoming capitalists. This aspect of the protests was played out symbolically, as noted by a *New York Times* article of May 25, 1989, "Upheaval in China; Chinese Take Umbrage at Attack on Mao's Portrait," which mentions that "lately some workers and students have taken to wearing Mao buttons and pins, apparently to suggest their longing for the Maoist days of egalitarianism, honesty and selflessness."[8]

Finally, let us consider two *New York Times* articles that appeared on June 6, 1989, two days after the Beijing massacres, when the question of civil war was being mooted: "Crackdown in Beijing; Civil War for Army" and "Crackdown in Beijing; An Army with Its Own Grievances." The first reported, "All of China's senior officials have had extensive contacts with the American military and have attended courses at American military schools." It continued, "Emerging Chinese military thinking is based on the American model and China's modernization program is largely dependent upon American technology and equipment." Meanwhile, there is discontent among the rank and file.[9] The second article pointed out that the Chinese Army has been ordered to become self-supporting. "As a consequence, some units have used their trucks to start transport companies, their repair depots to serve as commercial garages, and their hospitals to admit private paying patients." The article drily reported, "Sometimes, ill soldiers have been turned away to cater to patients who can pay. . . . This has created wide demoralization."[10]

Putting together the articles from media available on any well-stocked newsstand in the U.S. we can see that the student-worker movement in China is not the last episode of a dying socialism but the first manifestation of the post-socialist anticapitalist struggle in China. The student protest at Tiananmen Square opened the space for the workers and government to take up their much-anticipated confrontation. The U.S. found the repression a welcome and 'inevitable' result, for as the media had been commenting in the months prior to the crackdown, the question was not whether the anticapitalist proletarian demands were to be rejected, the question was how.

## Notes

1   Nicholas D. Kristof, "Socialism Grabs a Stick; Bankruptcy in China," *New York Times*, March 7, 1989, accessed May 20, 2018, https://www.nytimes.com/1989/03/07/business/socialism-grabs-a-stick-bankruptcy-in-china.html.
2   Nicholas D. Kristof, "Beijing Journal; Second Thoughts: Laissez Faire or Plain Unfair?" *New York Times*, April 6, 1989, accessed May 20, 2018, https://www.nytimes.com/1989/04/06/world/beijing-journal-second-thoughts-laissez-faire-or-plain-unfair.html.
3   Nicholas D. Kristof, "Chinese Face Epochal Wait for Housing," *New York Times*, March 1, 1989, accessed May 20, 2018, https://www.nytimes.com/1989/03/01/world/chinese-face-epochal-wait-for-housing.html.
4   Edward A. Gargan, "China Explains Policy Shift Retightening Economic Grip," *New York Times*, accessed July 13, 2018, https://www.nytimes.com/1988/10/28/world/china-explains-policy-shift-retightening-economic-grip.html.
5   Adi Ignatius, "China's Restructuring Is Enriching Peasants but Not City Dwellers," *Wall Street Journal*, October 10, 1988.
6   Fox Butterfield, "Aspiring Party Leaders at the Forefront of Revolt," *New York Times*, May 25, 1989, accessed May 20, 2018, https://www.nytimes.com/1989/05/25/world/aspiring-party-leaders-at-forefront-of-revolt.html.
7   Barbara Basler, "Upheaval in China; Canton's Prosperous Students March," *New York Times*, March 25, 1989, accessed May 20, 2018, https://www.nytimes.

com/1989/05/25/world/upheaval-in-china-canton-s-prosperous-students-march.html.

8    Sheryl Wudunn, "Upheaval in China; Chinese Take Umbrage at Attack on Mao's Portrait," *New York Times*, May 25, 1989, accessed May 20, 2018, https://www.nytimes.com/1989/05/24/world/upheaval-in-china-chinese-take-umbrage-at-attack-on-mao-portrait.html.

9    Bernard E. Trainor, "Crackdown in Beijing; Civil War for Army," *New York Times*, June 6, 1989, accessed May 20, 2018, https://www.nytimes.com/1989/06/06/world/crackdown-in-beijing-civil-war-for-army.html.

10   Fox Butterfield, "Crackdown in Beijing; An Army with Its Own Grievances," *New York Times*, accessed May 20, 2018, https://www.nytimes.com/1989/06/06/world/crackdown-in-beijing-an-army-with-its-own-grievances.html.

# From Commoning to Debt:
# Financialization, Microcredit,
# and the Changing Architecture
# of Capital Accumulation

**Introduction: Financialization and the Rise of the 'Debt Economy'**

Debt, as David Graeber so powerfully reminded us,[1] has a central place in the history of humanity and the class struggle. Debtors' revolts were frequent in ancient Athens as early as the sixth century BC, forcing debt cancellations and prohibitions against debt enslavement.[2] In Rome, in 63 BC, the head of the *populares*, Catilina, led an army of debtors against the patricians.[3] In modern times, public debt has become "one of the most powerful levers of primitive accumulation" as Marx pointed out in his chapter on the "Genesis of the Industrial Capitalist."[4] Shays' Rebellion of 1786, in Western Massachusetts, three years after the end of the War of Independence, had as its target the debt collectors.[5] A hundred years later, the Populist Party expressed the rage of the farmers at seeing their farms taken away by the bankers because they could not pay their debts.[6] Also the 'penny auctions' that spread from Wisconsin to much of the Midwest during the Great Depression were responses to the threat posed by debt and foreclosures. In sum, as a means of exploitation and enslavement, debt has been an instrument of class rule through the ages. It would be a mistake, however, to conceive of it as a sort of 'political universal.' Like the class societies in which it has thrived, debt itself has undergone significant transformations.

This is especially true of the contemporary situation, as a new 'debt economy'[7] has come into existence with the neoliberal turn in capitalist development that is changing not only the architecture of capitalist accumulation but the form of the class relationship and debt itself. Debt has become ubiquitous, affecting millions of people across the planet, who for the first time are indebted to banks, and it is now used by governments and financiers not only to accumulate wealth but to undermine social solidarity and the efforts movements are making worldwide to create social commons and alternatives to capitalism.

It was through the 'debt crisis'[8] triggered in 1979 when the Federal Reserve raised of interest rate on the dollar that the World Bank and the International Monetary Fund (IMF), as representatives of international capital, 'structurally adjusted' and de facto recolonized much of the former colonial world, plunging entire regions into a debt that over the years has continued to grow rather than being extinguished.[9] In many countries, due to the 'debt crisis,' the gains obtained by the anticolonial struggle were nullified and a new economic order was forced into existence that has condemned entire populations to a poverty never before experienced. On this basis, a restructuring of the world political economy has been set in motion that has systematically channeled the resources of Africa, Latin America, and every country in the grip of the 'debt crisis' toward Europe, the U.S., and more recently China.

So successful has the 'debt crisis' been in recolonizing much of the 'Third World' that its mechanisms have since been extended to the disciplining of North American and (more recently) European workers, as demonstrated by the drastic austerity measures imposed on the populations of Greece,[10] Spain, Italy, and the UK, among others, and the fact that public debt is now plaguing even the smallest municipalities[11] and "through [it] entire societies have become indebted."[12]

But the clearest expression of the logic that motivates the new debt economy is found in the new forms of individual debt that have proliferated with the neoliberal turn—student loan debt, mortgage, credit card debt, and above all microfinance debt now affecting millions across the planet.

What is specific about this new use of debt, considering that debt is the oldest means of exploitation? In what follows I investigate this question and argue that individual and group debt not only *amplify the economic effects of state debt* but change the relations between capital and labor and between workers themselves, placing exploitation on a more self-managed basis and turning the communities that people are building in search of mutual support into means of mutual enslavement. This is *why* the new debt regime is so pernicious and why it is so crucial for us to understand the mechanisms by which it is imposed.

## The End of the Welfare State and the Crisis of the Wage Common

Brought to public attention by the subprime crisis of 2008, individual and household debt is already the object of a large body of literature investigating its causes and social effects, its relation to the increasing financialization of everyday life[13] and reproduction,[14] its determination of new forms of subjectivity,[15] and above all the forms of mobilization most effective against it.[16]

There is a broad consensus that the institution of a 'debt-based' economy is an essential part of a neoliberal political strategy responding to the cycle of struggles that in the 1960s and 1970s put capitalist accumulation in crisis, and that it was triggered by the dismantling of the social contract that had existed between capital and labor since the Fordist period. Plausibly, the struggles of women, students, and blue-collar workers showed to the capitalist class that investing in the reproduction of the working class 'does not pay,' either in terms of a higher labor productivity or in terms of a more disciplined workforce. Hence not only the dismantling of the 'welfare state' but the 'financialization of reproduction,' in the sense that an increasing number of people (students, welfare recipients, pensioners) have been forced to borrow from the banks to purchase services (health care, education, pensions) that the state formerly subsidized, so that *many reproductive activities have now become immediate sites of capital accumulation.*

These developments are well understood. It is agreed that debt serves to impose social austerity, to privatize the means of reproduction, and to intensify the mechanism of domination.[17] It is also agreed that the financialization of reproduction by which much individual and household debt is produced is not something superimposed on the real economy, but *is the 'real economy,'* insofar as it is the direct organizer of people's labor. But what the new literature on debt has not sufficiently highlighted is the role that the new forms of debt play in the destruction of communal solidarity, an element that differentiates them from previous forms of proletarian debt. We must remember, in fact, that debt has always been one of the most common aspects of proletarian life. From the nineteenth century until the post–World War II period, working-class communities have lived for a good part of their year on credit, paying shopkeepers on payday and borrowing from each other to make ends meet. In this context, debt has often functioned as a sort of mutual aid, a means by which communities circulated their scarce resources to those most in need. Even in company towns, debt did not isolate those burdened with it, as the common bondage unified in the resentment against the exploiters. Debt began to change its connotation first with the creation of purchase by installment that became a habitual practice by the 1920s[18] and later, in the post–World War II period, with the extension of mortgages, especially to white male workers, with wages guaranteed by the state and the unions functioning as the collateral. Debt for mortgages and consumer spending were both a victory and a defeat. A victory because the extension of credit to workers reversed the ontological capitalist principle according to which you work first and then you get paid: that is, proletarians must work on credit. A defeat because to the extent that it was tied to the availability of wages, to performance, and in many cases to racial privilege, it contributed to diminishing communal cohesion.[19]

By the 1980s, however, workers' debt had become a sure measure of their loss of social power. The 1980s was the time of the 'Great Transformation' that built the infrastructure for the new debt economy. By this time, the extension of bank credit to workers through expanded access to credit cards, coupled with the precarization of work, the removal of anti-usury laws in most states, and the increasing commercialization of education and health care changed the nature of debt as a social relation. As credit grew in the face of both diminishing wages and of increasing incentives to turn to the market to acquire the necessities of life, the material bases of solidarity were further undermined. It is quite ironic that, while access to employment became more difficult to obtain and more insecure, indebtedness was immensely facilitated. As we know, much fraud was employed to bring multitudes under the control of the banks. But what matters, for my point at least, are not the manipulations of the financial world, but the fact that *a debt economy was consolidated that has disarticulated the social fabric, not least with the illusion that the financial means that the international banking system has manufactured could be used by workers as well, and not only to purchase the necessities of life but to get ahead in the system.*

It is not my intention here to examine the complex class dynamics that have enabled this process. Suffice it to say that mass indebtedness and the neoliberal assault on wages and 'social rights' would not have been possible without the acceptance by some workers of the neoliberal ideology of prosperity through the market. From this viewpoint, we can place the escalation of indebtedness to the banks on a continuum, with some workers' acceptance of company stocks in the place of wages and benefits and their attempt to improve their declining economic condition through equity raised on their homes in part explaining the lack of mass resistance in the face of the refusal by the state to use its accumulated resources to guarantee our reproduction.

But as the 2008 Wall Street crash so dramatically demonstrated, the hope that 'financialization' might provide a solution or an alternative to the vanishing jobs and wages has not been fulfilled. The decision to bail out banks but not working-class debtors has made it clear that debt is designed to be a standard condition of working-class existence, no less than in the early phase of industrialization, though with more devastating consequences from the viewpoint of class solidarity. For the creditor is no longer the local shopkeeper or the neighbor but the banker and, due to the high interest rates, debt, like a cancer, with time continuously increases. Moreover, since the 1980s, a whole ideological campaign has been orchestrated that represents borrowing from banks to provide for one's reproduction as a form of entrepreneurship, thus mystifying the class relation and the exploitation involved. Accordingly, instead of the capital-labor struggle mediated through the debt, *we have millions of microentrepreneurs 'investing' in their reproduction*, even if in possession of only a few hundred dollars, presumably 'free' to prosper or fail as their laboriosity and sagacity allows.

Not only is 'reproduction' presented as a 'self-investment.' As the lending-debt machine becomes the main means of reproduction, a new class relation is produced where the exploiters are more hidden, more removed, and the mechanisms of exploitation are far more individualized and guilt inducing. Instead of work, exploitation, and above all 'bosses,' so prominent in the world of smokestacks, we now have debtors confronting not an employer but a bank and confronting it alone, not as part of a collective body and collective relationship, as was the case with wage workers. In this way, workers' resistance is diffused, economic disasters acquire a moralistic dimension, and the function of debt as an instrument of labor extraction is masked, as we have seen, under the illusion of self-investment.

### Microfinance and Macro-debt

So far, I have described in broad outlines how working-class debt creation has functioned in the United States. But the workings of the lending/debt machine are best seen in the politics of *microcredit or microfinance*, the much publicized program launched in the late 1970s by the Bangladeshi economist Muhammad Yunus with the foundation of the Grameen Bank, and since then extended to every region of the planet. Promoted as a means to 'alleviate poverty' in the world, microfinance has actually proven to be a debt-creating engine, involving a vast network of national and local governments, NGOs, and banks, starting with the World Bank, mostly serving to capture the work, energies, and inventiveness of the 'poor,'[20] women above all. As María Galindo of Mujeres Creando[21] has written with reference to Bolivia in her Prologue to *La pobreza: un gran negocio*, microfinance, as a financial and political program, aimed to recuperate and destroy the survival strategies that poor women had created in response to the crisis of male employment produced by structural adjustment in the 1980s. Assuring women that even a small loan could solve their economic problems, it has subsumed their informal activities, made up of exchanges with poor unemployed women like themselves, to the formal economy, forcing them to pay a weekly amount as part of their loan repayment.[22] Galindo's observation that microfinance is a mechanism to place women under the control of the formal economy can be generalized to other countries, and so can her argument that loans are traps from which few women can profit or free themselves.

It is significant that loans, usually involving very small sums of money, are mostly given to women, and in particular to women's groups, although in many cases it is the husbands or other men in the families that use them.[23] Financial planners prefer women, because they recognize that they are more responsible in their economic transactions, being far more dependent on steady economic resources for the reproduction of their families and being more vulnerable to intimidation. They have also studied women's communities and "appropriated their system of social relations for their objectives,"[24] treating it like a *social capital*, so that when groups are not available women are encouraged to form them.

Microloans are given to groups because in this way each member becomes responsible for their repayment, and should anyone default each member can be expected to intervene. Joint responsibility, moreover, as Lamia Karim argues in her *Microfinance and Its Discontents* (2011), leads to a proliferation of disciplining technologies with women constantly monitoring and surveilling each other and notifying managers of potential problems.[25] "Through this system," as María Galindo also points out, "the social fabric that supports women in their everyday life is used to support the payment of the debt."[26] This has proven to be a very effective mechanism, since microloans are given in societies in which rural codes—tied to ancient survival tactics—make repayment a matter of honor, and women's honor in particular is essential to a family's standing in the community. Indeed, as Karim writes, women's honor operates as a sort of collateral.[27] Thus, the paradox is that although the borrowers are the poorest of the world, the rates of repayment are the highest.

Collective self-policing is only partially responsible for this 'success.' Equally important have been the strategies used in case of default. Banks, international agencies, and NGOs have been engaging in a true *ethnography of shame*, studying the mechanisms by which different communities culturally enforce their ethical mores, which they then apply accompanied by threats and physical intimidation. Home visits and a variety of vilifying methods are used to terrify debtors into payment. In some countries, like Niger, the pictures of women who have not repaid their debts are posted on the doors of the banks.[28] In Bolivia, some microfinance institutions have marked the houses of defaulters and put posters in the neighborhoods where they live.[29] In Bangladesh, a standard method to punish defaulters is *housebreaking*, the practice by which NGO officers enter into a house and rip out the doors, floor planks, and roofs to resell them as payment for the defaulted loan.[30] However, "Public punishments and sanctions also include ... flogging, pouring pitch over bodies, tonsuring women's hair ... publicly spitting on a person every time she or he walks by."[31] NGOs have also turned to the police, the courts, and the local elites. As a result, those in danger of default live in a state of terror that intensifies resentments and hostilities among the women themselves, who at times cooperate in the housebreaking. This explains why repayment rates are so high despite the fact that few can claim to have had much success with the capital acquired.

'Empowerment' through microcredits is not an easy feat, at least for the majority of recipients. The reality is that poverty and misery are not caused by lack of capital but by the unjust distribution of wealth, and this is a problem that a few hundred dollars cannot resolve or mitigate. A few hundred dollars, or even more, in the hands of families who live daily at the edge of disaster quickly vanish and are rarely invested to make more money. The husband gets sick, the goat dies, children have no shoes to go to school: soon loan recipients find themselves unable to meet their repayments and have borrow from moneylenders to pay back the loans they have taken. Far from lifting themselves out of poverty by some 'virtuous' investment, they plunge more deeply into it, going from a small debt to a bigger one in a sequence that often ends in a suicide.[32] Even when they do not die physically, many borrowers die socially. Some, full of shame for not being able to pay back their debts, leave their villages. In Bangladesh, defaulting women have been abandoned by their husbands after they were publicly shamed. That many default is guaranteed not only by their perennial state of crisis but also by the high interest rates imposed on the loans, usually 20 percent or more.[33] The justification given for these high rates is that lending to the poor is a laborious process, presumably requiring a substantial social/work machine to ensure that they do not escape the hold of their creditors, and if they cannot repay with money they will repay with their last drop of blood, be this in the form of a small piece of land, a tiny shack, a goat, or a pot and pan. In Bangladesh, defaulting women are punished by being deprived of the large pot for cooking rice that they use to feed her families, the ultimate shame a woman can suffer, an insufferable loss of face with respect to the community that can lead to abandonment by the husband and at times suicide.[34] Yet this is precisely what many women have been subjected to, their house being broken into and they themselves being at times physically assaulted.

This being the situation, why then are microloans still proliferating? What induces people to take them and what is achieved by this generalized extension of debt? The answer is that few people today worldwide can live purely on subsistence, even in predominantly agricultural areas. Land expropriations, currency devaluations, and cuts in jobs and social services, combined with the extension of market relations, are forcing even populations primarily engaged in agriculture to seek some form of monetary income. NGOs have also learned to combine lending with marketing schemes, offering together with loans a variety of goods, like medicines or foods the borrowers will be tempted to buy.[35] Some borrowers do succeed in improving their situation, but they are a minority and often do so by collaborating with NGOs in policing other borrowers and debt collecting.[36] We see here a parallel between the situation of female borrowers in Bolivia or Bangladesh and that of students in the USA, who are often ready to face very high rates of indebtment, convinced that the degree thus purchased will fetch them higher wages, although in reality many, upon graduating, will have a hard time finding employment or finding it at the expected wage rates or at rates enabling them to pay back their debts.

The reasons why investors insist on promoting this program, despite the growing criticism and evidence of its failure to end poverty,[37] are quite varied. The good return on the money invested is only one factor. Equally important are the changes in class relations and relations within the proletariat itself that debt is producing. Microfinance enables international capital to directly control and exploit the world proletariat, bypassing the mediation of the national states, thus ensuring that any profit made accrues directly to the banks instead of being appropriated by local governments. It also enables it to bypass the world of male relatives as mediators in the exploitation of women's labor and to tap the energies of a population of women who in the wake of 'structural adjustment' have been able to create new forms of subsistence outside or at the margins of the money economy, which microcredit attempts to bring under the control of monetary relations and the banks. Last but not least, like other debt-generating policies, microfinance is a means of experimentation with different social relations where the tasks of surveillance and policing are 'internalized' by the community, the group, or the family, and where exploitation appears to be self-managed and failure is more burning for being experienced as an individual problem and disgrace.

Here as well we can see a continuity between the experience of indebted women in Egypt, Niger, Bangladesh, or Bolivia and that of indebted students or victims of the subprime crisis in the U.S.

In both cases, the state and the employers disappear as the immediate beneficiary of the labor extracted and therefore as targets of demands and conflict. We also have the ideology of micro-entrepreneurship that hides the work and exploitation involved. We have the individualization of the reasons for success or failure, the individually suffered shame, the politics of guilt leading to hiding, self-imposed silence, and avoidance of disclosure.

This strategy has been very successful so far, but it is clearly unsustainable in the long run, and not only for the poor. In fact, it is already beginning to show its limits. It is significant that as pauperization due to microfinance is becoming ever more severe, and the ability to further squeeze the poor is reduced, microlending networks are redirecting their attentions to more affluent populations and increasingly moving to the global North. Significantly the Grameen Bank—literally the Village Bank—has opened branches in ten U.S. cities, starting with New York.[38] In the long term, the debt strategy puts capitalism in a bind, as in no part of the world can the absolute impoverishment of so many people be sustained if world production is not to further stagnate and retrench. Most important, capitalism is arguably reaching the point at which the advantage derived from the pauperization and expropriation of the world multitudes is offset by its inability to contain the resistance it is generating.

## Anti-Debt Movements Have Already Appeared in Latin America

The most powerful anti-debt movement in Mexico in the 1990s was El Barzon (the yoke), which in a few years extended nationwide, with the slogan "I owe, I don't deny it. But I pay what is right."[39] A debtors mobilization also took place in Bolivia, where in May 2001 thousands of people, mostly women, coming from different parts of the country, lay siege to the banks in the streets of La Paz for ninety-five days.[40] Meanwhile, the Grameen Bank has become a hated name in Bangladesh, its founders and administrators viewed as nothing better than moneylenders who have enriched themselves at the expense of the poor.[41] And an anti-debt movement is growing in the United States, as the formation of Strike Debt![42] in an increasing number of U.S. cities and the success of the Rolling Jubilee that was launched in New York in November of 2012 demonstrate.[43] While the outcome of these forms of resistance remains to be seen, it can be said that the formation of a 'liberation from debt' movement is a major victory in and of itself, as the power of the debt economy derives in good part from the fact that its consequences are suffered in isolation; as the *Debt Resisters' Operations Manual* states, "there is so much shame, frustration and fear surrounding our debt [that] we seldom talk about it openly with others."[44]

Indeed, the curtain of fear and guilt debt has generated all over the world must be torn open, as it was in Mexico by El Barzon in the 1990s and in Bolivia in 2001 when indebted women rallied in the streets of La Paz and besieged the banks. Students, especially in the United States, have a special role in this process, as many of the cultural tools used by NGOs and banking systems to convince women to contract a debt and to shame borrowers into repayment even at the cost of their lives are forged in our universities. Anthropologists in particular "have played the midwife role" bringing to the world's attention the ability of the poor to survive "in the face of alienation, deprivation, and marginalization."[45] As Julia Elyachar points out, it was anthropologists who alerted economic planners to the extraordinary ways in which the poor manage to survive against all odds and to the importance of networks of relationships to people's survival. She adds that some of the effects of microfinance may not have been what the researchers had intended. Nevertheless, it was a short step from the recognition of culture and social relations as economic resources to the definition of a 'program of action.'[46]

Elyachar's comments demonstrate the importance of our universities in the production of new models of disciplining and labor extraction.[47] Thus, from the viewpoint of an anti-student debt movement, the task is twofold. On the one hand, the movement must refuse the student loan debt as illegitimate, for education should not be a commodity to be bought and sold. On the other, it should refuse to collaborate in the production of the knowledge producing the debt, as well as knowledge usable as an instrument of debt repayment and an instrument of psychological torture for those who fail.

The struggle against microcredit is also intensifying. A No Pago (I won't pay) movement has developed in Nicaragua. Protests against microcredit have also spread to India, where by 2010 almost all borrowers had stopped repaying their loans, placing the industry in danger of collapse.[48] In Bangladesh, the birthplace of microfinance, as reported by the Economist, even Prime Minister Sheik Hasina Wazed has accused it of "sucking the blood of the poor in the name of poverty alleviation" and treating the people of Bangladesh as "guinea pigs."[49] In Bolivia, Mujeres Creando has made the cancellation of the debt one of the key tasks of the organization, accusing banks and NGOs of stealing women's work, time, and hope for the future and urging women to recuperate their traditional forms of borrowing in which "money passes from woman to woman on the basis of friendship and reciprocity relations."[50] More broadly, new movements are forming, like Strike Debt! in the United States, that view debt as a potential terrain of class recomposition, where those struggling against mortgages and foreclosures can meet indebted students, defaulting borrowers of microloans, and credit card holders. But as Galindo powerfully intuited, the success of these movements will very much depend on the degree to which they not only protest the debt but recreate and reinvent the commons the debt has destroyed.

## Notes
1    David Graeber, Debt: The First 5000 Years (Brooklyn: Melville House, 2011).
2    Graeber, Debt, 230–31, 427nn24–25.

3    George Caffentzis, "Two Cases in the History of Debt Resistance," unpub-
     lished manuscript based on a presentation at the Occupy University Fall
     Series on Debt, the Elizabeth Foundation for the Arts, October 17, 2012, 3.

4    "The only part of the so-called national wealth that actually enters into the
     collective possession of a modern nation is the national debt"; Marx, *Capital:
     A Critique of Political Economy*, Vol. 1, ed. Frederick Engels, trans. Ben Fowkes
     (London: Penguin, 1990), 919.

5    Howard Zinn, *A People's History of the United States: 1492–Present* (New York:
     HarperCollins, 1999 [1980]), 3.

6    Zinn, *A People's History of the United States*, 284.

7    I take the concept of a 'debt economy' from Maurizio Lazzarato, *The Making
     of the Indebted Man*, Semiotext(e) Intervention Series no. 13 (Cambridge, MA:
     MIT Press, 2012).

8    The literature on the debt crisis is now immense. For references, see Elmar
     Altvater et al., *The Poverty of Nations: A Guide to the Debt Crisis from Argentina
     to Zaire* (London: Zed Books 1991 [1987]); George Caffentzis, "The Fundamental
     Implications of the Debt Crisis for Social Reproduction in Africa," in *Paying
     the Price: Women and the Politics of International Economic Strategy*, eds.
     Mariarosa Dalla Costa and Giovanna F. Dalla Costa (London: Zed Books,
     1995), 153–87; Federici, "The Debt Crisis, Africa, and the New Enclosures," in
     this volume; Harry Cleaver, "Notes on the Origins of the Debt Crisis," *New
     Enclosures, Midnight Notes* no. 10 (Fall 1990).

9    The exception is Latin America where, on average, the external debt has
     declined from 59 percent of GDP in 2003 to 32 percent in 2008; "Database:
     *Latin Macro Watch*," accessed May 21, 2018, https://www.iadb.org/en/
     databases/latin-macro-watch/latin-macro-watch-country-profiles%2C18579.
     html.

10   On the 'debt crisis' in Greece, see TPTG (The Children of the Gallery),
     "Burdened with Debt: 'Debt Crisis' and Class Struggles in Greece," in *Revolt
     and Crisis in Greece: Between a Present Yet to Pass and a Future Still to Come*, eds.
     Antonis Vradis and Dimitris Dalakoglou (Oakland: AK Press, 2011), 245–78;
     David Graeber, "The Greek Debt Crisis in Almost Unimaginably Long-Term
     Historical Perspective," in Vradis and Dalaoglou, *Revolt and Crisis in Greece*,
     229–44.

11   Starting in the late 1970s, state and municipal debt has been created through
     the adoption of laws and provisions forbidding governments from address-
     ing their money problems by coining new money, forcing them to resort to
     private financial markets; Lazzarato, *The Making of the Indebted Man*, 18.

12   Lazzarato, *The Making of the Indebted Man*, 8.

13   Randy Martin, *Financialization of Daily Life* (Philadelphia: Temple University
     Press, 2002).

14   Christian Marazzi, *The Violence of Financial Capitalism*, Semiotext(e)
     Intervention Series no. 2 (Cambridge, MA: MIT Press, 2010).

15   Lazzarato, *The Making of the Indebted Man*.

16   Caffentzis, "Two Cases in The History of Debt Resistance."

17   Lazzarato, *The Making of the Indebted Man*.

18   See Gary S. Cross, *Time and Money: The Making of a Consumer Culture* (New York: Routledge, 1993), 148.

19   On the relationship between the growth of 'consumer spending' and the privatization of social relations in the working class, see Cross, *Time and Money*, 168–83.

20   I place 'poor' in quotes to highlight the mystification implicit in this concept. There are no 'poor'; they are people and populations who have been impoverished. This may appear a minor distinction, but it is a necessary one to prevent the normalization and naturalization of impoverishment that the concept of the 'poor' promotes.

21   Mujeres Creando is the most important autonomous feminist organization in Bolivia. Based in La Paz since 2002, it has been involved in the struggle against microfinance debt and has promoted the research on microfinance that was the origin of the book cited. On this subject, see María Galindo, "La pobreza: un gran negocio," *Mujer Pública* no. 7 (December 2012).

22   Galindo, "La pobreza: un gran negocio," 8.

23   This is the situation in Bangladesh as described by Lamia Karim, who found in her research that "95 per cent of women borrowers gave their loans to their husbands or other male borrowers"; Lamia Karim, *Microfinance and Its Discontents: Women in Debt in Bangladesh* (Minneapolis: University of Minnesota Press, 2011), 86.

24   María Galindo, "Prólogo," in Graciela Toro Ibáñez, *La pobreza, un gran negocio: un análisis crítico sobre oeneges, microfinancieras y banca* (La Paz: Mujeres Creando, 2010), 10.

25   Karim, *Microfinance and Its Discontents*, 73–74.

26   Galindo, "La pobreza: un gran negocio," 10.

27   Karim, *Microfinance and Its Discontents*, 198.

28   I have obtained this information in an interview with Professor Ousseina Alidou, director of the Center for African Studies at Rutgers University-New Brunswick, in September 2012.

29   Graciela Toro Ibáñez, *La pobreza: un gran negocio* (La Paz: Mujeres Creando, 2010), 135.

30   Karim, *Microfinance and Its Discontents*, 85, 117.

31   Karim, 85.

32   There have been many suicides, including of men who cosigned the debts of their wives. According to Vandana Shiva, many of the fifteen thousand and more Indian farmers who in recent years have killed themselves in India under the burden of debt belonged to this category; Vandana Shiva, "The Suicide Economy of Corporate Globalization," *crosscurrents.org*, April 5, 2004, accessed May 21, 2018, https://www.countercurrents.org/glo-shiva050404.htm.

33   Toro Ibáñez, *La pobreza*, 146–52.

34   Karim, *Microfinance and Its Discontents*, 91.

35   In Bangladesh, NGOs have made deals with various companies, such as Danone, promoting its yogurts as crucial for the health of children; Karim, *Microfinance and Its Discontents*, 67, 196. There was a great protest in India

when NGOs there tried to make a deal with Monsanto to combine giving loans with the marketing of its seeds; see UNIBIG, Policy Research Development Alternative, "The Monsanto Initiative: Promoting Herbicides Through Micro-Credit Institutions," 1998, inactive June 2, 2018, http://membres.multimania. fr/ubinig/monsanto.htm. See also "Vandana Shiva Responds to the Grameen Bank," *Synthesis/Regeneration* 17 (Fall 1998): accessed June 2, 2018, http://www. greens.org/s-r/17/17-15.html, a letter Shiva wrote on that occasion to the head of the Grameen Bank; Karim, *Microfinance and Its Discontents*, xx.

36   As María Galindo points out, those women who excel in their policing role take on a leadership role in the neighborhood and become collaborators of the NGOs. She adds that 'empowerment' has a specific policing content; Galindo, "Prólogo," 10.

37   See Barbara Crossette, "UN Report Raises Questions about Small Loans to the Poor," *New York Times*, September 3, 1998, A8; Milford Bateman, *Why Doesn't Microfinance Work? The Destructive Rise of Local Neoliberalism* (London: Zed Books, 2010); "In Micro-finance Boom Echoes of Subprime," *Bloomberg Business Week*, June 21–27, 2010; Sylvia Chant, ed., *The International Handbook of Gender and Poverty: Concepts, Research, Policy* (London: Edward Elgar Publishing, 2010); Kentaro Toyama, "Lies, Hype, and Profit: The Truth about Microfinance," *Atlantic*, January 28, 2011, accessed June 2, 2018, https://www.theatlantic.com/business/archive/2011/01/lies-hype-and-profit-the-truth-about-microfinance/70405/.

38   As advertised, Grameen America offers micro-loans, for a maximum of $1,500. It also offers savings accounts through commercial partner banks that members are required to make deposits into. Typically, in order to receive a loan an individual must be living below the poverty line, must be located in a community with a Grameen America branch, and must be willing to create or join a five-member group of 'like-minded individuals.' Borrowers must also attend weekly meetings at which they make repayments on their loans; "Grameen America," *Wikipedia*, accessed May 31, 2018, https://en.wikipedia. org/wiki/Grameen_America.

39   Ana Cristina Samperio, *Se nos reventó el Barzón: radiografía del movimiento barzonista* (Mexico, DF.: Edivision, 1996); Daniel Chávez, "El Barzón: Performing Resistance in Contemporary Mexico," *Arizona Journal of Hispanic Cultural Studies* 2 (1998): 87–112.

40   Toro Ibañez, *La pobreza*, 137–44.

41   Karim, *Microfinance and Its Discontents*, 192–93.

42   Strike Debt is an organization formed in New York as an offshoot of Occupy Wall Street. It is committed to challenging the legitimacy of the debt that people have contracted, on the premise that basic services like housing, education, and health care should not be commodities reserved for those who can pay; see Strike Debt and Occupy Wall Street, *The Debt Resisters' Operations Manual* (Oakland: PM Press, 2014); 2012 edition available at, http://strikedebt. org/The-Debt-Resisters-Operations-Manual.pdf.

43   Rolling Jubilee was a strategy of Strike Debt, buying hefty debts at discount rates on secondary markets, a move intended to raise consciousness of the

fact that millions of people are now enslaved to banks, sometimes for the rest of their lives. Strike Debt launched the second phase, the Debt Collective, in 2014; https://debtcollective.org.

44   Strike Debt and Occupy Wall Street, *The Debt Resistors' Operations Manual*, 2012, iv, http://strikedebt.org/The-Debt-Resistors-Operations-Manual.pdf.

45   Julia Elyachar, "Empowerment Money: The World Bank, Non-Governmental Organizations, and the Value of Culture in Egypt," *Public Culture* 14, no. 3 (Fall 2002): 499.

46   Elyachar, "Empowerment Money," 508.

47   Among the forms of knowledge instrumental to the management of debtors is what Lamia Karim calls "poverty research" producing "an archive of intimate knowledge about the poor"; Karim, *Microfinance and Its Discontents*, 164–77. The task here is "unmasking representations," making them legible to the broader public; Karim, 166.

48   Lydia Polgreen and Vikas Bajaj, "India Microcredit Sector Faces Collapse from Defaults," *New York Times*, November 17, 2010, accessed June 2, 2018, https://www.nytimes.com/2010/11/18/world/asia/18micro.html.

49   "Saint Under Siege: A Microfinance Pioneer Is Under Attack in His Homeland," *Economist*, January 6, 2011, accessed June 4, 2018, https://www.economist.com/node/17857429; see also Lydia Polgreen and Vikas Bajaj, "Microcredit Pioneer Ousted Head of Bangladeshi Bank Says," *New York Times*, March 2, 2011, accessed June 2, 2018, https://www.nytimes.com/2011/03/03/world/asia/03yunus.html.

50   Toro Ibañez, *La pobreza*.

# PART TWO
On the Commons

# Introduction to Part Two

Like the existing commons, the articles included in this section do not provide a unitary picture. Instead, they travel through different sites, attempting to clarify the principles involved in communitarian societies and the challenges the defense of existing commons and the construction of new ones encounter. Here too the picture I present is far from exhaustive. My objective is primarily to demonstrate the potential of communal relations, not only as a guarantee of survival and an increased capacity for resistance but also, above all, as a path to transform our subjectivity and gain the capacity to recognize the world around us—nature, other people, the animal world—as a source of wealth and knowledge and not as a danger. Although written at different points for different reasons the essays in this part should be read as a continuum, the primary unifying thread being the effort to apply the principle of the commons to the organization of social reproduction. Throughout this process I have never forgotten what people who already live a communitarian experience would say: "You live the commons, you cannot talk about them, and even less theorize them." That I imagine is because of the difficulty to give words to such a powerful and rare experience as that of being part of something larger than our individual lives, of dwelling on 'this earth of mankind' not as a stranger or a trespasser, which is the way capitalism wishes us to relate to the spaces we occupy, but as home. But words are necessary, especially for those of us who live in areas where social relations have been almost completely disarticulated.

# Beneath the United States,
# the Commons

Two fundamental facts, that arose spontaneously, govern the primitive history of all, or almost all, nations: the grouping of the people according to kindred and common property in the soil.
> —Frederick Engels, "The Mark"[1]

The ancient voice that speaks to us of community heralds another world as well. Community—the communal mode of production and life—is the oldest of American traditions, the most American of all. It belongs to the earliest days and the first people, but it also belongs to the times ahead and anticipates a new New World.
> —Eduardo Galeano, "Traditions of the Future"[2]

If American society judiciously modeled the traditions of the various Native Nations, the place of women in society would become central, the distribution of goods and power would be egalitarian, the elderly would be respected, honored and protected as a primary social and cultural resource.
> —Paula Gunn Allen, "Who Is Your Mother?
> Red Roots of White Feminism"[3]

## Introduction
Back in the late 1930s, communist historians like Paul Kosok, students of the origins of class society, discovered that the territory in the lands of the Nazca, a population of Central Peru, carried remarkable signs and plausible testimonies of an ancient irrigation system, whose discovery

they believed would throw new light on the origin of class relations and the state. Such marks would not appear to the naked eye, but flying over the territory immediately revealed intricate patterns that years of erosion had not effaced.

This example comes to mind, with all its metaphoric power, with the realization that a book on the commons written in the United States must start by acknowledging our debt to the first commoners on this continent: the Native American populations, the First Nations, who held the land in common for centuries, honoring, celebrating its bounty, taking from it just enough for their survival not to deplete its wealth, leaving the same abundance for the next seven generations as Native wisdom dictated. Today, in the eyes of the average American, little seems to remain of the First Nations' commons, beside a host of names, often encountered on the highways, designating communities that have long been displaced. Only the reservations seem to stand—these too violated by constant federal theft of Native land and the contamination caused by the extractivist activities imposed upon them. Yet, as with the grid historians have discovered in the land of the Nazca, much of the wealth of this country—its food, its medicines, its healing practices, even some of its institutions—as Paula Gunn Allen reminds us—have their origins in Native America. Most important, what remains alive of the First Nations' world is *a conception of people's relation to property and the land that still nourishes our imagination.*

The indigenous commons, moreover, are far from being extinguished. Not only in the South of the American continent are vast territories governed by communitarian regimes, but, as the Zapatista movement has shown, new communal forms of social organization are continually being produced.

Whereas private property was the condition of freedom in bourgeois political philosophy and the distinguishing mark between civilization and savagery, liberty for the Native nations depended on its absence.[4] Ownership of things in common was so universal throughout the American continent when the Europeans arrived that even the cooking pot, Columbus noted, was available to anyone who wanted to take from it, and this even in times of starvation. Two centuries later, Thomas Morton could also say of the Five Nations inhabiting New England that "although every proprietor knows his own . . . yet all things, so long as they will last, are used in common amongst them."[5] The idea of ownership of land was so alien among Native Americans that individuals made no effort to secure

79

for themselves the lands they occupied, frequently moving grounds, and readily sharing them with newcomers. As Kirkpatrick Sale writes, "Owning the land, selling the land, seemed ideas as foreign as owning and selling the clouds or the wind."[6] William Cronon too comments, "This relaxed attitude towards personal possession was typical throughout New England."[7] As we know, this willingness to part with personal possession was misinterpreted by Europeans as a sign that property did not exist. Thus, when the colonists came to New England they assumed that Indian territory was terra nullius, because they saw that the inhabitants had a loose attitude toward personal possessions and periodically moved their grounds. In reality, Indian families had a guaranteed use of their fields and of the land where their tents stood. But these were not permanent possessions. No effort was made to set permanent boundaries around a field that a family used, and fields were abandoned after some years and allowed to return to bushes. What people possessed was the use of the land and the crops; this is what was traded, and this usufruct right could not prevent trespassing. In fact, different groups of people could have claims on the same land, depending on the use they made of it, which might not be the same.[8] Several villages could fish in the same rivers recognizing their mutual rights. And when one left the clan they left everything they had possessed. Yet, these unattached, nomadic tribes had a far deeper communion with the land and agriculture than the privatizing Europeans and so much respect for it that though "they had taken their livelihood from the land for eons, hunting, foraging, planting, fishing, building, trekking," at the time of the Europeans' arrival "the land of North America was still by every account without exception a lush and fertile wilderness teeming with abundant wildlife in water, woods, and air."[9]

The result of this lack of attachment to private property among the Native peoples of America was a communal outlook that valued cooperation, group identity, and culture. In Indian land, for instance, at the time of the Europeans' arrivals, if one starved, everybody starved, making the help they gave to the colonists even more remarkable. The dislike for individual accumulation was so strong that they invented the ritual of the *potlatch*, that is, a periodic redistribution of wealth, to free themselves from it. Healing too was and continues to be a collective practice that fuses—in the sweat lodge—not only the bodies but fuses them with the earth, the fire, and the great force rising from this profoundly commoning experience.

To acknowledge this history and its legacy today is not—as it is at times argued—to romanticize an artificially constructed Indian subject or naturalize an ethnicized identity produced by the colonizers' gaze. It is to recognize the peoples that historically have most suffered and fought against the enclosures on the American continent and to refuse to be oblivious to the claims of those who once inhabited the land we think of as the site of future commons. No major political change will in fact be possible in the United States unless the two grand injustices on which this country is based—the dispossession and genocide of the Native Americans and the enslavement of millions of Africans, continued through the post-Reconstruction era and in many ways into the present—are confronted and reparations are provided. Furthermore, as Paula Gunn Allen has written, loss of memory is the root of oppression, for obliviousness to the past renders meaningless the world in which we move, strips the spaces in which we live of any significance, as we forget at what cost we tread the ground we walk upon and whose histories are inscribed in the stones, fields, and buildings that surround us.[10] Loss of memory makes for a silent environment in which our struggles have little chance of success, confronted with the cacophony of paid-up media and political lies under military protection.

Two more reasons make it imperative that in the beginning of a discussion of feminism and the commons we turn to the history of the commoning practices of the Native populations of the American continent. As the construction of the Keystone Pipeline in the territory of the Lakota has well demonstrated, the theft and destruction of the First Nations' commons continues.[11] Indeed, throughout Latin America, the communitarian regimes indigenous people have created are struggling to survive, yet holding on to the social institutions that have enabled them to maintain their relation to the land, govern themselves, and organize their communities according to a logic profoundly different from that of the state.[12] Thus, the question of our relationship to the Native commons is an urgent political one. Furthermore, as we have seen, in the history of the Native commons we find the best, most concrete example of a *commoning use of resources realized without any private property claim* or exclusionary regulations.

Especially important for the purpose of this book is the power that women had in Native communities, very likely related to the latter's lack of desire for private property and accumulation. As reported by Lewis

Henry Morgan,[13] such was the power of women among the five Iroquois nations that they could decide on peace or war. According to Allen, the value Native people placed on freedom, lack of hierarchies, and egalitarian relations has been a major source of influence on not only socialist thought in Europe and America, but especially American feminism, an influence symbolically evoked by the gathering of the first feminist conference in the United States on what had been Indian land: Seneca Falls.[14]

It is not, thus, a pure coincidence that the first reconstruction of a territory on the continent organized on the principle of the commons was realized by Native Americans—the Zapatistas—or that the Women's Revolutionary Law is central to their constitution, establishing a broad range of women's rights that is unprecedented in any country.[15] Similarly it is not a coincidence that throughout the Latin American continent—from Tierra del Fuego to the Amazon, from Chiapas to South Dakota, today it is women who are leading the struggle in defense of the commons, in this process creating new forms of communization. Whereas a broad coalition of forces met at Standing Rock to oppose the drilling on the reservation's sacred grounds, it was primarily women who built the infrastructure that enabled more than seven thousand people to camp for months in one of the coldest parts of the country, where temperature in the winter reaches far below zero, organizing food and clothing supplies and classes for children, as well as creating the slogans for the struggle. The courage and creativity that these 'water protectors' have demonstrated is certainly part of the reason for the support the encampment has received. Not only have representatives from four hundred tribes joined it, but activists, men and women of all ages, have also gone to it from every part of the country, breaking the isolation in which Native peoples have in the past confronted the White Man and recognizing a common interest in the defense and reclamation of the American commons.

## Notes

1   Frederick Engels, "The Mark," in *Socialism: Utopian and Scientific* (New York: International Publishers, 1935).

2   Eduardo Galeano, *The Book of Embraces* (New York: W.W. Norton, 1991), 135.

3   Paula Gunn Allen, "Who Is Your Mother? Red Roots of White Feminism," in *Multicultural Literacy: Opening the American Mind*, eds. Rick Simonson and Scott Walker (Saint Paul, MN: Graywolf Press, 1988), 3–12.

4   On this subject, see William Brandon, *New Worlds for Old: Reports from the New World and Their Effects on the Development of Social Thought in Europe*,

*1500–1800* (Athens: Ohio University Press, 1986), 23–24. Brandon argues that the very concept of liberty, understood as self-determination, entered European social thought in the seventeenth century, traveling from the 'New World,' brought by countless reports that pictured the indigenous populations as a people without masters living in a state of equality, oblivious to thine and mine.

5   Thomas Morton, quoted in William Cronon, *Changes in the Land: Indians, Colonists, and the Ecology of New England* (New York: Hill and Wang, 2011), 61. An early American colonist, Thomas Morton was the founder, in 1626, of Merrymount, a colony held to be scandalous by its Puritan neighbors because of his relaxed moral rules and its good disposition toward the surrounding Algonquian populations, whom Morton admired and held in great respect. A particular object of scandal in the eyes of the governing authorities of the Plymouth Colony was the celebration of May Day festivals, during which the colonists danced around the May Pole, according to an old English peasant tradition, joining in the dance with Native women. On Thomas Morton, see Peter Linebaugh, *The Incomplete, True, Authentic, and Wonderful History of May Day* (Oakland: PM Press, 2016), 15–17, 85–86.

6   Kirkpatrick Sale, *The Conquest of Paradise: Christopher Columbus and the Columbian Legacy* (New York: Knopf, 1990), 314.

7   Cronon, *Changes in the Land*, 61–63.

8   See Cronon, *Changes in the Land*, 62–63; John Hanson Mitchell, *Trespassing: An Inquiry into the Private Ownership of Land* (Reading, MA: Perseus Books, 1998).

9   Sale, *The Conquest of Paradise*, 315.

10  Allen, "Who Is Your Mother?," 18–20.

11  Owned by the TransCanada Corporation and advertised as the most advanced pipeline in North America, the Keystone Pipeline will run for nearly two thousand kilometers from Alberta, Canada, to Texas. It runs through the lands of indigenous people threatening their sacred sites and waters. It has also been protested by environmental groups who have accused TransCanada of providing false information concerning the project's impact on the environment.

12  On the struggle of communitarian regimes to maintain their relationship to the land and govern themselves, see the work of the K'iche' scholar activist Gladys Tzul Tzul, especially *Sistemas de gobierno comunal indígena: mujeres y tramas de parentesco* (Guatemala: Sociedad Comunitaria de Estudios Estratégicos, 2016) and "Gobierno comunal indígena y estado guatemalteco," *Departamento Ecuménico de Investigaciones*, April 25, 2018, accessed June 2, 2018, http://www.deicr.org/+presentacion-de-libro-gladys-tzul+. Tzul Tzul examines the communal institutions that have served to defend indigenous populations' relationship to the land, with specific reference to the K'iche' indigenous population of the forty-eight cantons of Totonicapán, in Guatemala. Tzul Tzul stresses the role of collective work, collective decision-making through communal assemblies, and long established rituals (like the fiestas) in the production of autonomous forms of life and social relations.

13    Lewis Henry Morgan, *Ancient Society* (Cambridge, MA: Harvard University Press, 1964 [1877]). What Morgan found in his study and contact with Native populations in New England, as well as in the territories of the Dakotas, is that at the epoch of the European arrival descent was through the female line (79). Women had a voice in the council, which he described as a democratic assembly in which "every adult female and male member had a voice upon all questions brought before it." He also found that women were entrusted with bestowing names for their children and for members of the clan, when in the course of their lives they would need to change them, and that all clan members traced their descent from a common female ancestor (65). But he noted that at the time of his encounter things were changing as a result of the influence and pressure of the Europeans—for instance, some tribes were shifting from the female line descent to the male line.

14    The reference is to the first women's rights conference in the United States, held at Seneca Falls, in northern New York State, in July 1848, in what had been the territory of the Six Nations.

15    The Women's Revolutionary Law was adopted in the 1992 at the time of the Zapatista uprising. It stipulates seven key women's rights, including the right to participate in the revolutionary struggle as they desire and need to, to work and receive a just salary, to decide how many children they will have and care for, to participate in the affairs of the community and hold positions of authority, if freely and democratically elected, to education, to choose their partner, and to primary attention in matters of health and nutrition. For the text of the law, see *Zapatistas! Documents of the New Mexican Revolution* (Brooklyn: Autonomedia, 1994). For a discussion of the process that led to the adoption of the law, see Hilary Klein, *Compañeras: Zapatista Women's Stories* (New York: Seven Stories Press, 2015).

# Commons against and beyond Capitalism
## (with George Caffentzis)

> In our view, we cannot simply say, "No commons without community."
> We must also say, "No commons without economy," in the sense of
> *oikonomia*, i.e., the reproduction of human beings within the social
> and natural household. Hence, reinventing the commons is linked
> to the reinvention of the communal and a commons-based economy.
> —Maria Mies and Veronika Bennholdt-Thomsen,
> *The Subsistence Perspective*

'Commons' have become a ubiquitous presence in the political, economic,
and even real estate language of our time. Left and right, neoliberals and
neo-Keynesians, conservatives and anarchists use the concept in their
political interventions. The World Bank has embraced it requiring, in
April 2012, that all research conducted in-house or supported by its grants
be "open access under copyright licensing from Creative Commons—a
nonprofit organization whose copyright licenses are designed to accom-
modate the expanded access to information afforded by the Internet."[1]
Even that titan of neoliberalism, the *Economist*, has proven to have a
soft spot for it, in its praise of Elinor Ostrom, the doyenne of commons
studies and critic of market totalitarianism, as indicated by the eulogy in
its obituary:

> It seemed to Elinor Ostrom that the world contained a large body of
> common sense. People, left to themselves would sort out rational
> ways of surviving and getting along. Although the world's arable
> land, forests, fresh water and fisheries were all finite, it was possible

to share them without depleting them and to care for them without fighting. While others wrote gloomily of the tragedy of the commons, seeing only over-fishing and over-farming in a free-for-all of greed, Mrs Ostrom, with her loud laugh and louder tops, cut a cheery and contrarian figure.[2]

Finally, it is hard to ignore the prodigal use of 'common' or 'commons' in the real estate discourse of university campuses, shopping malls, and gated communities. Elite universities that cost students $50,000 a year call their libraries 'information commons.' *It is almost a law of contemporary society that the more commons are attacked, the more they are celebrated.*

In this essay we examine the reasons for these developments and respond to some of the main questions facing anticapitalist commoners today: What do we mean by 'anticapitalist commons'? How can we create a new mode of production no longer built on the exploitation of labor out of the commons that our struggles bring into existence? How can we prevent the commons from being co-opted and, instead of providing an alternative to capitalism, becoming platforms on which a sinking capitalist class can reconstruct its fortunes?

## History, Capitalism, and the Commons

We start with a historical perspective on the commons, keeping in mind that *history itself is a common*, even when it reveals the ways in which we have been divided, provided it is narrated through a multiplicity of voices. History is our collective memory, our extended body connecting us to a vast expanse of struggles that give meaning and power to our political practice.

History shows us that 'commoning' is the principle by which human beings have organized their existence on this earth for thousands of years. As Peter Linebaugh has reminded us, there is hardly a society that does not have the commons at its heart.[3] Even today, communal systems of property and commoning social relations continue to exist in many parts of the world, especially among of the indigenous peoples of Latin America, Africa, and Asia.

When we speak of commons, then, we do not only speak of one particular reality or a set of small-scale experiments, like the rural communes of the 1960s in Northern California, however important they may have been.[4] We speak of large-scale social formations that at times were continent-wide, like the networks of commons that in precolonial America stretched from present-day Chile to Nicaragua and Texas, connected by a vast array of exchanges, including gift and barter. In Africa, as well, communal land tenure systems have survived to the present, even in the face of an unprecedented 'land grabbing' drive.[5] In England, common land remained an important economic factor until the beginning of the twentieth century. Linebaugh estimates that in 1688 one-quarter of the total area of England and Wales was common land.[6] After more than two centuries of enclosures involving the privatization of millions of acres, according to the eleventh edition of the *Encyclopaedia Britannica*, the amount of common land remaining in 1911 was 1,500,000 to 2,000,000 acres, roughly 5 percent of English territory. By the end of the twentieth century common land was still 3 percent of the total of the territory.[7]

These considerations are important not because we wish to model our concept of the commons and attending practices on the past. We will not construct an alternative society by nostalgic returns to social forms that have already proven unable to resist the attack of capitalist relations against them. The new commons will have to be a product of our struggle. Looking back through the ages serves, however, to rebut the assumption that the society of commons we propose is a utopia or a project that only small groups can realize, rather than the commons being a political frame for thinking of alternatives to capitalism.

Not only have commons existed for thousands of years, but elements of a communally based society are still around us, though subject to a constant attack that recently has intensified. Capitalist development requires the destruction of communal properties and relations. With reference to the sixteenth- and seventeenth-century 'enclosures' that expelled the peasantry in Europe from the land—the act of birth of modern capitalist society—Marx spoke of 'primitive accumulation.' But we have learned that this was not a one-time affair, spatially and temporally circumscribed, but a centuries-long process that continues into the present. Primitive, or better originary, accumulation is the strategy the capitalist class always resorts to in times of crisis, since expropriating workers and expanding the labor available for exploitation are the most effective methods to reestablish the 'proper balance of power' and gain the upper hand in the class struggle.

In the era of neoliberalism and globalization this strategy has been developed in the extreme and normalized, making primitive accumulation and the privatization of the 'commonwealth' a permanent process, now extending to every area and aspect of our existence. Not only are lands, forests, and fisheries appropriated for commercial uses in what appears to be a new 'land grab' of unprecedented proportions, we now live in a world in which everything, from the water we drink to our body's cells and genomes, has a price tag or is patented and no effort is spared to ensure that companies have the right to enclose all the remaining open space on earth and force us to pay to gain access to it. From New Delhi and New York to Lagos and Los Angeles, urban space is being privatized. Street vending or sitting on the sidewalks or stretching on a beach without paying are being forbidden. Rivers are damned, forests logged, waters and aquifers bottled away and put on the market, traditional knowledge systems are sacked through intellectual property regulations, and public schools are turned into for-profit enterprises. *This is why the idea of the commons exercises such an attraction on our collective imagination; their loss expands our awareness of the significance of their existence and increases our desire to learn more about them.*

## Commons and the Class Struggle

For all the attacks on them, commons have not ceased to exist. As Massimo De Angelis has argued, there have always been commons 'outside' of capitalism that have played a key role in the class struggle, feeding both the utopian/radical imagination and the bellies of many commoners.[8] The mutual aid associations that workers had organized, which were later displaced by the welfare state, are key examples of this 'outside.'[9] More important for us is the fact that new commons are constantly created. From the free software movement to the solidarity economy movement, a whole world of new social relations is coming into existence based on the principle of communal sharing,[10] sustained by the realization that capitalism has only more work in store for us, more wars, more misery and divisions. Indeed, at a time of permanent crisis and constant assaults on our jobs, wages, and social spaces, the construction of commons is becoming a necessary means of survival. It is not a coincidence that in the last few years, in Greece, as wages and pensions have been cut on average by 30 percent and unemployment among youth has reached 50 percent, several forms of mutual aid have appeared, including free medical services, free distributions of produce by farmers in urban centers, and the 'repair' by electricians of wires that were cut because the bills were not paid.

We must stress, however, that the commoning initiatives we see pro-liferating around us—'time banks,' urban gardens, community-supported agriculture, food co-ops, local currencies, Creative Commons licenses, bartering practices, information sharing—are more than dikes against the neoliberal assault on our livelihood. They are experiments in self-provisioning and the seeds of an alternative mode of production in the making. This is also how we should view the squatters' movements that have formed in many urban peripheries throughout the world since the 1980s, products of land expropriations but also signs of a growing popula-tion of city dwellers 'disconnected' from the formal world economy, now organizing their reproduction outside of state and market control.[11] As Raúl Zibechi suggests, these urban land squats are better envisioned as a "planet of commons," in which people exercise their "right to the city,"[12] rather than as the "planet of slums" that Mike Davis has described.[13]

The resistance of the indigenous peoples of the Americas to the increasing privatization of their lands has given the struggle for the commons a new impulse. While the Zapatistas' call for a new Mexican constitution recognizing collective ownership has gone unheeded, the right of indigenous people to use the natural resources in their territories was sanctioned by the new Venezuelan constitution of 1999. In 2009, in Bolivia, as well, a new constitution recognized communal property. We cite these examples not to propose that we rely on the state's legal appa-ratus to promote the society of commons that we call for, which would be a contradiction, but to stress how powerful is the demand coming from the grassroots for the creation of new forms of sociality and provision-ing under communal control and organized on the principle of social cooperation.

### Co-opted and Gated Commons

In the face of these developments, the task before us is to understand how we can connect these different realities and, above all, how we can ensure that the commons we create are truly transformative of our social relations. We have commons in fact that are co-opted by the state, others that are closed and 'gated' commons, and still others that are commodity-producing and ultimately controlled by the market.

Consider two examples of co-opted commons. For years now, part of the capitalist international establishment (especially the World Bank) has been promoting a softer model of privatization that appeals to the principle of the commons. In the name of protecting the 'global commons,' for example, the World Bank has expelled from forests people who had lived there for generations, while giving access to those who can pay, arguing that the market (in the form of a game park or an ecotourism zone) is the best instrument of conservation.[14] The UN also advocates the right to manage access to the world resources, like the atmosphere, the oceans, or the Amazon forests, again in the name of preserving 'the common heritage of humanity.'

Communalism is also the jargon under which volunteer labor is recruited by governments. For instance, former British Prime Minister Cameron's 'Big Society' program proposed to mobilize people's energies for a variety of volunteer programs presumably compensating for the cuts in social services introduced in the name of the economic crisis. In an ideological break with the tradition that Margaret Thatcher initiated in the 1980s when she proclaimed, "There is no such thing as Society," proceeding to cut even the glass of milk out of the children's school lunch, the 'Big Society' is now ensconced in a series of laws, including the Public Services (Social Value) Act. This legislation instructs government sponsored organizations (from daycare centers to libraries and clinics) to recruit local artists and young people who, without pay, will engage in activities increasing the 'social value,' defined as contribution to social cohesion and reduction of the cost of social reproduction. In other words, nonprofit organizations providing programs for the elderly will qualify for government funding, if they can show they create social cohesion and 'social value,' measured according to a special arithmetic factoring in the advantages of a socially and environmentally sustainable society embedded in a capitalist economy.[15] In this way communal efforts to build solidarity and cooperative forms of existence outside the control of the market are subsumed by a program intent on cheapening the cost of social reproduction and contributing to accelerate the layoffs of paid public employees.

These are two examples of states (national and global) using the commons form to achieve their un-common aims. But there is a wide spectrum of commons (ranging from closed residential communities through consumer co-ops to certain kinds of land trusts and housing co-ops) where people share access to common resource fairly and democratically but are indifferent to or even hostile to the interests of 'outsiders.' We call these commons 'gated' commons and argue they are quite compatible capitalist relations. In fact, many operate as if they were corporations, with the commoners being something like shareholders. They constitute a fast growing sector of the institutions that self-identify as commons.

Such commons are rooted in the recognition that in this neoliberal period when the ideology of the market is triumphant, it is crucial for individuals to protect themselves against its 'failures' and 'catastrophes.' Commons can strengthen our collective power to intervene in markets. Thus, many 'gated' communities feature common swimming pools, golf courses, libraries, woodworking shops, theaters, and computer rooms. 'Gated' commoners share resources that would be difficult, expensive or impossible for any individual to purchase and enjoy. But these resources are jealously guarded from the use of 'outsiders,' especially those who would be unable to pay the often-hefty fee for buying into the common.

An example of 'gated' commons are housing co-ops. There are more than a million housing units organized as co-ops in the U.S. Though a majority of them embrace commons principles for their 'shareholders,' they are often legally obliged to attend to their monetary interests alone. Their cooperation remains on the instrumental plane and rarely takes on a transformative character.

Together these 'gated' commons satisfy the basic needs (for food, housing, recreation) of millions of people on a daily basis. This is power of collective action. But they do not construct different social relations and may even deepen racial and intra-class divisions.

## Commodity-Producing Commons

Along with gated commons, there are commons producing commodities for the market. A classic example are the unenclosed Alpine meadows of Switzerland, which every summer become grazing fields for dairy cows, providing milk for the dairy industry. Assemblies of dairy farmers manage these meadows. Indeed, Garrett Hardin could not have written his "Tragedy of the Commons" had he studied how Swiss cheese came to his refrigerator.[16]

Another often cited example of commons producing for the market are the more than one thousand lobster fishers of Maine, operating along hundreds of miles of coastal waters, where millions of lobsters live, breed, and die every year. Over more than a century, lobster fishers have built a communal system of sharing the lobster catch on the basis of agreed upon divisions of the coast into separate zones managed by local 'gangs' and

91

self-imposed limits on the number of lobsters to be caught. This has not always been a peaceful process. Mainers pride themselves on their rough individualism, and agreements between different 'gangs' have occasionally broken down. Violence has then erupted in competitive struggles to expand the allotted fishing zones or to bust the limits on catch. But the fishers have quickly learned that such struggles destroy the lobster stock and in time have restored the commons regime.[17]

Even the Maine state fishery management department now accepts this commons-based fishing, which was outlawed for decades as a violation of antitrust laws. One reason for this change in official attitude is the contrast between the state of the lobster fisheries compared to that of the 'groundfishing' (i.e., fishing for cod, haddock, flounder, and similar species) that is carried out in the Gulf of Maine and in Georges Bank, where the Gulf connects with the ocean. Whereas in the last quarter century the former has reached sustainability and maintained it (even during some severe economic downturns), since the 1990s, one species after another of groundfish has been periodically overfished, leading to the official closure of Georges Bank for years at a time.[18] At the heart of the matter are (1) the difference in the technology used by groundfishing and lobster fishing and, above all, (2) the difference in the site where the catches are taken. Lobster fishing has the advantage of having its common pool resource close to the coast and within the territorial waters of the state. This makes it possible to demarcate zones for the local lobster gangs, whereas the deep waters of Georges Bank are not easily amenable to a partition. The fact that Georges Bank is outside the twenty-mile territorial limit also meant that outsiders using big trawlers were able to fish until 1977, when the territorial limits were extended to two hundred miles. They could not have been kept out before 1977, contributing in a major way to the depletion of the fishery. Finally, the rather archaic technology lobster fishers uniformly employ discourages competition. By contrast, starting in the early 1990s, 'improvements' in the technology of groundfishing—'better' nets and electronic equipment capable of detecting fish more 'effectively'— have created havoc in an industry that is organized on an open-access principle (get a boat and you will fish). The availability of a more advanced and cheaper detection and capture technology has clashed with the competitive organization of the industry that had been ruled by the motto: "Each against each and nature against all," ending in the "Tragedy of the Commons" Hardin envisioned in 1968.

This contradiction is not unique to Maine groundfishing. It has plagued fisher communities across the world, who now find themselves increasingly displaced by the industrialization of fishing and the hegemonic power of the great trawlers, whose dragnets deplete the oceans.[19] Fishers in Newfoundland have thus faced a similar situation those of Georges Bank, with disastrous results for the livelihood of their communities.

The lobster commons are an important alternative to the logic of competition. At the same time, they are embedded in the international seafood market and their fate is ultimately determined by it. If the market for lobster collapses or the state decides to allow for offshore oil drilling in the Gulf of Maine, the lobsters commons will be dissolved, as they do not have any autonomy with respect to market relations.

## Defining Commons

The existence of 'gated' and commodity-producing commons demonstrates that there are many forms of commons and challenges us to see what aspects of commoning activities identify them as other from state and market and the principle of a social organization alternative to capitalism. To this end, keeping in mind Massimo De Angelis's recommendation against setting up 'models' of commons,[20] we propose some criteria drawn from discussions with comrades and practices we have encountered in our political work:

i) To contribute to the long-term construction of a new modes of production, commons should be autonomous spaces and should aim to overcome the divisions existing among us and build the skills necessary for self-government. Today we see only fragments of the new society potentially in the making, in the same way as we can spot fragments of capitalism in urban centers like Florence in late medieval Europe, for example, where broad concentrations of workers already existed in the textile industry by the mid–fourteenth century.

ii) Commons are defined by the existence of a shared property, in the form of a shared natural or social wealth—lands, waters, forests, systems of knowledge, capacities for care—to be used by all commoners, without any distinction, but which are not for sale. Equal access to the necessary means of (re)production must be the foundation of life in the commons. This is important because the existence of hierarchical relations makes commons vulnerable to enclosures.

93

iii) Commons are not things but social relations. This is the reason why some (e.g., Peter Linebaugh) prefer to speak of 'commoning,' a term that underscores not the material wealth shared but the sharing itself and the solidarity bonds produced in the process.[21] Commoning is a practice that appears inefficient to capitalist eyes. It is the willingness to spend much time in the work of cooperation, discussing, negotiating, and learning to deal with conflicts and disagreement. Yet only in this way can a community in which people understand their essential interdependence be built.

iv) Commons function on the basis of established regulations, stipulating how the common wealth is to be used and cared for, that is, what the commoners' entitlements and obligations should be.

v) Commons require a community, the principle being "no community, no commons." This is why we cannot speak of 'global commons,' a concept that presumes the existence of a global collectivity.

In the name of protecting the 'global commons' and the 'common heritage of humanity,' the World Bank launched a new privatization drive expelling from forests people who had lived there for generations.[22] Indeed, the World Bank has taken on the role of representing the global collectivity, because it is a part of the United Nations system set up in the post–World War II era to represent collective capitalism in all its varieties (including the statist versions of the Soviet Union and the People's Republic of China). The UN presents itself not as the voice of a collective capital that does exist but as a stand-in for a collective humanity that does not exist! On this basis, it claims to manage access to common resources like the atmosphere and the oceans in lieu of the nonexistent (but coming?) humanity.

Evidence of the fraud involved in the concept of the 'global commons' was the debate that took place on June 14, 2012, during the hearing at the U.S. Senate Committee on Foreign Relations concerning the ratification of the Law of Sea, which was meant to codify the use of the oceans beyond the two-hundred-mile economic exclusion zone claimed by most nations with oceanic coast lines. This hearing pitted former secretary of defense Donald Rumsfeld against Senators John Kerry and Richard Lugar. Rumsfeld was against the treaty because it required companies that mined the ocean 'commons' (i.e., beyond the two-hundred-mile limit) to contribute to a fund that would compensate 'less developed countries,' whose companies do not have the technological or capital requirements to do such mining. He claimed that this type of wealth redistribution is a "novel principle that has, in my view, no clear limits" and that "could become a precedent for the resources of outer space."

Kerry and Lugar instead argued in favor of the ratification of the Law of the Sea treaty not to protect the seas from capitalist exploitation, but because they believed the treaty gave mining companies an unequivocal legal claim to the ocean floor. "Accession to the Law of the Sea Convention is the only means to protect and advance the claims of U.S. entities to the vast mineral resources contained on the deep seabed floor," reads a June 13 letter to Mr. Kerry and Mr. Lugar from organizations including the American Petroleum Institute and the U.S. Chamber of Commerce.[23] The 'debate' among the global commoners, Rumsfeld, Kerry, and Lugar, was over whether or not it was necessary to bribe capitalists who cannot scramble for the riches made available by the greatest spatial enclosure in history! This is what the principle of the 'common heritage of humanity' came to on June 14, 2012.

The 'global commons' designation is a fraudulent maneuver that must be rejected. The same applies to the United Nations' designation of selected cities and geographical areas as 'heritage of humanity,' which required municipalities and government to adopt 'protection' and valorization measures that benefit the tourist industry, while diverting resources away from more works that would improve the conditions of the local populations.

vi) Commons are constituted on the basis of social cooperation, relations of reciprocity, and responsibility for the reproduction of the shared wealth, natural or produced. Respect for other people and openness to heterogeneous experiences provided the rules of cooperation are observed distinguishes them from gated communities that can be committed to racist, exclusionary practices, while fostering solidarity among their members.

vii) Commons are shaped by collective decision-making, through assemblies and other forms of direct democracy. Grassroots power, power from the ground up, power derived from tested abilities, and continual rotation of leadership and authority through different subjects, depending on the tasks to be performed, is the source of decision-making. This distinguishes commons from communism, which consigned power to the state. Commoning is reclaiming the power of making basic decisions about our lives and doing so collectively. This aspect of the commons is akin to the concept of *horizontalidad* that was coined during the revolt in Argentina that began on December 19–20, 2001, which has since become popular among social movements, especially in South America. It eschews the hierarchical structure of political parties, with decisions made by general assemblies (instead of by predefined central committees), where issues are discussed with the goal of achieving consensus.[24]

viii) Commons are a perspective fostering a common interest in every aspect of life and political work and are therefore committed to refusing labor hierarchies and inequalities in every struggle and prioritizing the development of a truly collective subject.

ix) All these characteristics differentiate the *common* from the *public*, which is owned, managed, controlled, and regulated by and for the state, constituting a particular type of private domain. This is not to say that we shouldn't fight to ensure that the public is not privatized. As an intermediate terrain it is in our interest that commercial interests do not engulf the public, but we should not lose sight of the distinction. We cannot abandon the state, since it is the site of the accumulation of the wealth produced by our past and present labor. Similarly, most of us still depend on capital for our survival, as most of us do not have land or other means of subsistence. But we should work to ensure that we go beyond the state and capital.

## Conclusion

The notion of the commons is today the object of much debate and experimentation. There are many issues that are still unsolved, but it is clear that commoning will be a growing practice as neither state nor market can guarantee our reproduction. The challenge that we face in this context is not how to multiply commons initiatives but how to place at the center of our organizing the collective reappropriation of the wealth we have produced and the abolition of social hierarchies and inequalities. Only by responding to these imperatives can we rebuild communities and ensure that commons are not created at the expense of the well-being of other people and do not rest on new forms of colonization.

## Notes

1    World Bank, "Bank Publications and Research Now Easier to Access, Reuse," April 10, 2012, accessed May 23, 2018, https://tinyurl.com/7axc7j3.

2    "Elinor Ostrom, Defender of the Commons, Died on June 12th, Aged 78," *Economist*, accessed May 31, 2018, http://www.economist.com/node/21557717.

3    Peter Linebaugh, *The Magna Carta Manifesto: Liberties and Commons for All* (Berkeley: University of California Press, 2008).

4    Iain Boal et al., *West of Eden: Communes and Utopia in Northern California* (Oakland: PM Press, 2012).

5    Fred Pearce, *The Land Grabbers: The New Fight Over Who Owns the Earth* (Boston: Beacon Press, 2012).

6    Peter Linebaugh, "Enclosures from the Bottom Up," in *The Wealth of the Commons: A World beyond Market and State*, eds. David Bollier and Silke Helfrich (Amherst, MA: Levellers Press, 2012), 114–24.

7    "Common Land," *naturenet*, accessed May 23, 2018, http://naturenet.net/law/commonland.html.

8    Massimo De Angelis, *The Beginning of History: Value Struggles and Global Capitalism* (London: Pluto Press 2007).

9    David T. Beito, *From Mutual Aid to the Welfare State: Fraternal Societies and Social Services, 1890–1967* (Chapel Hill: University of North Carolina Press, 2000).

10   Bollier and Helfrich, *The Wealth of the Commons*.

11   Raúl Zibechi, *Territories in Resistance: A Cartography of Latin American Social Movements* (Oakland: AK Press, 2012), 190.

12   Zibechi, *Territories in Resistance*.

13   Mike Davis, *Planet of Slums* (New York: Verso, 2006).

14   Ana Isla, "Who Pays for the Kyoto Protocol?" in *Eco-Sufficiency & Global Justice: Women Write Political Economy*, ed. Ariel Salleh (London: Pluto Press, 2009).

15   Emma Dowling, "The Big Society, Part 2: Social Value, Measure and the Public Services Act," *New Left Project*, July 30, 2012, accessed May 31, 2018, https://tinyurl.com/yamy6evv.

16   Robert McC. Netting, *Balancing on an Alp: Ecological Change and Continuity in a Swiss Mountain Community* (Cambridge: Cambridge University Press, 1981); Garrett Hardin, "The Tragedy of the Commons," *Science* 162, no. 3859 (December 1968): 1243–48, http://science.sciencemag.org/content/sci/162/3859/1243.full.pdf.

17   Colin Woodward, *The Lobster Coast: Rebels, Rusticators, and the Struggle for a Forgotten Frontier* (New York: Penguin Books, 2004).

18   Woodward, *The Lobster Coast*, 230–31.

19   Mariarosa Dalla Costa and Monica Chilese, *Our Mother Ocean: Enclosure, Commons, and the Global Fishermen's Movement* (Brooklyn: Common Notions, 2015).

20   Massimo De Angelis, *Omnia Sunt Communia: On the Commons and the Transformation to Postcapitalism* (London: Zed Books, 2017).

21   Linebaugh, *The Magna Carta Manifesto*, 50–51.

22  Isla, "Who Pays for the Kyoto Protocol?"

23  Kristina Wong, "Rumsfeld Still Opposes Law of the Sea Treaty: Admirals See It as a Way to Settle Maritime Claims," *Washington Times*, June 14, 2012, accessed June 2, 2018, http://www.washingtontimes.com/news/2012/jun/14/rumsfeld-hits-law-of-sea-treaty/?page=all.

24  Marina A. Sitrin, *Everyday Revolutions: Horizontalism and Autonomy in Argentina* (London: Zed Books, 2012).

# The University:
# A Knowledge Common?

When, in April 2011, I was invited to give a talk at the University of Minnesota at a conference entitled "Beneath the University, the Commons" I wondered what that title could mean. At the conference itself there were different interpretations. Jason Read reminded us that the university is already potentially a common, as students go there leaving the individualizing environment of their families to join a community and engage in collective activities. George Caffentzis spoke of knowledge commons, ranging from physical spaces like libraries to philosophical principles, such as the long-standing ban, dating back to Plato, against the commodification of knowledge.

For me the title of the conference brought a flood of images not the least of which was literally that of the grass and the land under the cement on which classrooms and libraries have been built, suggesting that building a university may be a sort of enclosure. My response was partly motivated by my memories of the universities of Port Harcourt, where I taught from 1984 to the end of 1986, and the nearby University of Calabar, which I frequently visited during my stays at Port Harcourt.

Three images in particular stood out. Uniport had been recently built with money coming from the oil boom of the late 1970s. It was built on land expropriated from the nearby village of Alu, but the villagers still held on to it. Every morning bicycling to my classes I saw women farming along the road on any patch of land the university had not cemented. In January, the time of slash and burn, the smoke coming from the burning stubs filled the campus, but no one, to my knowledge, ever protested. Possibly the students who trekked to their classrooms looked at these women bent on their machetes as people without knowledge, ignorant, with nothing to contribute to their education. Yet I soon learned that these same women knew better than me and better than many students all that was taking place on the campus, and they reported it to that great female common that in Africa is the market. When, for instance, a student was murdered in the spring of 1986, the market women asked me what I thought, and when they heard what I learned from my colleagues they shook their head with contempt.

Another image I still recall from the University of Port Harcourt is going to the bush in the evening to watch the sun setting among the palms. As I pedaled I would see the cars of some colleagues passing along, and I soon realized that they were going to check the progress of the food crops they had planted on the university's land. They did not own the land and did not cultivate it themselves, but they could not imagine not taking advantage of the availability of good land and being completely dependent on a wage. Again, everybody knew and no one complained.

Then, there were the cows. Every spring at the neighboring University of Calabar, the cows arrived. They came from the north to graze, driven by cattle raisers who brought them south in order to sell them, but before doing so they wanted to fatten them up with the rich grass of the rain forest belt. And the university accommodated itself to this need and hosted the cows.

These images of commons refusing to vanish, even in a university built on an expropriated village with money from the short-lived oil boom, receded, however, when I began investigating what might be underneath the university that hosted the conference. What I was told was that the land trust university that hosted the conference was constructed near the site of what once had been a market place belonging to the Sioux populations that had inhabited the area and that homesteaders had displaced, to then suffocate their rebellion in a bloodbath, including the execution of thirty-eight of their leaders on December 26, 1862—selected by President Lincoln a few days before his Emancipation Declaration from a list of more than three hundred originally presented for his approval.

I have not been able to verify if what I was told concerning the site of the St. Paul campus is true. But the story made me realize how easy it is to go through a university and work on a campus without knowing anything of its history or of the material infrastructure on which it depends and the people who work in it.

My contribution to the conference was to stress that if we want to change the university and construct a 'knowledge commons' we need to be concerned not only with the content of the curricula and, most important, the cost of studying, as crucial as these undoubtedly are. We need to question the material conditions of the production of a university, its history, and its relation to the surrounding communities. Especially in the U.S., where so much of the land used by institutions was appropriated following the bloody dispossession of its former inhabitants, such a reckoning is essential.

We must also change our conception of what knowledge is and who can be considered a knowledge producer. Currently, knowledge production on the campuses is insulated from the broad infrastructural work that sustains academic life, which requires a multiplicity of subjects (cleaners, cafeteria workers, groundkeepers, etc.) making it possible for students and teachers to return to the classroom every day. Yet, like women's reproductive work, this work too is mostly invisible. Every day "those who work by the hands" (Brecht) make it possible for "those who work with the head" and for the megamachine to start off again, but at best they are only recognized when they refuse to work. It is also assumed that they cannot be producers of knowledge, although increasingly the staff of U.S. campuses is made of immigrant workers or asylum seekers bringing to their work a rich international and political experience. This was the case of many workers at Hofstra University, where I have taught, which is located in the midst of the second largest Salvadoran community in the United States: so politically important that when, after the end of the war, the FMLN—now the party in power—had to take strategic decisions they would come to consult with them. To make a university a common we need to overcome the hierarchies existing within it on the basis of its division of labor. This is especially important today, as many of these university workers face deportation.

# Feminism and the Politics
# of the Commons in an Era of
# Primitive Accumulation

Our perspective is that of the planet's commoners: human beings with bodies, needs, desires, whose most essential tradition is of cooperation in the making and maintenance of life; and yet have had to do so under conditions of suffering and separation from one another, from nature and from the common wealth we have created through generations.

> —Emergency Exit Collective, "The Great Eight Masters and the Six Billion Commoners," Bristol, May Day 2008

The way in which women's subsistence work and the contribution of the commons to the concrete survival of local people are both made invisible through the idealizing of them are not only similar but have common roots. . . . In a way, women are treated like commons and commons are treated like women.

> —Marie Mies and Veronika Bennholdt-Thomsen,
> *The Subsistence Perspective*

Reproduction precedes social production. Touch the women, touch the rock.

> —Peter Linebaugh, *The Magna Carta Manifesto*

## Introduction: Why Commons?

At least since the Zapatistas took over the Zócalo in San Cristóbal de las Casas on December 31, 1993, to protest legislation dissolving the *ejidal* lands of Mexico, the concept of 'the commons' has been gaining popularity among the radical left internationally and in the U.S., appearing as a basis for convergence among anarchists, Marxists, socialists, ecologists, and ecofeminists.[1]

There are important reasons why this apparently archaic idea has come to the center of political discussion in contemporary social movements. Two in particular stand out. On one hand, there is the demise of the statist model of revolution that for decades had sapped the efforts of radical movements to build an alternative to capitalism. On the other, the neoliberal attempt to subordinate every form of life and knowledge to the logic of the market has heightened our awareness of the danger of living in a world where we no longer have access to seas, trees, animals, and our fellow beings except through the cash nexus. The 'new enclosures' have also made visible a world of communal properties and relations that many had believed to be extinct or had not valued until threatened with privatization.[2] Ironically, the new enclosures have demonstrated not only that the common has not vanished but also that new forms of social cooperation are constantly being produced, including in areas of life where none previously existed, for example, the internet.

In this context, the idea of the common/s has offered a logical and historical alternative to both the state and private property and the state and the market, enabling us to reject the fiction that they are mutually exclusive and exhaustive of our political possibilities. It has also served an ideological function as a unifying concept prefiguring the cooperative society that the radical left is striving to create. Nevertheless, ambiguities and significant differences remain in the interpretations of this concept that we need to clarify if we want the principle of the commons to translate into a coherent political project.[3]

What, for example, constitutes a common? We have land, water, and air commons and digital commons; our acquired entitlements (e.g., social security pensions) are often described as commons, and so are languages, libraries, and collective products of past cultures. But are all these commons equivalent from the viewpoint of their political potential? Are they all compatible? And how can we ensure that they do not project a unity that remains to be constructed? Finally, should we speak of 'commons' in the plural or 'the common,' as autonomist Marxists propose we do, this concept designating in their view the social relations characteristic of the dominant form of production in the post-Fordist era?

With these questions in mind, in this essay I look at the politics of the commons from a feminist perspective, where 'feminist' refers to a standpoint shaped by the struggle against sexual discrimination and over reproductive work, which, to paraphrase Linebaugh's comment above, is the rock upon which society is built and by which every model of social organization must be tested. This intervention is necessary, in my view, to better define this politics and clarify the conditions under which the principle of the common/s can become the foundation of an anticapitalist program. Two concerns make these tasks especially important.

## Global Commons, World Bank Commons

First, since at least the early 1990s, the language of the commons has been appropriated by the World Bank and the United Nations and put at the service of privatization. Under the guise of protecting biodiversity and conserving the global commons, the bank has turned rain forests into ecological reserves and expelled the populations that for centuries had drawn their sustenance from them, while ensuring access to those who can pay, for instance, through ecotourism.[4] For its part, the United Nations has revised the international law governing access to the oceans in ways that enable governments to concentrate the use of seawaters in fewer hands, again in the name of preserving the common heritage of mankind.[5]

The World Bank and the UN are not alone in their adaptation of the idea of the commons to market interests. Responding to different motivations, a revalorization of the commons has become trendy among mainstream economists and capitalist planners; witness the growing academic literature on the subject and its cognates: social capital, gift economies, altruism. Witness also the official recognition of this trend through the conferral of the Nobel Prize for Economics in 2009 to the leading voice in this field, the political scientist Elinor Ostrom.[6]

Development planners and policymakers have discovered that under proper conditions a collective management of natural resources can be more efficient and less prone to conflict than privatization and that commons can be made to produce very well for the market.[7] They have also recognized that carried to the extreme the commodification of social relations has self-defeating consequences. The extension of the commodity form to every corner of the social factory promoted by neoliberalism is an ideal limit for capitalist ideologues, but it is a project not only unrealizable but undesirable from the viewpoint of long-term reproduction of the capitalist system. Capitalist accumulation is structurally dependent on the free appropriation of immense quantities of labor and resources that must appear as externalities to the market, like the unpaid domestic work that women have provided, upon which employers have relied for the reproduction of the workforce.

It is no accident, then, that long before the Wall Street meltdown, a variety of economists and social theorists warned that the marketization of all spheres of life is detrimental to the market's smooth functioning, for markets too, the argument goes, depend on the existence of nonmonetary relations like confidence, trust, and gift giving.[8] In brief, capital is learning about the virtues of the common good.

We must be very careful, then, not to craft the discourse on the commons in such a way as to allow a crisis-ridden capitalist class to revive itself, posturing, for instance, as the environmental guardian of the planet.

## What Commons?

A second concern is that, while international institutions have learned to make commons functional for the market, how commons can become the foundation of a noncapitalist economy is a question still unanswered. From Peter Linebaugh's work, especially *The Magna Carta Manifesto* (2008), we have learned that commons have been the thread that has connected the history of the class struggle into our time, and indeed the fight for the commons is all around us. Mainers are fighting to preserve access to their fisheries against the attack of corporate fleets; residents of Appalachia are organizing to save their mountains threatened by strip mining; open source and free software movements are opposing the commodification of knowledge and opening new spaces for communications and cooperation. We also have the many invisible commoning activities and communities that people are creating in North America, which Chris Carlsson has described in his *Nowtopia* (2007). As Carlsson shows, much creativity is invested in the production of 'virtual commons' and forms of sociality that thrive under the radar of the money/market economy.

Most important has been the creation of urban gardens, which spread across the country in the 1980s and 1990s, thanks mostly to the initiatives of immigrant communities from Africa, the Caribbean, or the South of the United States. Their significance cannot be overestimated. Urban gardens have opened the way to a 'rurbanization' process that is indispensable if we are to regain control over our food production, regenerate our environment, and provide for our subsistence. The gardens are far more than a source of food security: they are centers of sociality, knowledge production, and cultural and intergenerational exchange. As Margarita Fernandez writes of urban gardens in New York, they as places where people come together not just to work the land but to play cards, hold weddings, and have baby showers or birthday parties, they "strengthen community cohesion."[9] Some have partner relationships with local schools, providing children with environmental education after school. Not least, gardens are "a medium for the transport and encounter of diverse cultural practices," so that African vegetables and farming practices, for example, mix with those of the Caribbean.[10]

Still, the most significant feature of urban gardens is that they produce for neighborhood consumption, rather than for commercial purposes. This distinguishes them from other reproductive commons that either produce for the market, like the fisheries of Maine's 'Lobster Coast,'[11] or are bought on the market, like the land trusts that preserve open spaces. The problem, however, is that urban gardens have remained a spontaneous grassroots initiative and there have been few attempts by movements in the U.S. to expand their presence and to make access to land a key terrain of struggle. More generally, the left has not posed the question of how to bring together the many proliferating commons that are being defended, developed, and fought for, so that they can form a cohesive whole and provide a foundation for a new mode of production.

An exception is the theory proposed by Antonio Negri and Michael Hardt in Empire (2000), Multitude (2004), and Commonwealth (2009), which argues that a society built on the principle of 'the common' is already evolving from the informatization and 'cognitivization' of production. According to this theory, as production presumably becomes production of knowledge, culture, and subjectivity organized through the internet, a common space and common wealth are created that escape the problem of defining rules of inclusion or exclusion. For access and use multiply the resources available on the net, rather than subtracting from them, thus signifying the possibility of a society built on abundance—the only remaining hurdle confronting the 'multitude' being how to prevent the capitalist 'capture' of the wealth produced.

The appeal of this theory is that it does not separate the formation of 'the common' from the organization of work and production but sees it immanent to it. Its limit is that its picture of the common absolutizes the work of a minority possessing skills not available to most of the world population. It also ignores that this work produces commodities for the market, and it overlooks the fact that online communication and production depends on economic activities—mining and microchip and rare-earth production—that, as currently organized, are extremely destructive, socially and ecologically.[12] Moreover, with its emphasis on knowledge and information, this theory skirts the question of the reproduction of everyday life. This, however, is true of the discourse on the commons as a whole, which is mostly concerned with the formal preconditions for the existence of commons and less with the material requirements for the construction of a commons-based economy enabling us to resist dependence on wage labor and subordination to capitalist relations.

## Women and the Commons

In this context a feminist perspective on the commons is important. It begins with the realization that, as the primary subjects of reproductive work, historically and in our time, women have depended on access to communal natural resources more than men and have been most penalized by their privatization and most committed to their defense. As I wrote in *Caliban and the Witch* (2004), in the first phase of capitalist development, women were at the forefront of the struggle against land enclosures both in England and in the 'New World,' and they were the staunchest defenders of the communal cultures that European colonization attempted to destroy. In Peru, when the Spanish conquistadores took control of their villages, women fled to the high mountains where they recreated forms of collective life that have survived to this day. Not surprisingly, the sixteenth and seventeenth centuries saw the most violent attack on women in the history of the world: the persecution of women as witches. Today, in the face of a new process of primitive accumulation, women are the main social force standing in the way of a complete commercialization of nature, supporting a noncapitalist use of land and a subsistence-oriented agriculture. Women are the subsistence farmers of the world. In Africa, they produce 80 percent of the food people consume, despite the attempts made by the World Bank and other agencies to convince them to divert their activities to cash cropping. In the 1990s, in many African towns, in the face of rising food prices, they have appropriated plots in public lands and planted corn, beans, and cassava "along roadsides . . . in parks, along rail-lines" changing the urban landscape of African cities and breaking down the separation between town and country in the process.[13] In India, the Philippines, and across Latin America, women have replanted trees in degraded forests, joined hands to chase away loggers, made blockades against mining operations and the construction of dams, and led the revolt against the privatization of water.[14]

The other side of women's struggle for direct access to means of reproduction has been the formation across the Third World, from Cambodia to Senegal, of credit associations that function as money commons.[15] Under different names, the *tontines* (as they are called in parts of Africa) are autonomous, self-managed, women-made banking systems that provide cash to individuals or groups that have no access to banks, working purely on a basis of trust. In this, they are completely different from the micro-credit systems promoted by the World Bank, which function on a basis of mutual policing and shame, reaching the extreme (e.g., in Niger) of posting in public places pictures of the women who fail to repay the loans, driving some women to suicide.[16]

Women have also led the effort to collectivize reproductive labor, both as a means to economize the cost of reproduction and to protect each other from poverty, state violence, and the violence of individual men. An outstanding example is that of the *ollas comunes* (common cooking pots) that women in Chile and Peru set up in the 1980s, when, due to stiff inflation, they could no longer afford to shop alone.[17] Like land reclamations or the formation of tontines, these practices are the expression of a world where communal bonds are still strong. But it would be a mistake to consider them something pre-political, 'natural,' or simply a product of 'tradition.' After repeated phases of colonization, nature and customs no longer exist in any part of the world, except where people have struggled to preserve them and reinvent them. As Leo Podlashuc has noted in "Saving Women: Saving the Commons," grassroots women's communalism today leads to the production of a new reality, shapes a collective identity, constitutes a counterpower in the home and the community, and opens a process of self-valorization and self-determination from which there is much that we can learn.

The first lesson we can gain from these struggles is that the 'commoning' of the material means of reproduction is the primary mechanism by which a collective interest and mutual bonds are created. It is also the first line of resistance to a life of enslavement and the condition for the construction of autonomous spaces, undermining from within the hold that capitalism has on our lives. Undoubtedly the experiences I have described are models that cannot be transplanted. For us, in North America, the reclamation and commoning of the means of reproduction must necessarily take different forms. But here too, by pooling our resources and reappropriating the wealth that we have produced, we can begin to de-link our reproduction from the commodity flows that, through the world market, are responsible for the dispossession of millions across the world. We can begin to disentangle our livelihood not only from the world market but also from the war machine and prison system on which the U.S. economy now depends. Not least, we can move beyond the abstract solidarity that so often characterizes relations in the movement, and which limits our commitment, our capacity to endure, and the risks we are willing to take.

In a country where private property is defended by the largest arsenal of weaponry in the world, and where three centuries of slavery have produced profound divisions in the social body, the recreation of the common/s appears as a formidable task that can only be accomplished through a long-term process of experimentation, coalition building, and reparations. Though this task may now seem more difficult than passing through the eye of a needle, it is also the only possibility we have for widening the space of our autonomy and refusing to accept that our reproduction occurs at the expense of the world's other commoners and commons.

## Feminist Reconstructions

What this task entails is powerfully expressed by Maria Mies, when she points out that the production of commons requires first a profound transformation in our everyday life, in order to recombine what the social division of labor in capitalism has separated.

The distancing of production from reproduction and consumption leads us to ignore the conditions under which what we eat, wear, or work with have been produced, their social and environmental cost, and the fate of the population on whom the waste we produce is unloaded.[18] In other words, we need to overcome the state of irresponsibility concerning the consequences of our actions that results from the destructive ways in which the social division of labor is organized in capitalism; short of that, the production of our life inevitably becomes a production of death for others. As Mies points out, globalization has worsened this crisis, widening the distances between what is produced and what is consumed, thereby intensifying, despite the appearance of an increased global interconnectedness, our blindness to the blood in the food we eat, the petroleum we use, the clothes we wear, and the computers we communicate with.[19]

Overcoming this state of oblivion is where a feminist perspective teaches us to start in our reconstruction of the commons. No common is possible unless we refuse to base our life and our reproduction on the suffering of others, unless we refuse to see ourselves as separate from them. Indeed, if commoning has any meaning, it must be the production of ourselves as a common subject. This is how we must understand the slogan "no commons without community." But 'community' has to be intended not as a gated reality, a grouping of people joined by exclusive interests separating them from others, as with communities formed on the basis of religion or ethnicity, but rather as a quality of relations, a principle of cooperation, and of responsibility to each other and to the earth, the forests, the seas, the animals.

Certainly, the achievement of such community, like the collectivization of our everyday reproductive work, can only be a beginning. It is no substitute for broader anti-privatization campaigns and the reclamation of our common wealth. But it is an essential part of our education to collective government and our recognition of history as a collective project, which is perhaps the main casualty of the neoliberal era of capitalism. On this account, we too must include in our political agenda the communalization of housework, reviving that rich feminist tradition that in the U.S. stretches from the utopian socialist experiments of the mid-nineteenth century to the attempts that 'materialist feminists' made from the late nineteenth century to the early twentieth century to reorganize and socialize domestic work, and thereby the home and the neighborhood, through collective housekeeping—attempts that continued until the 1920s when the Red Scare put an end to them.[20] These practices and, most importantly, the ability of past feminists to look at reproductive labor as an important sphere of human activity not to be negated but to be revolutionized must be revisited and revalorized.

One crucial reason for creating collective forms of living is that the reproduction of human beings is the most labor-intensive work on earth and, to a very large extent, is irreducible to mechanization. We cannot mechanize childcare, health care, or the psychological work necessary to reintegrate our physical and emotional balance. Despite the efforts that futuristic industrialists are making, we cannot robotize care except at a terrible cost for the people involved. No one will accept nursebots as caregivers, especially for children and the ill. Shared responsibility and cooperative work not given at the cost of the health of the providers are the only guarantees of proper care. For centuries, the reproduction of human beings has been a collective process. It has been the work of extended families and the communities upon which people could rely, especially in proletarian neighborhoods, even when they lived alone, so that old age was not accompanied by the desolate loneliness and dependence with which so many of our elderly live. It is only with the advent of capitalism that reproduction has been completely privatized, a process that is now extended to a degree that destroys our lives. This trend must be reversed, and the present time is propitious for such a project.

As the capitalist crisis destroys the basic elements of reproduction for millions of people across the world, including in the United States, the reconstruction of our everyday life is a possibility and a necessity. Like strikes, social/economic crises break the discipline of wage work, forcing new forms of sociality upon us. This is what occurred during the Great Depression, which produced a movement of hoboes who turned the freight trains into their commons, seeking freedom in mobility and nomadism.[21] At the intersections of railroad lines, they organized hobo jungles, prefigurations, with their self-governance rules and solidarity, of the communist world in which many of the hoboes believed.[22] But except for a few Boxcar Berthas,[23] this was predominantly a masculine world, a fraternity, and in the long term it could not be sustained. Once the economic crisis and the war came to an end, the hoboes were domesticated by the two great engines of labor power fixation: the family and the house. Mindful of the threat of working-class recomposition during the Depression, American capital excelled in its application of the principle that has characterized the organization of economic life: cooperation at the point of production, separation and atomization at the point of reproduction. The atomized, serialized family house that Levittown provided, compounded by its umbilical appendix, the car, not only made the worker sedentary but put an end to the type of autonomous workers' commons that hobo jungles had represented.[24] Today, as millions of American houses and cars are being repossessed, as foreclosures, evictions, and massive loss of employment are again breaking down the pillars of the capitalist discipline of work, new common grounds are again taking shape, like the tent cities that sprawl from coast to coast. This time, however, it is women who must build the new commons, so that they do not remain transient spaces, temporary autonomous zones, but become the foundation of new forms of social reproduction.

If the house is the *oikos* on which the economy is built, then it is women, historically the houseworkers and house prisoners, who must take the initiative to reclaim the house as a center of collective life, one traversed by multiple people and forms of cooperation, providing safety without isolation and fixation, allowing for the sharing and circulation of community possessions, and, above all, providing the foundation for collective forms of reproduction. As has already been suggested, we can draw inspiration for this project from the programs of the nineteenth-century materialist feminists who, convinced that the home was an important "spatial component of the oppression of women," organized communal kitchens and cooperative households, calling for workers' control of reproduction.[25]

These objectives are crucial at present. Breaking down the isolation of life in the home is not only a precondition for meeting our most basic needs and increasing our power with regard to employers and the state. As Massimo De Angelis has reminded us, it is also a protection from ecological disaster. For there can be no doubt about the destructive consequences of the 'uneconomic' multiplication of reproductive assets and the self-enclosed dwellings that we now call our homes, dissipating warmth into the atmosphere during the winter, exposing us to unmitigated heat in the summer. Most importantly, we cannot build an alternative society and a strong self-reproducing movement unless we redefine our reproduction in a more cooperative way and put an end to the separation between the personal and the political and between political activism and the reproduction of everyday life.

It remains to be clarified that assigning women this task of commoning/collectivizing reproduction is not to concede to a naturalistic conception of femininity. Understandably, many feminists view this possibility as a fate worse than death. It is deeply sculpted in our collective consciousness that women have been designated as men's common, a natural source of wealth and services to be as freely appropriated by them as the capitalists have appropriated the wealth of nature. But, to paraphrase Dolores Hayden, the reorganization of reproductive work, and therefore the reorganization of housing and public space, is not a question of identity; it is a question of labor and, we can add, a question of power and safety.[26] I am reminded here of the experience of the women members of the Movimento dos Trabalhadores Rurais Sem Terra (Landless People's Movement of Brazil—MST), who, after their communities won the right to maintain the land that they had occupied, insisted that the new houses be built to form one compound so that they could continue to communalize their housework, wash together, cook together, take turns with men, as they had done in the course of the struggle, and be ready to run to give each other support when abused by men. Arguing that women should take the lead in the collectivization of reproductive work and housing is not to naturalize housework as a female vocation. It is refusing to obliterate the collective experiences, the knowledge, and the struggles that women have accumulated concerning reproductive work, whose history has been an essential part of our resistance to capitalism. Reconnecting with this history is a crucial step for women and men today, both to undo the gendered architecture of our lives and to reconstruct our homes and lives as commons.

## Notes

1   A key source on the politics of the commons and its theoretical foundations is the UK-based online journal *The Commoner*, the fifteenth issue of which was published in 2012. The contents of past issues, reviews, and more are accessible at www.commoner.org.uk.

2   A case in point is the struggle taking place in many communities in Maine against Nestlé's appropriation of Maine's waters for its Poland Spring bottled water. Nestlé's theft has made people aware of the vital importance of these waters and the supporting aquifers and has truly reconstituted them as a common; "Nestlé's Move to Bottle Community Water," *Food and Water Watch Fact-Sheet*, July 2009, accessed May 31, 2018, https://www.foodandwaterwatch.org/sites/default/files/nestle_bottle_community_water_fs_july_2009_1.pdf. Food and Water Watch is a (self-described) "non-profit organization that works to ensure clean water and safe food in the United States and around the world."

3   An excellent site for current debates on the commons is the UK-based movement journal *Turbulence: Ideas for Movement* (December 5, 2009): accessed June 2, 2018, http://www.turbulence.org.uk/wp-content/uploads/2009/11/turbulence_05.pdf.

4   For more on this subject, see the important article "Who Pays for the Kyoto Protocol?" by Ana Isla, in *Eco-Sufficiency and Global Justice*, ed. Ariel Salleh (New York, London: Macmillan Palgrave, 2009), in which the author describes how the conservation of biodiversity has provided the World Bank and other international agencies with the pretext to enclose rain forests on the grounds that they represent 'carbon sinks' and 'oxygen generators.'

5   The United Nations Convention on the Law of the Sea, adopted in November 1994, establishes a two-hundred-mile offshore limit, defining an Exclusive

Economic Zone in which nations can exploit, manage, and protect the resources it contains, from fisheries to natural gas. It also regulates deep-sea mining and the use of the resulting revenues. On the development of the concept of the "common heritage of mankind" in United Nations debate, see Susan J. Buck, *The Global Commons: An Introduction* (Washington, DC: Island Press, 1998).

6   Ostrom's work focuses on common pool resources and "on how humans interact with ecosystems to maintain long-term sustainable resource yields"; "Elinor Ostrom," *Wikipedia*, accessed May 24, 2018, https://en.wikipedia.org/wiki/Elinor_Ostrom.

7   For more on this topic, see Calestous Juma and J.B. Ojwang, eds., *In Land We Trust: Environment, Private Property and Constitutional Change* (London: Zed Books, 1996), an early treatise on the effectiveness of communal property relations in the context of capitalist development and efforts.

8   David Bollier, *Silent Theft: The Private Plunder of Our Common Wealth* (New York: Routledge, 2002), 36–39.

9   Margarita Fernandez, "Cultivating Community, Food and Empowerment," unpublished manuscript, 2003, 23–26. An early, important work on urban gardens is Bill Weinberg and Peter Lamborn Wilson, ed., *Avant Gardening: Ecological Struggle in the City and the World* (Brooklyn: Autonomedia, 1999).

10   Wilson, *Avant Gardening.*

11   The fishing commons of Maine are currently threatened with a new privatization policy, justified in the name of preservation and ironically labeled 'catch shares.' This is a system, already applied in Canada and Alaska, whereby local governments set limits on the amount or fish that can be caught by allocating individual shares on the basis of the amount of fishing that boats have done in the past. This system has proven to be disastrous for small, independent fishers who are soon forced to sell their share to the highest bidders. Protest against its implementation is now mounting in the fishing communities of Maine. See Laurie Schreiber, "Catch Shares or Share-Croppers?" *Fishermen's Voice* 14, no. 12 (December 2009): accessed June 2, 2018, http://www.fishermensvoice.com/archives/1209index.html.

12   It has been calculated, for example, that 33,000 liters of water and 15–19 tons of material are required to produce a personal computer; see Saral Sarkar, *Eco-Socialism or Eco-Capitalism? A Critical Analysis of Humanity's Fundamental Choices* (London: Zed Books, 1999), 126; Elizabeth Dias, "First Blood Diamonds, Now Blood Computers?" *Time*, July 24, 2009, accessed May 31, 2018, http://content.time.com/time/world/article/0,8599,1912594,00.html. Dias cites claims made by Global Witness—an organization campaigning to prevent resource related conflicts—to the effect that the trade in the minerals at the heart of the electronic industry feeds the civil war in the Democratic Republic of Congo.

13   Donald B. Freeman, "Survival Strategy or Business Training Ground? The Significance of Urban Agriculture for the Advancement of Women in African Cities," *African Studies Review* 36, no. 3 (December 1993): 1–22; Federici, "Witch-Hunting, Globalization and Feminist Solidarity in Africa

Today," *Journal of International Women's Studies* 10 no. 1 (October 2008): 29–35, reprinted in Federici, *Witches, Witch-Hunting, and Women* (Oakland: PM Press, 2018), 60–86.

14    Vandana Shiva, *Staying Alive: Women, Ecology and Development* (London: Zed Books, 1989).

15    Leo Podlashuc, "Saving Women: Saving the Commons," in *Eco-Sufficiency and Global Justice: Women Write Political Ecology*, ed. Salleh, Ariel (London: Macmillan Palgrave, 2009).

16    I owe this information to Ousseina Alidou, director of the Center for African Studies at Rutgers University in New Jersey.

17    Jo Fisher, *Out of the Shadows: Women, Resistance and Politics in South America* (London: Latin America Bureau, 1993); Carol Andreas, *When Women Rebel: The Rise of Popular Feminism in Peru* (Westport, CT: Lawrence Hill, 1985).

18    Maria Mies and Veronika Bennholdt-Thomsen, *The Subsistence Perspective: Beyond the Globalized Economy* (London: Zed Books, 1999).

19    Mies and Bennholdt-Thomsen, *The Subsistence Perspective*.

20    Dolores Hayden, *The Grand Domestic Revolution: A History of Feminist Designs for American Homes, Neighborhoods, and Cities* (Cambridge, MA: MIT Press, 1985 [1981]); Hayden, *Redesigning the American Dream: The Future of Housing, Work and Family Life* (New York: W.W. Norton, 1986).

21    George Caffentzis, "Three Temporal Dimensions of Class Struggle," paper presented at the International Studies Association annual meeting, San Diego, CA, March 2006.

22    Nels Anderson, *On Hobos and Homelessness* (Chicago: University of Chicago Press, 1998); Todd DePastino, *Citizen Hobo* (Chicago: University of Chicago Press, 2003); Caffentzis, "Three Temporal Dimensions of Class Struggle."

23    *Boxcar Bertha* (Los Angeles: American International Pictures, 1972), 88 min., is Martin Scorsese's adaptation of Ben Reitman's *Sister of the Road* (Oakland: AK Press, 2002 [1937]), a fictionalized account presented as the autobiography of a radical and transient named Bertha Thompson.

24    Hayden, *The Grand Domestic Revolution*.

25    Hayden, *Redesigning the American Dream*.

26    Hayden, *The Grand Domestic Revolution*, 230.

# Women's Struggles for Land in Africa and the Reconstruction of the Commons

[W]hen [in 1956] hunters killed the last elephant that strayed into Gusii territory . . . and, for the last time, people from the surrounding area helped themselves to free meat [the] event was memorialized in a folk song . . . "'the mother of commodities for free' has died in Gesabakwa." From that time on, commodities began to be sold for cash so that anybody expecting otherwise would be reminded rhetorically, "have you not heard that 'the mother of commodities for free' has died in Gesabakwa?

Justus M. Ogembo, *Contemporary Witch-Hunting in Gusii,*
*Southwestern Kenya*

## Introduction

The concept of the 'commons' has become a major theme in the literature of social justice movements internationally, proving very useful for expanding the scope of political analysis beyond the confines of the wage struggle. Lodged halfway between the 'public' and the 'private,' but irreducible to either category, the idea of the commons expresses a broader conception of property, referring to social goods—lands, territories, forests, meadows, and streams, or communicative spaces—that a community, not the state or any individual, collectively owns, manages, and controls. Unlike the 'public,' which presuppose the existence of market economy and private property and is "typically administered by the state,"[1] the idea of the commons evokes images of intense social cooperation. Through this concept, moreover, the history of the class struggle can be rewritten so that the indigenous peoples' resistance to colonial expropriation in the Americas can be seen on a continuum with peasant resistance against the English enclosures, and farmers' struggles in India can be described as the complement to the struggles of anti–intellectual property programmers in the free software movement. All are 'commoners,' after all.[2]

As with the real commons, however, the concept itself has been the object of many manipulations and appropriations, mostly by the institutions that have made the abolition of communal property their mission. Witness the World Bank's definition of seas, water resources, and forests as 'global commons,' which serves to legitimize new enclosures, presumably in the interest of 'conservation,' driving aboriginal people off their lands and giving access to them on a monetary basis. Similarly, the World Bank has promoted 'community-based' land reforms in Africa that purport to guarantee a more equitable allocation of communal lands but actually promote commercial interests and reduce the resources that people can claim. A further problem is that with the expansion of capitalism, the existing commons have become home to many of the divisions and conflicts that we find in the rest of society, which international financial institutions exploit to their ends.

With these concerns in mind, I look at two kinds of women's movements that have a direct impact on the future of communal lands in Africa. First, the women's movement that developed in the 1990s to fight for land rights, which has declared its opposition to customary land tenure because of its frequent discrimination against women. Second, the movement of women in urban areas who opt for direct action, taking over and farming public lands, subverting the neoliberal attempt to put a monetary gate around all natural resources, and reaffirming the principle the earth is our common.

I discuss these movements because there is much that we can learn from them about the role that women play in defense of communal wealth, and because they show that egalitarianism is for the commons a question of survival, since gender-based disparities lead many women to demand a strengthening of the very legal machine upon which land privatization depends.[3]

## Africa: Still the Land of Commons
Africa is a good test case for a discussion of communal land tenure—the material foundation of all other communal forms of property (woods,

forests, waters)—because it is the region where this form of property has survived longer than in any other part of the world, despite repeated attempts to put an end to this 'scandal.' As Liz Alden Wily, a Nairobi-based 'expert on land tenure and rural development,' writes, "Despite a century of purposeful penetration of non-customary tenure ideology and legislation... unregistered, customary tenure not only persists, but also is by far the majority form of tenure in the region. None of the strategies adopted to ignore or diminish it have been successful."[4] Indeed, most people in rural Africa live under communal tenure systems,[5] though they may have individual titles to land under statutory law, as many African countries have dual or plural legal regimes.[6]

Today's African commons bear little resemblance, however, to the 'traditional' models, to the degree that these can be reconstructed through oral histories and what we know of precolonial African societies.[7] As a vast literature has documented, the shift from subsistence farming to cash crops and the colonial introduction of private property regimes, based on titling and the enclosure of individual holdings, have increasingly undermined what used to be "an egalitarian pattern of social organization."[8] Decolonization did not counter this trend. Whether the goal was capitalist or socialist development, the independent African nations contributed to undermining communal land systems by making all land the property of the state, thus establishing its right to appropriate it for public projects. As a result of these developments, by the late 1970s, landlessness in rural areas was growing and so was class differentiation.

It is generally agreed that those most harmed by these developments were women. For, as land became more scarce and valuable, men often devised new rules to restrict women's access to it, something the traditional systems had always guaranteed. I will return to this point. Here I want to stress that the 'debt crisis' and the liberalization of African political economies were a turning point with regard to land tenure relations. As we have seen, the World Bank and other international capitalist institutions saw the crisis as a historic opportunity to end Africa's communal land tenure systems.[9] This was to be the first objective of the structural adjustment programs.[10] All the conditionalities written into them—the shift from food production to export-oriented agriculture, the opening of African lands to foreign investment, the privileging of cash crops over subsistence agriculture—were premised on a land privatization drive to be implemented through individual titling and registration.

But these expectations have only been partly satisfied. A new 'scramble for Africa' has taken place, which has expropriated the most fertile and most mineral-rich of the African commons and transferred them to business ventures. By the 1990s, however, only a small percentage of African communal land had been registered, in some areas less than 1 percent. Small farmers saw no need for registration, assuming that they already owned their land and being unwilling to pay the high fees and taxes title and registration required. People also resisted "giving all rights over to one person."[11] Worse yet, from the viewpoint of prospective investors, even in the areas where land had been registered, customary regulations continue to be observed, as people could not be convinced the land was no longer a collective asset.[12]

In response to such findings and aware of a growing peasant mobilization inside and outside of Africa since the 1990s, taking the form of land takeovers, African governments and the World Bank have adopted a softer, less conflictual road to land privatization. Confident that much of the task of privatizing land can be left to the market, they have sponsored a reform model that recognizes communal tenure but ensures that land can be alienated and land markets can expand.[13]

Already implemented in several African countries, and typically promoted as a 'pro-poor, rural development policy,' the new reform is based on four innovations. It decentralizes the administration and management of communal lands, placing them in the hands of politically appointed boards or elected 'village councils' responsible to the central government. It introduces 'group titling,' so that land can be registered in the name of land associations as well as individuals. It makes it possible for local management bodies or associations to sell land to outsiders for business purposes, provided it is under the guise of joint ventures.[14] In sum, it introduces a two-tier system that avoids a head-on confrontation with small farmers, while enabling the local capitalist elite to pursue their interests and open the door to foreign investors.

The new land reforms also contain provisions against discrimination on the basis of gender through the introduction of the right of co-tenancy between husbands and wives.[15] Gender equity is a key theme in the ideological presentation of the reform. But these provisions have failed to satisfy the women's organizations that formed in the 1990s to fight for women's land rights. In their view placing the decision-making process with regard to land management in the hands of local bodies and validating local customs makes women vulnerable to abuse. What these organizations demand is that customary tenure be eradicated and a rights-based system be instituted through legal and legislative reform, so that women can buy, own, sell, and obtain titles to land—entitlements, they claim, that under customary law women can obtain only through the goodwill of men.[16]

In a detailed article on this matter, the Ugandan feminist Aili Mari Tripp defends this strategy, stating that it represents the dominant position among women's organizations, especially in East Africa, and that it has also won the support of some pastoralist groups. But she acknowledges that women's land rights groups are accused of promoting the agenda of foreign investors.[17] In fact, a debate is taking place in Africa that questions whether the consolidation of private ownership can benefit women and whether customary tenure can be abolished without serious consequences for the livelihood of the rural and urban populations.[18]

Across differences, however, there is a consensus that the discrimination that women face in customary law has less to do with 'tradition' than with the pressures resulting from the commercialization of agriculture and the loss of communal land.

## Women, Customary Law, and the Masculinization of the Commons

As it is the case today, in precolonial times, customary laws gave men priority with regard to landownership and management, on the assumption that women would eventually marry and leave the clan and the clan's land should be protected.[19] Thus, despite variations, depending on whether the system was matrilineal or patrilineal and other historical and cultural factors, even in precolonial times, women had access to land through their relations with husbands and kin. 'Ownership,' however, had a very different meaning than in statutory law, as customary law worked "on a principle of inclusion" rather than exclusion.[20] The owner had the right of occupancy and held the land in trusteeship for the other members of the family, including the generations to come. Ownership did not confer absolute proprietorship nor the right to sell. Thus, either through their own families or through their husbands, women always had fields of their own, their own crops, and controlled the income they earned from the sale of the produce they farmed.[21]

Things changed, however, with the commercialization of agriculture and the beginning of production for the international market. As a rule, the more the demand for land has increased, the stricter the "constraints [placed] on women's access to it."[22]

Several strategies have been used for this purpose. In parts of East Africa, men have refused to pay the bride price, opting for marriage by elopement, which makes it easier for them to dissolve the relationships with their wives and refuse them any transfer or donation of land. A study conducted in Gusii land in Southwestern Kenya, showed that by the 1980s, 80 percent of marriages in that area were by elopement, with the consequent creation of "a whole category of landless women," something unprecedented in the region.[23] A similar study found that in a Rwandan village, in the late 1990s, two-thirds of the couples had married without the payment of the bride price, again a proof that rural women are losing one of their main forms of protection, for without this payment they have no claim to land and can be asked to leave their husbands' homes at any time.[24]

Another tactic used to deny women's land rights has been the redefinition of what constitutes kinship and, therefore, who 'belongs' to the clan and who does not. As the recent conflicts in Kenya's Rift Valley have shown, the politics of 'othering' and 'belonging' have been used to expel different ethnic or religious groups from the land. But the same politics have been used to curtail women's access to land, by defining wives as outsiders and nonfamily members. Witchcraft accusations—the ultimate 'othering' strategy—have served this purpose.[25] In Mozambique, in recent years, women who have demanded their deceased husbands' land or their share of the crops have been accused of being witches and of having murdered their husbands to inherit their belongings.[26]

Lands and crops too have been reclassified—along with increases in their monetary values—to demonstrate that men have unique title to them.[27] But, aside from these expedients, women's access to land is increasingly precarious because the dual legal system enables men to strip women of their due. As Judy Adoko and Simone Levine from the Land and Equity Movement of Uganda explain, "The fact that customarily a woman gained access to land via her husband is now (deliberately) confused with notions of individualized ownership. Thus, 'men are now claiming rights that under customary law they never had,' like selling land without consulting the family and even their wives."[28]

Widows, divorcees, and women without male children have been particularly penalized. Often widows cannot even hold on to the property that the couple acquired together.[29] For they are threatened with expropriation by their in-laws, who can claim what he had, making some concessions only if the widow has sons and holds the property in their name.[30]

The literature on women's 'land rights' is filled with stories of widows stripped of their belongings and forced to leave their homes by the relatives of the deceased. In an apparently typical case, one widow had hardly buried her husband, when she had to fight her in-laws trying to dig up their brother's yams from her fields, despite her pleas that they leave some for her children. In another case, a Ugandan widow found out that her in-laws had sold her husband's land behind her back when the new buyer came to evict her.[31] Mary Kimani reports that in Zambia more than one-third of widows lost access to the family land when the husband died.[32] Women in polygamous families are also among the losers, for men usually register only one wife, and in case of divorce or death the others have no rights.

In sum, there is little doubt that customary laws, as currently defined, discriminate against women, despite the fact that they are the bulk of the African farmers, the main producers of food—in many countries providing up to 70 percent of the food people consume—and they perform the majority of agricultural tasks: sowing, weeding, harvesting, storing, processing, and marketing.[33]

Because of these contradictions, women's position on the African commons has been compared to that of 'servants' or 'bonded laborers,' being expected to provide various types of unpaid work to their male relations, without having control over the land they farm or security of access to it.[34]

Lack of control over land implies for women also lack of control over their sexuality and reproductive functions. Access to land is often conditioned on irreproachable sexual behavior, and, at the same time, a willingness to accept a husbands' extramarital relations and, most important, the ability to have sons.[35] Some women have more children than they desire hoping to gain more secure access to land. More broadly, lack of control over land makes it difficult for women farmers to have some autonomy, and it lessens their bargaining power in the family, making them more vulnerable to sexual harassment and domestic violence.[36] It also has serious implications for people's food security. Women are the bulk of subsistence farmers. In an economic environment where food is exported, land is taken out of production for mining and other business ventures or is devoted to the cultivation of nonedible crops, and where international institutions are pressuring African governments to convince them to import staple crops, women's farming activities are essential to people's survival.

## Land Is Women's Right: A Women's Movement for Land Privatization?

Given this situation, it is not surprising that women's relation to land and communal tenure has become a central issue in African feminist politics. But it was the United Nations campaign for women's rights that put the land question on the feminist agenda, and not in Africa alone.[37] Movements similar to those that formed in Africa in the 1990s have also developed in Latin America, with similar strategies and demands.[38] By the 1990s, international policymakers and developers had concluded that many rural development schemes intended to boost cash crop production had failed to materialize because they had 'ignored women's contribution.' They had assumed that male farmers could easily recruit their wives as unpaid helpers, overlooking the fact that African women have always had their own economic activities, separate from those of their husbands, and that lack of secure access to land and other resources strengthened their reluctance to work at their husbands' dependence for free. The United Nations campaign for women's rights was to remedy this situation, its efforts doubled by those of the World Bank, which, in the same years, was discovering the need to 'genderize' its agenda. Hence the prominence that the land question was given at the World Conference on Women in Beijing in 1995, which was the spark for women's land rights movements across the planet.

In Africa, due to the support from the UN organizations and international NGOs, scores of organizations have formed and conferences, workshops, and publications on women's land rights have proliferated. Meanwhile, the women who could afford it have pooled resources to purchase land, often using women's informal saving systems, not wanting to be dispossessed in case of their husbands' deaths.

So far, despite institutional backing, the movement has scored few successes and even those have been "more declamatory than real."[39] Only in Ethiopia and Eritrea have women been made "owners of the land they till."[40] But here too the movement has faced an uphill battle. For even when statutory laws strengthen women's rights, there is resistance to their implementation. How entrenched opposition to granting women broader land rights is can be measured by the fact that a mobilization of women's associations in Uganda could not secure the introduction of a clause giving wives co-ownership of land when a Land Act was passed in that country in 1998. This defeat, in which President Museveni played a crucial role, may explain why many women have been adamant about the need for stronger legal and constitutional provisions.[41]

The problem, however, is that by advocating for laws that strengthen private ownership and the elimination of communal tenure, women's land rights organizations have given support to the very liberalization program that has served to transfer thousands of acres of African land to foreign investors and dispossess millions of farmers, many of them women. As Ambreena Manji wrote in *The Politics of Land Reform in Africa* (2006), by seeking social change through legal reform of land tenure, the women's land rights movement has embraced the language of international financial institutions and contributed to obliterating the question of land redistribution, the African people's most crucial demand since the end of colonialism. It has also underwritten the use that international financial institutions are making of the law as a means for the globalization of capitalist relations and for placing African localities under the control of a transnational power structure.[42]

What Manji suggests is that African women should fight for more land, rather than for more law; buttressing individual land property is of little use when landlessness becomes a general condition. Manji is not alone in her criticism. There is a widespread sense that the campaign for women's right to land represents the interests and viewpoint of a limited group of formally educated, economically better-off, mostly urban middle-class women, who have the money to buy land, pay the taxes that the acquisition of legal titles requires, and perhaps invest in some agricultural business.[43]

There is also a justified concern that the demise of what remains of communal land tenure will tear apart rural African societies and intensify land disputes. Land for the majority of African people, women in particular, is still the main means of production and subsistence. It is Africa's 'social security system,' more important than money and wages are for Americans or Europeans, who have become used to the infinite precariousness and abstractness of monetary relations. Having some land at the village or the prospect of it at the end of a life of work away from it makes the difference for many between life and death or, increasingly, between life in Africa or migration. Not surprisingly, land conflicts are the most bitter, most murderous ones, often resembling true wars. In this context, a key question is whether a privatizing legal reform will worsen the social and economic position of rural women, who are the population that would be most directly affected by it. This is an important question, keeping in mind that communal land tenure often involves access to a broader range of resources, like trees—the pastoralists' 'saving bank'—grazing grounds, forests, lakes, and ponds.[44]

Significantly, both as individuals and through their organizations, rural women have demonstrated little interest in formal landownership for much the same reason that male peasants have dismissed the importance of titling and registration. Rural women know that the land is scarce, that it belongs to the community, and that only wealthy people can buy it, and they do not want to nor can they pay the taxes that acquiring formal ownership entails. Thus, though they are vitally interested in having more land and more security, they do not think of individual titling as the means to obtain it. Some women also fear that if they bought land their husbands might feel threatened, seeing it as an attack on their power.

In view of these resistances, some women's organizations think that they can negotiate a better deal working 'within' the customary legal system and outside the 'rights' framework, while engaging in educational campaigns to change the power relations on the ground. As political theorists Winnie Bikaako and John Ssenkumba put it: "The solution seems to lie in a compromise position, away from completely abolishing customary law and practices and away from leaving land to the market."[45]

Presumably, by increasing women's participation in rural committees and decision-making processes, much can be gained, without resorting to policies that risk expropriating the bulk of female farmers. But if the commercialization of land continues and land redistribution remains a dead letter, it is doubtful that negotiations at the community level can make a significant difference in women's land security. For the defining problem is that the commons are shrinking and the premise for a peaceful road to communal egalitarianism is more land.

### Women against Enclosures: Land Appropriation and Urban Farming in Africa

What, then, is the destiny of the Africa's land commons from the viewpoint of women? Are continuing privatization and masculinization the inevitable outcomes of the present balance of forces on the land? Undoubtedly, as recent land conflicts in Kenya and South Africa have demonstrated, the picture is not optimistic. As an African proverb has it, "When elephants fight, the grass underneath gets trampled upon," which begs the question: How can women gain more land when their communities are destroyed because the competition for land is driving people to despair? Land disputes and land expropriations are also at the root of the witch hunts that have taken place in Africa in the 1980s and 1990s, in conjunction with the 'adjustment' of African economies.[46]

Under these circumstances, feminists would agree that a broad-based mobilization is needed to build the power of women in every sphere of life: health, education, employment, and reproductive work, as well as to ensure women's access to land. Short of it, all gains would be temporary and most would be hard to win. In the meantime, a different type of struggle has taken place that has been ignored by the literature and the initiatives in the field, which are largely dominated by institutionally supported NGOs working within a neoliberal framework.

While women land rights organizations have fought for stronger private property laws, rural movements have grown in Africa, resisting dispossession and struggling to deprivatize land by taking it over and squatting on it. An example is the Landless People's Movement in South Africa, whose backbone is women and youth. While negotiating with the government for the implementation of a redistributive land reform, the movement also favors land occupations, as articulated in its 2004 plan, which includes a 'Take Back the Land Campaign.'[47] Rural movements using direct action tactics have also been active in other parts of Southern Africa.[48]

But perhaps the most significant land movement is one that does not present as such, appearing as a set of spontaneous and separate initiatives. This is the 'movement' of landless women who have migrated to the towns and, using direct action tactics, appropriate and farm vacant plots of public land. This practice is not new. A communistic culture is so engrained in African societies that even today, after decades of commercialization, a use is made of public space that would be unthinkable in Europe or the United States. Not only is roadside selling the norm, crops are grown on university campuses; in some southern Nigerian universities, at some points in the year, one can see cows pasturing on campus grass before being brought to the market.

Women, the bulk of subsistence farmers, have always cultivated any vacant land available to them. But since the 1980s, as economic conditions have deteriorated, this practice has become more widespread, especially in the urban areas to which many have migrated. Urban farming has evolved into an important economic activity for landless women and some men as well, providing the means by which many families manage to survive. In Accra, Ghana, urban gardens supply the city with 90 percent of its vegetables. In Dar es Salaam, Tanzania, one adult in five grows fruits or vegetables. In Guinea-Bissau, in the capital city and other towns, in the early 1980s, women began to surround their houses with vegetable gardens, planting cassava and fruit trees, in times of scarcity preferring to renounce the earnings they might have made selling their produce to ensure that their families would have enough food. In the Democratic Republic of Congo too there has been an explosion of 'rurbanization.' As Theodore Trefon describes it, "manioc is planted all over the city, while goats graze along a central boulevard that is considered the Champs Elysees of Kinshasa."[49] This picture is confirmed by Christa Wichterich, who, calling subsistence farming and urban gardening "cooking pot economics," writes:

> There were onions and papaya trees, instead of flower borders, in front of the housing estates of underpaid civil servants in Dar es Salaam; chickens and banana plants in the backyards of Lusaka; vegetables on the wide central reservations of the arterial roads of Kampala, and especially of Kinshasa, where the food supply system had largely collapsed. . . . In [Kenyan] towns green roadside strips, front gardens and wasteland sites, were immediately occupied with maize, plants, sukum wiki, the most popular type of cabbage which literally means 'push the week.'[50]

Most of the land that women farm is public or private land that they have appropriated along roadsides, rail lines, and in parks, without asking anyone's permission or paying anyone a fee. In this sense, we can say that this land is the beginning of a common, in that its appropriation produces a different relationship to public space—a relationship of direct management and responsibility, restoring people's symbiosis with the natural environment.

Keeping the land clean and farming it is a big addition to women's workloads, particularly when the plot is not near their homes. There are also many risks involved: theft or destruction of the crops, police harassment, and, of course, urban pollution. As Donald B. Freeman describes it, on the basis of the interviews he conducted with female farmers in Nairobi in the early 1990s, women use many devices to confront these problems and hide their crops. But the difficulties they meet are compensated by the satisfaction they gain from being able to provide their families with extra food and a more varied diet and from being self-supporting. For women, urban farming is also an assertion of autonomy, as it gives them some independence from their families and the market. Some women build subsidiary activities out of it, like processing and selling the food they grow.[51] Not surprisingly, Freeman found that urban farming is an activity that many women continue even when they have a job, proof that something more than pure survival is at stake.

What is at stake can be described in Fantu Cheru's words as the "silent revolution of the poor,"[52] by which he means the growth of self-help activities among peasants and urban poor, who, seeing that the state is "becoming irrelevant to them," are reclaiming "the self-reliance that was theirs until the advent of the modern nation state."[53] It is a revolution that is not organized, though it requires careful, strategic thinking and planning and a readiness to battle to defend land and crops. It also appears as a proliferation of individual initiatives rather than a collective process. But this appearance is misleading. Women urban farmers learn from each other and gain from each other's example the courage to become more self-supporting. There are also unspoken rules establishing which land can be taken and who has precedence. And there is a collective transformation of the social and physical reality of the cities. In disobedience of city laws and to the disappointment of urban planners, who, from colonial times, have tried to reserve Africa cities for the elite, urban farmers are breaking down the separation between town and country and converting African cities into gardens.[54] They are also putting limits on urban development plans and commercial housing that destroys communities and their residents' ability to support themselves with farming.

An example is the struggle that women have carried out in the Kawaala neighborhood of Kampala, Uganda, where, in 1992–1993, the World Bank, in conjunction with the City Council, sponsored a large housing project that would have destroyed much subsistence farmland around or near people's homes. Women strenuously organized against it, forming a residents' committee and eventually forcing the bank to withdraw from the project. As one of the women leaders put it:

Women were more vocal [than men] because they were directly affected. It is very hard for women to stand without any means of

income.... [M]ost of these women are people who basically support
their children and without any income and food they cannot do it....
You come and take their peace and income and they are going to fight,
not because they want to, but because they have been oppressed and
suppressed.[55]

The struggle in the Kawaala neighborhood is not unique. Similar
struggles have been reported in different parts of Africa and Asia, where
peasant women's organizations have opposed the development of industrial zones threatening to displace them and their families or contaminate
the environment. What these struggles show is that in defending land
from assault by commercial interests and affirming the principle that
'land and life are not for sale,' women are also defending their history and
culture. In the case of Kawaala, residents on the disputed land had been
living there for generations and had buried their kin there—for many
Ugandans the ultimate proof of landownership. Reflecting on this, Tripp
comments:

> the residents, especially the women involved, were trying to institu-
> tionalize some new norms for community mobilization, not just in
> Kawaala but more widely in providing a model for other community
> projects. They had a vision of a more collaborative effort that took
> the needs of women, widows, children, and the elderly as a starting
> point and recognized their dependence on the land for survival.[56]

It is this implicit vision that gives significance to African women's
land takeovers and struggles. By appropriating land, they are in fact
voting for a different 'moral economy' from that promoted by the World
Bank and other international developers that, for years, have been trying
to eradicate subsistence farming on the grounds that land becomes productive only when brought as collateral for credit to the bank. It is an
economy built on a noncompetitive, solidarity-centered mode of life.
Veronika Bennholdt-Thomsen and Maria Mies call it the "other" economy
saying that it "puts everything necessary to produce and maintain life on
this planet at the centre of economic and social activity and not the never-
ending accumulation of dead money."[57]

African women's struggle for the commons has also taken the form
of a mobilization against the destruction of natural resources. The best
known initiative in this context is the 'Green Belt Movement,' which under

the leadership of Wangari Maathai has been planting a green belt around the main Kenyan cities and, since 1977, has planted several million trees to prevent deforestation, soil loss, and desertification.[58] But the most striking struggle for the survival of the forests is taking place in the Niger Delta, where the mangrove tree swamps are being threatened by oil production. Opposition to this has been growing for twenty years, beginning in Ogharefe, where in 1984 several thousand women from the area laid siege to Pan Ocean's production station, demanding compensation for the destruction of the water, the trees, and the land. To show their determination, the women threatened to disrobe themselves should their demands be frustrated—a threat which they soon put into action. When the company's director arrived, he found himself surrounded by thousands of naked women, a serious curse in the eyes of the Niger Delta communities, which convinced him to accept the reparation claims.[59]

## Conclusion

While a new scramble for Africa is underway, it is evident that African women are not passive observers of the expropriation of their communities, and their struggle for more land and more security will play a key role in shaping the future of the African commons. But their strategies seem to move in opposite directions. Thus, an important conclusion to be drawn from an analysis of these struggles is that communalism in Africa is in crisis, undermined not only by outside forces but by the divisions among the commoners, starting with the divisions between women and men and continuing with those among women themselves.

At the same time, new commons are being created, and we can be sure that the efforts to deprivatize land will continue to grow. As the 'food crisis,' among other 'disasters,' demonstrates, the reappropriation of land and the creation of alternatives to the money economy and the market are today for millions of people across the planet the condition not only of personal and collective autonomy but of physical survival.

## Notes
1    Anatole Anton, "Public Goods as Common Stock: Notes on the Receding Commons," in *Not for Sale: In Defense of Public Goods*, eds. Anatole Anton, Milton Fisk, and Nancy Holmström (Boulder, CO: Westview Press, 2000), 4.
2    George Caffentzis, "The Fundamental Implications of the Debt Crisis for Social Reproduction in Africa," in *Paying the Price: Women and the Politics of International Economic Strategy*, eds. Mariarosa Dalla Costa and Giovanna

Dalla Costa (London: Zed Books, 1995), 15–41; Massimo De Angelis, *The Beginning of History: Value Struggles and Global Capital* (London: Pluto Press, 2007); Peter Linebaugh. *The Magna Carta Manifesto: Liberties and Commons for All* (Berkeley: University of California Press, 2008).

3    L. Muthoni Wanyeki, ed. *Women and Land in Africa: Culture, Religion and Realizing Women's Rights* (London: Zed Books, 2003); Aili Mari Tripp, "Women's Movements, Customary Law, and Land Rights in Africa: The Case of Uganda," *African Studies Quarterly* 7, no. 4 (Spring 2004): 1–19; Judy Adoko, "Land Rights: Where We Are and Where We Need to Go," *Mokoro*, September 2005, accessed May 31, 2018, http://mokoro.co.uk/wp-content/uploads/lemu_land_rights_where_we_are_and_where_we_need_to_go.pdf.

4    Liz Alden Wily, "Reconstructing the African Commons," *Africa Today* 48, no. 1 (Spring 2001): 85, accessed May 31, 2018, https://pdfs.semanticscholar.org/3 1e4/4633588b0c258364e7e82c8785e166d7fd25.pdf.

5    Customary law is the complex of traditions that governed life and the management and distribution of land in precolonial African societies. In the majority of African countries, it is still part of the legal system, coexisting with statutory law, and often with British law and Sharia law.

6    Lorenzo Cotula, Camilla Toulmin, and Ced Hesse, *Land Tenure and Administration in Africa: Lessons of Experiences and Emerging Issues* (London: International Institute for Environment and Development, 2004), 2.

7    An example of how customary laws were reconstructed is G.S. Snell, *Nandi Customary Law* (Nairobi: Kenya Literature Bureau, 1986 [1954]), xii. A British anthropologist, Snell conducted extensive interviews with local chiefs, trying to assess how the laws had changed under British colonial rule. He pointed out that only with time did customary laws evolve into static codes, for abundance of land and other resources made their provisions originally very flexible and not in need of great detailing.

8    Ron J. Lesthaeghe, "Production and Reproduction in Sub-Saharan Africa: An Overview of Organizing Principles," in *Reproduction and Social Organization in Sub-Saharan Africa*, ed. Ron J. Lesthaeghe (Berkeley: University of California Press, 1989), 13–59; Snell, *Nandi Customary Law*, 112–13.

9    *Sub-Saharan Africa: From Crisis to Sustainable Growth* (Washington, DC: World Bank, 1989).

10   Caffentzis, "The Fundamental Implications of the Debt Crisis for Social Reproduction in Africa," 28.

11   Adoko, "Land Rights," 6.

12   Bondi D. Ogolla and John Mugabe, "Land Tenure Systems and Natural Resource Management," in *In Land We Trust. Environment, Private Property and Constitutional Change*, eds. Calestous Juma and J.B. Ojwang (London: Zed Books, 1996), 102–3.

13   Masao Yoshida "Land Tenure Reform Under the Economic Liberalization Regime: Observation from the Tanzanian Experience," *African Development* 30, no. 4 (2005): 141; Tripp, "Women's Movements," 11.

14   Wily, "Reconstructing the African Commons," 88; Cotula, Toulmin, and Hesse, *Land Tenure and Administration in Africa*, 5.

15   Wily, "Reconstructing the African Commons," 92–93.

16   Tripp, "Women's Movements," 2.

17   Tripp, 13.

18   Yoshida, "Land Tenure Reform Under the Economic Liberalization Regime,"; Ambreena Manji, *The Politics of Land Reform in Africa* (London: Zed Books, 2006).

19   Wanyeki, *Women and Land in Africa*; Tripp, Women's Movements, Customary Law, and Land Rights in Africa, 2, 10.

20   E.G.C. Barrow, "Customary Tree Tenure in Pastoral Land," in Juma and Ojwang *In Land We Trust*, 264.

21   Wanyeki, *Women and Land in Africa*, 187–88.

22   Tripp, "Women's Movements," 2.

23   Thomas Hakansson, "Landless Gusii Women: A Result of Customary Land Law and Modern Marriage Pattern," Working Papers in African Studies no. 29, African Studies Programme, Department of Cultural Anthropology, University of Uppsala, 1988; Leslie Gray and Michael Kevane, "Diminished Access, Diverted Exclusion: Women and Land Tenure in Sub-Saharan Africa," *African Studies Review* 42, no. 2 (September 1999): 15–39.

24   Gray and Kevane, "Diminished Access," 21.

25   Silvia Federici, "Witch Hunts in Africa," *WAGADU* (June 2008).

26   Liazzat Bonate, "Women's Land Rights in Mozambique: Cultural, Legal and Social Contexts," in Wanyeki, *Women and Land in Africa*, 115, 122.

27   Gray and Kevane, "Diminished Access," 22.

28   Adoko, "Land Rights," 11.

29   Gray and Kevane, "Diminished Access," 18.

30   Fenella Mukangara and Bertha Koda, *Beyond Inequalities: Women in Tanzania* (Harare: Southern Africa Research and Documentation Centre, 1997); Tripp, "Women's Movements"; Wanyeki, *Women and Land in Africa*, 267.

31   Mary Kimani, "Women Struggle to Secure Land Rights: Hard Fight for Access and Decision-Making Power," *Africa Renewal* 22, no. 1 (April 2008): 10, accessed May 24, 2018, http://www.un.org/en/africarenewal/vol22no1/221-women-struggle-to-secure-land-rights.html.

32   Kimani, "Women Struggle to Secure Land Rights."

33   Margaret C. Snyder and Mary Tadesse, *African Women and Development: A History* (London: Zed Books, 1995), 17.

34   Winnie Bikaako and John Ssenkumba, "Gender, Land and Rights: Contemporary Contestations in Law, Policy and Practice in Uganda," in Wanyeki, *Women and Land in Africa*, 262; Robin Palmer, "Gendered Land Rights—Process, Struggle, or Lost C(l)ause?" *Mokoro*, November 28, 2001, accessed June 2, 2018, http://mokoro.co.uk/wp-content/uploads/gendered_land_rights.pdf.

35   Bikaako and Ssenkumba, *Gender*, 263.

36   Bikaako and Ssenkumba, 246.

37   Tripp, "Women's Movements."

38    Carmen Diana Deere and Magdelena León de Leal, *Empowering Women: Land and Property Rights in Latin America* (Pittsburgh: University of Pittsburgh Press, 2001).

39    Wily, Reconstructing the African Commons, 88; Cotula, Toulmin, and Hesse, *Land Tenure and Administration in Africa*, 85.

40    Cotula, Toulmin, and Hesse, *Land Tenure and Administration in Africa*.

41    Tripp, "Women's Movements," 9.

42    Manji, *The Politics of Land Reform in Africa*, 67–68, 99–121.

43    Sam Moyo, "Land in the Political Economy of African Development: Alternative Strategies for Reform," *Africa Development* 32, no. 4 (2007): 1–34; Palmer, "Gendered Land Rights."

44    Barrow, *Customary Tree Tenure in Pastoral Land*, 267.

45    Bikaako and Ssenkumba, *Gender*, 276.

46    Justus M. Ogembo, *Contemporary Witch-Hunting in Gusii, Southwestern Kenya* (Lewiston, NY: Edwin Mellen Press, 2006); Federici, "Witch Hunts in Africa."

47    Bongani Xezwi, "The Landless People Movement," Research Report no.10, Center for Civil Society, *RASSP Research Reports 2005* 1, 185–87.

48    Moyo, "Land in the Political Economy of African Development," 16–18.

49    Theodore Trefon, "The Political Economy of Sacrifice: *Kinois* and the State," *Review of African Political Economy* 29, no. 93–94 (2002): 490.

50    Christa Wichterich, *The Globalized Woman: Reports from a Future of Inequality* (London: Zed Books, 2000), 73.

51    Donald B. Freeman, "Survival Strategy or Business Training Ground? The Significance of Urban Agriculture for the Advance of Women," *Africa Studies Review* 36, no. 3 (December 1993): 14.

52    Fantu Cheru, "The Silent Revolution and the Weapons of the Weak: Transformation and Innovation from Below," in *The Global Resistance Reader*, ed. Louise Amoore (New York: Routledge, 2005), 78.

53    Cheru, "The Silent Revolution and the Weapons of the Weak."

54    Freeman, "Survival Strategy or Business Training Ground?" 19–20.

55    Quoted in Tripp, "Women's Movements," 183.

56    Tripp, 194.

57    Maria Mies and Veronika Bennholdt-Thomsen, *The Subsistence Perspective: Beyond the Globalized Economy* (London: Zed Books, 1999), 5.

58    Wangari Maathai, *Unbowed: One Woman's Story* (London: Arrow Books, 2008).

59    Terisa E. Turner and M.O. Oshare, "Women's Uprising against the Nigerian Oil Industry," in *Arise Ye Mighty People! Gender, Class and Race in Popular Struggles*, eds. Terisa E. Turner and Brian J. Ferguson (Trenton, NJ: Africa World Press, 1994), 140–41.

# Women's Struggles for Land and the Common Good in Latin America

The impeachment of Dilma Rousseff in Brazil, the deep economic and political crisis in Venezuela, and the victory of a right-wing candidate in Argentina's elections all indicate that a phase in Latin American politics is coming to an end. What is ending is the illusion that many harbored that the emergence of 'progressive,' left-leaning governments could transform the politics of the region, implement the reforms that social movements for decades have been fighting for and promote social justice. On the balance, these objectives have not been achieved. Following the example of Venezuela's 'Bolivarian Revolution,' the governments of Morales, Correa, Kirchner, and Lula da Silva have transferred part of their country's revenues to the popular sectors, with the institution of welfare programs (*Bolsas Familiales*) providing subsidies to children's education and other basic necessities. In this way, the most extreme forms of poverty have been alleviated. But these measures have been a far cry from what social movements had expected. Taking Brazil as an example, it is calculated that at least thirty million people have benefitted from the welfare programs that the Lula government adopted. Still, social expenses have claimed a tenth of the money transferred to mining and agribusiness companies, which have continued to play a hegemonic role in the politics of the country. As extractivism has continued to be the model of economic development, the land reform advocated by the movements that brought the Partido de los Trabajadores (PT) to power has not been realized. Instead, the concentration of land in a few hands, one of the highest levels on the continent, has continued to increase, and for the first time indigenous peoples' lands have come under a direct attack, in the name of modernization.[1] Meanwhile, police violence has not been reined in, so, according to official statistics, thousands of people, mostly black homeless youth, are killed every year by the police, 4,224 in 2016. This may explain why relatively few proletarians have gone to the streets to demand the reinstatement of Dilma Rousseff after her final impeachment, although its unconstitutional and fraudulent character has been widely condemned. As Débora Maria da Silva, one of the founders and leader of the movement of the Mães de Maio declared in a meeting held in Sao Paulo on September 13, 2016: "I will not cry for Dilma, because for us in the favelas the dictatorship never ended."[2]

With local variations, the Brazilian model of 'progressive' development, with its mixture of welfarism and extractivism and its reliance on an export-oriented economy as the basis for a more egalitarian distribution of wealth is also the path adopted by the governments of Bolivia, Ecuador, and, before the last elections, Argentina. Chavism too, though more supportive of popular power, has relied on oil extraction to subsidize its social programs, failing to give the country a long-term material basis not dependent on the vagaries of the global commodities market.

But while 'progressivism' has failed to maintain its promises, and we are now witnessing an institutional takeover by the right, it would be a mistake to conclude that radical change has come to an end in Latin America. Social mobilization has reached such a level of intensity—and not only across the region—that as acute a theorist as Raúl Zibechi has spoken of "societies in movement."[3] What is especially significant is that resistance to this onslaught and the extension of capitalist relations is creating more cooperative forms of existence and providing a vision of what a noncapitalist society might be like. As I argue in this article, women are the main protagonists of this change. Indeed, women's activism is currently the main force for social change in Latin America. Seventy thousand women from different parts of the region met in Chaco, Argentina, in 2017 for the thirty-second edition of the National Encounter of Women, held every year in the week of October 11, to discuss what had to be done, what strategies to adopt to change the world.

Such massive mobilizations—coming at the moment of a realignment in Latin American institutional politics—are not surprising. Women play a central role in social struggles because they are those most affected by dispossession and environmental degradation, suffering directly the effects of public policy in their everyday life. It is women who must deal with those who become sick because of petroleum contamination or because the water they use to cook, wash, and clean is toxic, and who cannot feed their families because of the loss of land and the destruction of local agriculture.[4] Thus, women today stand on the front lines against the transnational mining and agribusiness corporations that invade rural areas and devastate the environment. As the Ecuadorian scholar-activist Lisset Coba Meja has pointed out, it is women who in the Amazonian region lead the struggle in defense of water.[5] They also are the main opponents of petroleum extraction, aware that it undermines their productive activities and, in the words of Ecuadorian activist Esperanza Martínez of Acción Ecologica, it "exacerbates machismo"; the wages that the oil companies pay to the men they employ deepen gender inequalities, boost alcohol consumption, and intensify violence against women.[6] Her words are echoed by the complaints of many Amazonian women who are fighting against oil extraction. "We cannot feed oil to our children," says the Kichwa leader Patricia Gualinga, from Sarayaku, a village in the Amazonian forest. "We don't want alcoholism, we do not want prostitution, we do not want men who beat us. We do not want this life, because even if they give us schools, bathrooms and houses with zinc, it takes away our dignity."[7]

In recent years, such opposition has brought women into a direct confrontation with then-president Rafael Correa, peaking on October 16, 2013, when one hundred leaders of indigenous women's organizations walked from their lands in the rainforest to Quito, their children in their arms, in response to Correa's decision to abandon his conservation plan and begin petroleum extraction in the Yasuní National Park, home to one of the most diverse ecosystems on earth. They were following the example of thousands of other women who, one year earlier, had likewise marched to the capital to defend the waters of their territories against a mining project contracted by the Correa government with the Chinese company EcuaCorriente. But in a show of arrogance and disrespect, consistent with his reputation as the most misogynous of Ecuadorian presidents, Correa refused to receive them.[8]

In Bolivia too, indigenous women have contested the government's 'progressivism' and in particular President Evo Morales's proclaimed defense of Pachamama (Mother Nature), leading marches in 2011 and 2012 against the construction of a highway that, according to the government's plans, would traverse the Parque Nacional Isiboro Sécure, in indigenous territory. As it is often the case, the women provided the support infrastructure necessary for the marches, from food to blankets, and organized the cleaning of the camps built along the road, in an arrangement that ensured that the men participating would do their share.[9] Peasant/indigenous women, together with feminist networks like the Marcha Mundial de Mujeres, were also at the heart of the Cumbre de los Pueblos, a gathering of social movements held in Rio de Janeiro, in June 2012, on the occasion of Rio+20, the United Nations Conference on Sustainable Development held twenty years after the UN Earth Summit of 1992.[10]

One characteristic of these new women's movements is the process of political radicalization they reflect. Increasingly, women are aware that their activism must not only protect the lives of their communities against the activities of transnational companies and fight for food sovereignty or against the genetic engineering of seeds by building seed banks, for example. It must also transform the model of economic development into one respectful of human beings and the earth. They see that the problems they face stem not solely from specific policies or companies but are rooted in the mercenary logic of capitalist accumulation, which even through the promotion of a 'green economy' is turning the cleaning of the environment into a new source of speculation and profit.

A further aspect of this radicalization is the growing assimilation by rural/indigenous women of the issues raised by popular feminism, such as the devaluation of domestic work, women's right to control their bodies and reproductive capacity, and the need to resist the growing violence against them. This process was not sparked off by ideological considerations but by the very contradictions that women have experienced in their everyday lives, including within the organizations in which they participate.[11]

Typical is the case of Zapatista women, whose crucial role in the depatriarchalization of their communities is becoming ever more apparent. As Hilary Klein's *Compañeras* (2015) and Márgara Millán's *Des-ordenando el género/¿Des-centrando la nación?* (2014) well document, women have directed the course of Zapatism from the first days of its existence, joining the first groups that gathered in the mountains of Chiapas when the movement was still very young, in order to change their living conditions as much as to fight institutional oppression. It was through their initiative and on the basis of their ideas and demands that the movement's Women's Revolutionary Law was adopted in 1993, which, as Klein points out, "given indigenous women's reality in rural Chiapas at the time represented a radical stance and … implied a series of dramatic changes."[12]

The law's ten points established women's right to participate in the revolutionary struggle in any way they desired, according to their capacity; the
right to decide the number of children they have and care for; to choose
their partners and not enter into marriage; to participate in community
affairs and hold positions of authority, if they are freely and democratically elected; to occupy positions of leadership in the organization and
hold military ranks in the revolutionary armed forces.[13] In the words
of Klein, the adoption of the law was a "watershed moment" that "transformed public and private life in Zapatista communities."[14] The women
realized, however, that their work was not over. After the Law was made
public, some traveled throughout the Zapatista territories to promote its
application and impose a ban on alcohol consumption in Zapatista territories, convinced it was a major cause of violence against them.[15]

A further sign of a rising feminist consciousness is the emergence
of a new critical stance among indigenous women who are questioning
the patriarchal structures that govern their communities, especially the
transmission of land, which often occurs in a patrilineal fashion. This
"differential inclusion"[16] has major consequences, as Gladys Tzul Tzul,
an indigenous scholar/activist from the Totonicapán area of Guatemala,
points out, as it affects "the registration of the family's property, the
guardianship of children, and the symbolic meaning of having children
outside of marriage."[17] For instance, women who marry outside their
ethnic groups risk their children being excluded from access to the clan's
communally shared land. The challenge, Tzul Tzul argues, is to change
this custom without resorting to the individual titling of land, which legit-
imizes the trend toward land privatization, the strategy advocated by the
World Bank since the Beijing Conference of 1995.

A strategy that women in the indigenous movements have used
to end their marginalization has been the creation of autonomous
women's spaces. One example is the Hijas del Maíz, described as "a space
of encounter for women from peasant and indigenous communities
of the Ecuadorian coast, mountain range, and Amazonía."[18] "Much has
changed in the lives of our people," says Blanca Chancosa, one of its founders. "[Men] have migrated . . . [and] those who have remained . . . are the
women. This means that we need to know more to move on. . . . This is why
we need a women's space in which we can discuss our ideas."[19] A similar
autonomy seeking strategy to boost women's social participation has been
the formation of peasant movements consisting exclusively of women.

An example is the Movimento de Mujeres Campesinas de Brasil, which, according to Roxana Longo, "recuperates the theory and practice of the feminist movement."[20] Formed in 1983, as the rural populations began to feel the negative effects of the 'Green Revolution,'[21] this alliance of women variously involved in agricultural work has fought to change the social identity of peasant women—to have them recognized as workers and gain for them the right to social security. In 1995, it formed a national network of peasant women's groups and women from mixed peasant movements that won paid maternity leave and struggled to defend public health care.[22] It also engaged in protest actions against the activities of transnational corporations, knowing that their presence would be the end of their communities.

As political participation has increased, so too has women's awareness of the need for self-education and political formation. These are now common elements in many women's organizations, as they confront social forces whose logic is shaped at an international level and requires an understanding of international politics. Combined with the self-confidence gained through social activism, these practices generate new forms of subjectivity that contrast with the image of the peasant woman propagated by international institutions—anchored to the past, cognizant only of outdated knowledges on the way to extinction. Peasant women in South America are far from being concerned solely with their local cultivation rights or their families' well-being. They participate in assemblies, challenge the government and police, and see themselves as the custodians of the land, as they are less easily co-opted than men, who are often seduced by the wages promised by transnational corporations—wages that give them more power over women, feeding into a macho culture that instigates violence against them.[23]

One factor that encourages women's role as custodians of the land and communal wealth is their greater role in preserving and transmitting traditional knowledge. As *tejedoras de memoria*, 'weavers of memory,'[24] as Mexican theorist/activist Mina Navarro puts it, they form an important instrument of resistance, because the knowledge they sustain and share produces a stronger collective identity and cohesion in the face of dispossession.[25] The participation in the new movements of indigenous women, who bring with them a vision of the future shaped by a connection with the past and a strong sense of the continuity between human being and nature, is crucial in this context. With reference to the 'cosmovisions' that

139

typify indigenous cultures in Latin America some feminists have coined the term 'communitarian feminism,' where the concept of the common is understood to express a specific conception of space, time, life, and the human body. As Francesca Gargallo reports in her *Feminismos desde Abya Yala* (2013), communitarian feminists, such as the Xinka feminist Lorena Cabnal of Guatemala, have contributed new concepts such as the *body-territory*, which looks at the body as on a continuum with the land, where the placenta of the newborns is often buried, both possessing a historical memory and both equally implicated in the process of liberation.[26] While they champion their ancestral origins, however, communitarian feminists nevertheless reject the patriarchalism of many indigenous cultures as much as that planted by the colonizers and what they describe as "ethnic fundamentalism."[27]

## Women's Struggle and the Production of the Urban Commons

The struggle in the rural areas continues in the city; the men and women who are displaced from the land form new communities in urban areas. They take over public spaces, constructing shelters, roads, and bodegas, all through collective labor and communal decision-making. Again, women have taken a leading role. As I have written elsewhere,[28] in the peripheries of the sprawling megacities of Latin America, in areas mostly occupied through collective action, and in the face of permanent economic crisis, women are creating a new political economy based on cooperative forms of social reproduction, establishing their 'right to the city' and laying the groundwork for new practices of resistance and reclamation.[29]

Equally important has been the socialization of reproductive activities, like shopping, cooking, and sewing. These activities have a long history. In 1973, in Chile, after the military coup, women in proletarian settlements, paralyzed by fear and subjected to a brutal austerity program, pooled their labor and resources. They began to shop and cook together in teams of twenty or more in the barrios where they lived. Born out of necessity, these initiatives produced far more than an expansion of limited resources. The act of coming together and rejecting the isolation into which the Pinochet regime was forcing them qualitatively transformed their lives, giving them self-esteem and breaking the paralysis induced by the government's strategy of terror. It also reactivated the circulation of information and knowledge that is essential to resistance. And it transformed the concept of what it means to be a good mother and wife, contributing to its redefinition as going outside the home and participating in social struggles.[30] The work of social reproduction ceased to be a purely domestic and individual activity; housework went into the streets alongside the big *ollas* (cooking pots) and acquired a political dimension.

These politics did not escape the notice of the authorities, who came to view organizing popular kitchens as a subversive, communist activity. In response to this threat to their power, police launched olla smashing raids into the barrios. As some of the women involved in the popular kitchen recalled:

> Sara: [W]ith 300 people involved it was difficult to hide what was going on. They came and turned the food stores upside down, they made us stop cooking and took all the leaders prisoner. . . . They came many times, but the kitchen went on. . . .
>
> Olga: The police came: "What's going on here? A communal kitchen? So why are you doing it if you know it is prohibited?" "Because we are hungry." "Stop cooking!" They said it was political. The beans were half-cooked and we had to throw them all away. . . . The police came many times, but we managed to keep the kitchen going, one week in one house, the next week in another.[31]

It is generally agreed that such survival strategies boosted the community's senses of solidarity and identity and demonstrated women's capacity to reproduce their lives without having to be completely dependent on the market, helping in the post-coup period to keep alive the popular movement that had brought Allende to power. By the 1980s, it was strong enough to mount a successful resistance to the dictatorship.

Collective forms of social reproduction have also proliferated in Peru, Argentina, and Venezuela. According to the Uruguayan social theorist Raúl Zibechi, in the 1990s, in Lima alone, there were fifteen thousand popular organizations providing glasses of milk or breakfasts for children and organizing soup kitchens and neighborhood councils.[32]

In Argentina, the *piqueteras*, proletarian women, who together with their children and many young men, took an important role in response to the catastrophic 2001 economic crisis that for months paralyzed the country. They organized roadblocks, built encampments, and assembled barricades—*piquetes*—that lasted at times more than a week. Paraphrasing what Zibechi writes concerning the famous Madres of the Plaza de Maio,[33] we can say that the piqueteras "understood the importance of occupying a public space." They reorganized their social reproductive activities in the street, cooking, cleaning, taking care of children, and maintaining social relations, and in the process communicated to the struggle a passion and courage that strengthened and enriched it.[34] The testimony of the Cuban social science researcher Isabel Rauber is significant:

> From the beginning, from the first pickets . . . the presence of women and their children was crucial. Determined not to go back home without something to put in their pots, the women went to piquetes to defend their lives with teeth and nails. Determined to achieve their objectives they immediately participated and guaranteed the organization of daily life on the barricades, which often lasted more than a day. If tents had to be set up, if it was necessary to take turns watching over the security of the piquetes, to prepare food—for sure, together with the men—to construct barricades and defend the positions taken, there were the women.[35]

What Rauber underlines—which I would argue applies to many women's struggles today in Latin America and beyond—is that, as neoliberalism unleashes a genocidal attack on people's means of subsistence, the role of women in the struggle becomes more fundamental. The struggle against it must be rooted in the activities that reproduce our lives, because, in the words of a male militant Rauber quotes, "Everything begins in our daily life and then is translated into political terms. Where there is no everyday life, there is no organization, and where there is no organization, there is no politics."[36]

Her view is confirmed by the account of the piqueteras movement by Natalia Quiroga Díaz and Verónica Gago, who have argued that the economic crisis of 2001 induced "a feminization of the economy, and together with it a deprivatization of the resources necessary for reproduction."[37] As soon as the official economy collapsed, with many companies and even the banks shutting down and people unable retrieve their savings, a different, 'feminine' economy surfaced. It was inspired by the logic of domestic work but organized collectively in public spaces in ways that made visible the political character and social value of reproductive work. As women occupied the streets, bringing their pots and pans to the roadblocks and their neighborhood assemblies, as barter networks and various types of cooperatives were set up, a subsistence economy emerged. It enabled thousands to survive and, at the same time, redefined what value is and where it is produced, increasingly identifying it with the capacity to collectively manage the reproduction of our life, whose rhythms and needs reshape urban space and time.

Although the piqueteras movement has since demobilized, its lesson has not been forgotten. On the contrary, what was a response to an immediate crisis has become, in many Argentinian proletarian neighborhoods, a broad social reality and part of a more lasting social fabric. As Marina Sitrin has documented, years after the rebellion of 2002, neighborhood assemblies and the forms of collective action and cooperation that were born in the piquetes continue.[38] In the villas of Buenos Aires, we can best see how the refusal of immiseration and dispossession that animated the piquetes can turn into the construction of a new world.[39] Here one meets women who live in a situation in which every moment of their everyday lives becomes an instance of political choice, as nothing is due them and nothing is guaranteed; everything is gained through negotiation or struggle, and everything must be continuously defended. Potable water and electricity must be contracted with the state, as must some of the material necessary to build the roads needed to prevent rain from turning the streets into rivers of mud. But the women who struggle to obtain these resources do not expect or indeed allow the state to organize their lives. Cooperating with each other, determined not to be defeated and to escape social and economic impoverishment, they are creating new spaces that belong to no one, in which to collectively make decisions concerning the reproduction of everyday life, including the provision of services for all who contribute. As Zibechi describes the situation in Villa Retiro Bis, one of the twenty-one villas in Buenos Aires:

> Here you have neighbors who have lunch in the popular kitchens . . .
> at night study in a primary school, and socialize in the houses of
> women. . . . Certainly they are precarious spaces that have some ties
> with the state and the market, but they are minimal, marginal. The
> main thing is that they are undertakings sustained by mutual aid,
> self-management, cooperation, and fraternization.[40]

When I visited the same villa in April 2015, the women, part of the Corriente Villera Independiente, were proud of what they have achieved. "Everything you see," they told me, "we have built with our hands." And I could see, walking in streets that they had helped pave, visiting the *comedores populares* (popular kitchens), where they serve hundreds of meals daily, working on a rotating basis, attending a performance of the Theatre of the Oppressed they had organized,[41] that this space where they walked was their space, not the alien territory we usually traverse where we have no stake and no means of control. When, prior to my visit, the city of Buenos Aires constructed a wall to prevent a further expansion of the villa, the women immediately tore part of it down, because, they said, "We want to be able to move freely and refuse to be enclosed."

While the crisis of the subsistence agriculture that neoliberal politics has produced has often resulted in the formation of partially self-managed encampments like those found in the villas, in Bolivia a more common phenomenon has been the proliferation of street vendors, who, in "incalculable numbers," have occupied urban areas and transformed them into *ciudades mercado*, "market cities," mostly through the "incessant work of thousands and thousands of women."[42] Confronted with displacement from rural lands and the impoverishment of their communities, many proletarian women have taken their reproductive work outside their home and "transformed the markets into their daily living space" where "they cook, take care of their children, iron their clothes, watch TV, visit each other, all in the bustle of buying and selling."[43]

As María Galindo of the Bolivian anarcho-feminist organization Mujeres Creando points out, Bolivian women's struggle for survival has ruptured the universe of the home and domesticity. It has broken the isolation characteristic of domestic work, so that the figure of the woman shut away in the home is now a thing of the past. In response to the precarization of labor and the crisis in male wages, a culture of resistance has emerged. Women have appropriated the streets, "converting the city into a domestic space"[44] where they spend most of their time selling wares (food, smuggled goods, pirated music, etc.) that "cheapen the cost of living for all the population," organizing with other women, and confronting the police, and in this process "reinventing their relationship to society."[45] Mujeres Creando has contributed to this new female appropriation of the urban space, opening a social center, the Virgen de los Deseos (the Virgin of Desires)—which Galindo has described as "a reproductive machine," owing to the manifold activities that take place there—and providing services that are especially intended for street women, such as daycare, food vending, a radio transmitter that women use to broadcast news about their struggles or denounce abuses they have suffered, and the publication of political-educational materials.

Selling goods in the streets may not seem a radical activity. But anyone who is familiar with the intricate social relations that have to be created, especially in our time, to be able to occupy public space in a way not authorized by the state knows that this impression is mistaken. For the women who make up the majority of *vendidores ambulantes*, creating the conditions that enable them to spend much of their day in the street, ensure the safety of their wares—especially from attack by the police—and work peacefully with each other, coordinating the shared use of space and time, as well as cleaning activities and pricing, a substantial amount of negotiation and policy making is required. Once accomplished, these efforts create a counterpower that the authorities cannot ignore. It is for this reason that, across the world, governments mount 'clean-up' campaigns, using the pretexts of sanitary improvement and beautification to destroy presences that threaten their urban plans and by their occupation of public space and their very visibility pose a threat to governmental authority.

One example of the threats to which *ambulantes* are exposed is the criminalization of the Union Popular de Vendedores Ambulantes 28 de Octubre,[46] an organization of market sellers based in the Mexican city of Puebla that was recently declared a public enemy by President Enrique Peña Nieto. With the male leaders of the organization mostly in jail or threatened with death in a country sadly famous for its high level of political assassinations, it is the women of 28 Octubre who now carry on the political work. They function as mothers, wives, and street vendors, caring for those imprisoned and for their children, while also spending long hours at work, and through it all taking on the work of political organization. The scenario makes for a life of constant worry, with no time for rest or any form of recreation. Yet, as is common in women's organizations, what one hears in their words is pride for what they are accomplishing and for the individual and collective growth they experience in their understanding of the world, their capacity to resist intimidation, and their respect for themselves and other women. It is in the words of such women that one sees the possibility of a different world, where commitment to social justice and cooperation merge in a new conception of politics that is the antithesis of the one generally recognized. A measure of the difference are the organizational practices the women of 28 Octubre have adopted, which are inspired by the principle of *horizontalidad* and an insistence on collective decision-making, often realized through neighborhood assembles in which all can participate.

Will these new women's movements be able to resist the onslaught of the expansion of capitalist relations? Will they have the power to contest the attempts to recolonize their lands and communities? There are no sure answers to these questions. What is certain, however, is that in moments of acute crisis, when the constitutive mechanisms of the capitalist political economy have collapsed, women have stepped forth and, through a collective effort, have guaranteed basic forms of social reproduction and broken the wall of fear that had imprisoned their communities. When a political and economic crisis 'normalizes,' the alternative economy that women create is often slowly dismantled, but never without leaving behind new forms of communal organization and a broader sense of possibility.

Thus, as Raúl Zibechi has often noted, in the villas of Argentina, Mexico, Peru, as in the peasant/indigenous and Afro-descendent communities of Latin America, a new world and a new politics are in the making. It is a world that gives a new vitality to the much abused notion of the commons, resignifying it as not only a wealth to be shared but as a commitment to the principle that this life we have should be a *vida digna de ser vivida*; a life, that is, worthy of being lived. At its center, as Raquel Gutiérrez, has written, are the reproduction of material life, its care, and the reappropriation of wealth collectively produced, organized in a way that is subversive; for it is based on the possibility to "articulate human activity and creativity for autonomous ends."[47]

The promoter of an investigative research writing group of women scholar-activists based at the Autonomous University of Puebla, in Mexico, Gutiérrez is today one of the main contributors in Latin America to the articulation of the experiences I have described, in all their capacity to recuperate the practices, knowledges, values, and visions sedimented by generations of indigenous communities and their continuous production of new meaning and forms of existence. Her work, like that that of the group of women with whom she has collaborated—Mina Lorena Navarro, Gladys Tzul Tzul, Lucia Linsalata—is an important part of the struggle, both as an example of a 'common of knowledge,' working within an academic context but in ways that run against the principles that academia imposes on the production of knowledge and as an effort to give voice to that powerful though mostly invisible, unarticulated complex of affects and emotions that are the substance and soil on which communitarian relations are produced. Today, such work is more indispensable than ever, for making visible how deeply rooted commoning relations are in our affective life, how essential they are to our survival and the valorization of our life, and gives us courage and strength in the face of the most violent, brutal attack capitalism has waged on every form of social solidarity since the heyday of colonization. It demonstrates that commoning is an irreducible aspect of our life, one that no violence can destroy, as it is continually recreated as a necessity of our existence.

## Notes

1    On the agricultural politics of the Lula government, see Raúl Zibechi, *Brasil potencia: entre la integración regional y un nuevo imperialismo* (Malaga: Badre y Zambra, 2012), especially 307–11. Zibechi writes that "the extraordinary expansion of agribusiness, strongly supported by the governments of Lula and Dilma has put into crisis the struggle for agrarian reform."

2    The movement of the Mães de Maio was founded in May 2006, one week after hundreds of people were killed by the police in a favela in São Paulo—six hundred according to official records, more than a thousand according to the mother of one of the victims of this mass killing. On the origin and work of the movement of the Mães de Maio 10, see *Fala Guerreira* no. 3, "Especial Mães de Maio 10 anos," March 22, 2016, accessed June 23, 2018, https://issuu.com/falaguerreira/docs/03_revistafala_guerreira.

3    Raúl Zibechi, *Territories in Resistance: A Cartography of Latin American Social Movements* (Oakland: AK Press, 2012).

4    See Colectivo Miradas Críticas del Territorio Desde el Feminismo, *La vida en el centro y el crudo bajo tierra: El Yasuní en clave feminista* (Quito: Colectivo Miradas Críticas del Territorio Desde el Feminismo, 2014).

5    Lisset Coba Mejía, "Agua y aceite: La sostenibilidad de la vida en crisis en la Amazonía," *Flor del Guanto* no. 5 (January 2016): 7.

6    Interview with Esperanza Martínez, "La actividad petrolera exacerba el machismo," in Colectivo Miradas Críticas, *La vida en el centro y el crudo bajo tierra*, 42–45.

7    Interview with Patricia Gualinga, "La voz y la lucha de las mujeres han tratado de ser minimizada," in Colectivo Miradas Críticas, *La vida en el centro*, 48–50.

8    On the march of the Amazonian women leaders to Quito, see "Conversatorio con Ivonne Ramos," in Colectivo Miradas Críticas, *La vida en el centro*, 82–85; see also 69–76.

9    Helen Álvarez, "La Marcha de la Mujeres," *Mujer Pública* (La Paz: Casa Virgen de Los Deseos), issue dedicated to the theme "Mujer globalizada, riqueza aniquilada."

10   On the participation of women's organizations in the Cumbre de los Pueblos, see SOF (Sempreviva Organização Feminista), *En lucha contra la mercantilización de la vida: la presencia de la Marcha Mundial de las Mujeres en la Cumbre de los Pueblos* (São Paulo, 2012).

11   On the relation between capitalist development and violence against women, see SOF, *En lucha contra la mercantilización de la vida*, 24 ff.

12   Hilary Klein, *Compañeras: Zapatista Women's Stories* (New York: Seven Stories Press, 2015), 72.

13   Klein, *Compañeras*, 71; see also Márgara Millán, *Des-ordenando el género/¿Descentrando la nación? El Zapatismo de las mujeres indígenas y sus consequencias* (México City: Ediciones del Lirio, 2014), 74–81.

14   Klein, *Compañeras*, 72.

15   On the Zapatista women's mobilization against alcohol, see Klein, *Compañeras*, 61–66. The significance of this initiative is summed up by a group of women interviewed by Klein at the *Caracol* in Morelia, one of the five sites of the Zapatista government: "When women began organizing it was because we were suffering so much with our husbands. We saw many women being abused and beaten by their husbands, and we had to do something about this situation…. In the organization women's lives have changed and we are not as oppressed. Before when men drank being abused was part of women's lives, but not anymore…. We marched with banners and we went to the town hall to pressure them to enact a dry law. There were about 250 women from different communities. We yelled and shouted"; Klein, *Compañeras*, 62.

16   Gladys Tzul Tzul, *Sistemas de gobierno comunal Indígena: mujeres y tramas de parentesco en Chuimeq'ena'* (Puebla: Sociedad Comunitaria de Estudios Estratégicos, 2016), 71–76.

17   Tzul Tzul, *Sistemas de gobierno comunal Indígena*, 168.

18   Colectivo Miradas Críticas, *La vida en el centro*, 51.

19   Blanca Chancosa, "Saramanta Warmikuna (Hijas del Maíz) un espacio de aliadas naturales," in Colectivo Miradas Críticas, *La vida en el centro*, 51–53.

20   Roxana Longo, *El protagonismo de las mujeres en los moviminentos sociales: Innovaciones y desafíos* (Buenos Aires: America Libre, 2012), 151ff.

21   The 'Green Revolution' is a broad agricultural program, sponsored by the United Nations, the United States, and the Food and Agriculture Organization as the solution to agricultural improvement in the Third World. It extends to former colonial territories the industrialized agricultural methods already applied in Europe and the U.S. It requires the construction of dams to boost irrigation and the extensive application of fertilizers, pesticides, and genetically modified seeds in the countries that adopt it (Mexico, the Philippines). The Green Revolution has deepened class divisions and has led to a further concentration of land and the expulsion from the rural areas of many small landowners, who could not sustain the expenses required for the purchase of the new agricultural technologies. For a critique of the Green Revolution see, among others, Vandana Shiva, *Monocultures of the Mind: Perspectives on Biodiversity and Biotechnology* (London: Zed Books, 1993), 39–49; Shiva, *Staying Alive: Women, Ecology and Development* (London: Zed Books, 1989), 96–98, 135–40, 143–45.

22   Longo, *El protagonismo de las mujeres en los moviminentos sociales*, 156–57.

23   Mirabel Álvarez, "Las Actividades extractivas convierten a la gente en esclavos," in Colectivo Miradas Críticas, *La vida en el centro*, 57.

24 Mina Navarro, *Luchas por lo común: Antagonismo social contra el despojo capitalista de los bienes naturales en Mexico* (Puebla: Bajo Tierra Ediciones, 2015), 264.

25 Navarro, *Luchas por lo común*, 248.

26 Francesca Gargallo, *Feminismos desde Abya Yala* (Buenos Aires: America Libre, 2013), 227.

27 Gargallo, *Feminismos desde Abya Yala*, 230–37, 245.

28 Federici, "Commoning the City," *Journal of Design Strategies* 9, no. 1 (Fall 2017): 33–37; published by the Parsons New School for Design, New York State.

29 The reference here is to David Harvey, *Rebel Cities: From the Right to the City to the Urban Revolution* (London: Verso, 2012).

30 See Jo Fisher, "'The Kitchen Never Stopped': Women's Self-Help Groups in Chile's Shanty Towns," in *Out of the Shadows: Women, Resistance, and Politics in Latin America* (London: Latin America Bureau, 1993), 17–43.

31 Fisher, "The Kitchen Never Stopped," 32–33.

32 Zibechi, *Territories in Resistance*, 236–39.

33 Raúl Zibechi, *Genealogía de la revuelta: Argentina: la sociedad en movimiento* (La Plata: Letra Libre, 2003).

34 Isabel Rauber, "Mujeres piqueteras: El caso de Argentina," in *Economie mondialiseé et identités de genre*, ed. Fenneke Reysoo (Geneva: Institut Universitaire d'Études du Développement, 2002), 115.

35 Rauber, "Mujeres piqueteras," 113.

36 Rauber, 115.

37 Natalia Quiroga Díaz and Verónica Gago, "Los comunes en femenino: cuerpo y poder ante la expropiación de las economías para la vida," *Economía y Sociedad* 19, no. 45 (June 2014): 13.

38 See Marina A. Sitrin, *Everyday Revolutions: Horizontalism and Autonomy in Argentina* (London: Zed Books, 2012), 81–83.

39 In Argentina, city encampments generally set up by people expelled from the rural areas and immigrants are known as *villas*.

40 Raúl Zibechi, *Descolonizar el pensamiento crítico y las práticas emancipatorias* (Bogotá: Edíciones Desde Abajo, 2015), 108.

41 The Theatre of the Oppressed was created in the 1960s by Brazilian actor, educator, and theatre director Augusto Boal. It is a political theatre in which the spectators become protagonists, helping to resolve the problems posed by the actors by acting them out.

42 Lucia Linsalata, *Cuando manda la asamblea: lo comunitario popular en Bolivia* (Mexico City: SOCEE, 2015), 64–65.

43 Linsalata, *Cuando manda la asamblea*, 65.

44 María Galindo, "La pobreza, un gran negocio," *Mujer Pública*, no. 7 (December 2012): 111–12.

45 Galindo, "La pobreza, un gran negocio," 114.

46 The group took the name 28 Octubre to commemorate those injured and killed in a violent raid the police conducted against the vendors of open-air street market on that date in 1973, which led to torching of dozens of stalls and an infant burning to death. An account of the raid and the activities of the

organization is given by Sandra C. Mendiola García, "Vendors, Mothers, and Revolutionaries: Street Vendors and Union Activism in 1970 Puebla Mexico," *Oral History Forum*, Special Issue on Oral History and the Working Class (2013): 1–26, accessed May 25, 2018, http://www.oralhistoryforum.ca/index. php/ohf/article/view/463/542.

47  Raquel Gutiérrez Aguilar, "Políticas en Femenino: Transformaciones y sub-versiones no centradas en el estado," *Contrapunto* no. 7 (December 2015): 126–27.

# Marxism, Feminism, and the Commons

> Communism is for us not a state of affairs which is to be established, an ideal to which reality will have to adjust itself. We call communism the real movement which abolishes the present state of things. The conditions of this movement result from the premises now in existence.
>
> —Karl Marx and Frederick Engels, *The German Ideology*[1]

## Introduction

What tools, principles, and ideas can Marxism bring to feminist theory and politics in our time? Can we think today of a relationship between Marxism and feminism other than the 'unhappy marriage' that Heidi Hartman depicted in a much quoted essay of 1979?[2] What aspects of Marxism are most important for reimagining feminism and communism in the twenty-first century? And how does Marx's concept of communism compare with the principle of the commons, the political paradigm inspiring so much radical feminist thinking today?

In asking these questions, I join a conversation on the construction of alternatives to capitalism that has begun in encampments and squares across the planet where, in ways replete with contradictions but creative of new possibilities, a society of 'commoners' is coming into existence, striving to build social spaces and relations not governed by the logic of the capitalist market.

Assessing the legacy of Marx's vision of communism for the twenty-first century is not an easy task, however. Added to the complexity of Marx's thought is the fact that in the last period of his life, after the defeat of the Paris Commune, Marx apparently abandoned some of his political axioms, especially with regard to the material preconditions for the construction of a communist society.[3] It is also agreed that there are important differences between his two major works, *Capital* and the *Grundrisse*,[4] and that Marx is not a writer whose thought can be grasped through any set of formulations, as "his level of analysis [was] continuously changing with his political design."[5]

## Two Things, However, Are Certain

The political language that Marx has given us is still necessary to think of a world beyond capitalism. His analysis of surplus value, money, and the commodity form, and, above all, his method—giving history and the class struggle a material foundation and refusing to separate the economic from the political—are still indispensable, though not sufficient, for understanding contemporary capitalism. Not surprisingly, with the deepening of the global economic crisis there has been a revival of interest in Marx that many could not have anticipated in the 1990s, when the dominant wisdom declared his theory defunct. Instead, amid the debris of realized socialism, broad debates have emerged on the questions of 'primitive accumulation,' the modalities of the 'transition,' and the historical and ethical meaning and possibility of communism. Mixed with feminist, anarchist, antiracist, and queer principles, Marx's theory continues to influence the disobedients of Europe, the Americas, and beyond. An anticapitalist feminism, then, cannot ignore Marx. Indeed, as Stevi Jackson has argued, "in the early 1980s the dominant perspectives within feminist theory were generally informed by, or formulated in dialogue with, Marxism."[6] Yet there is no doubt that Marx's categories must be given new foundations and we must go "beyond Marx."[7] This is not only because of the socioeconomic transformations that have taken place since Marx's time, but because of the limits in his understanding of capitalist relations—limits whose political significance has been made visible by the social movements of the last half century, which have brought to the world stage social subjects that Marx's theory ignored or marginalized.

## Feminism and the Viewpoint of Social Reproduction

Feminists have made an important contribution to this process, but they have not been alone. In the 1950s and 1960s, in the wake of the anticolonial struggle, political theorists like Frantz Fanon[8] questioned analyses like

Marx's that almost exclusively focused on wage labor and assumed the vanguard role of the metropolitan proletariat, thus marginalizing the enslaved, the colonized, and the unwaged, among others, in the process of accumulation and anticapitalist struggle. These political theorists realized that the experience of the colonies called for a rethinking "of Marxism as a whole," and that either Marxist theory could be reframed to incorporate the experiences of 75 percent of the world population or it would cease to be a liberating force and become instead an obstacle to it.[9] The peasants, the peons, and the lumpen, who made the revolutions of the twentieth century, showed no intention of waiting for a future proletarianization, or for 'the development of the productive forces,' to demand a new world order, as orthodox Marxists and the parties of the left would advise them to do.

Ecologists, including some ecosocialists, have also taken Marx to task for promoting an asymmetrical and instrumental view of the man-nature relationship, presenting human beings and labor as the only active agents and denying nature any intrinsic value and self-organizing potential.[10] But it was with the rise of the feminist movement that a more systematic critique of Marxism could be articulated, for feminists brought to the table not only the unwaged of the world but the vast population of social subjects (women, children, occasionally men) whose work in fields, kitchens, bedrooms, and streets daily produces and reproduces the workforce, and with them a set of issues and struggles concerning the organization of social reproduction that Marx and the Marxist political tradition have barely touched upon.

It is starting from this critique that I consider the legacy of Marx's vision of communism, concentrating on those aspects that are most important for a feminist program and for the politics of the commons, by which I refer to the many practices and perspectives embraced by social movements across the planet that today seek to enhance social cooperation, undermine the market's and state's control over our lives, promote the sharing of wealth, and, in this way, set limits to capital accumulation. Anticipating my conclusions, I argue that Marx's vision of communism as a society beyond exchange value, private property, and money, based on associations of free producers, and governed by the principle 'to each according to their needs from each according to their abilities' represents an ideal that no anticapitalist feminist can object to. Feminists can also embrace Marx's inspiring image of a world beyond the social division of labor, although they may want to ensure that between hunting in the morning, fishing in the afternoon, and criticizing after dinner, there would remain some time for everyone to share cleaning and childcare. But feminist politics teach us that we cannot accept Marx's conception of what constitutes work and the class struggle, and even more fundamentally we must reject the idea—permeating most of Marx's published work—that capitalism is or has been a necessary stage in the history of human emancipation and a necessary precondition for the construction of a communist society. This must be firmly stated, as the idea that capitalist development enhances workers' autonomy and social cooperation and thereby works toward its own dissolution has proven remarkably intractable.

Far more important for feminist politics than any ideal projection of a postcapitalist society are Marx's relentless critique of capitalist accumulation and his method, beginning with his reading of capitalist development as the product of antagonistic social relations. In other words, as Roman Rosdolsky[11] and Antonio Negri,[12] among others, have argued, more than the visionary revolutionary projecting a world of achieved liberation, the Marx who most matters to us is the theorist of class struggle, who refused any political program not rooted in real historical possibilities and throughout his work pursued the destruction of capitalist relations, seeing the realization of communism in the movement that abolishes the present state of things. From this point of view, Marx's historical materialist method, which posits that in order to understand history and society we must understand the material conditions of social reproduction, is crucial for a feminist perspective. Recognizing that social subordination is a historical product rooted in a specific organization of work has had a liberating effect on women. It has denaturalized the sexual division of labor and the identities built upon it, projecting gender categories not only as social constructs but as concepts whose content is constantly redefined, infinitely mobile, open-ended, and always politically charged. Indeed, many feminist debates on the validity of 'women' as an analytic and political category could be more easily resolved if this method were applied, for it teaches us that it is possible to express a common interest without ascribing fixed and uniform forms of behavior and social conditions.

Analyzing the social position of women through the prism of the capitalist exploitation of labor also discloses the continuity between discrimination on the basis of gender and discrimination on the basis of race and enables us to transcend the politics of rights that assumes the permanence of the existing social order and fails to confront the antagonistic social forces standing in the way of women's liberation. As many feminists have shown, however, Marx did not consistently apply his own method, not at least to the question of reproduction and gender relations. As both the theorists of the Wages for Housework movement—Mariarosa Dalla Costa,[13] Selma James,[14] and Leopoldina Fortunati[15]—and ecofeminist theorists, like Maria Mies[16] and Ariel Salleh,[17] have demonstrated, there is a glaring contradiction at the center of Marx's thought. Although it takes the exploitation of labor as the key element in the production of capitalist wealth, it leaves untheorized some of the activities and social relations that are most essential for the production of labor power, like sexual work, procreation, the care of children, and domestic work. Marx acknowledged that our capacity to work is not a given but is a product of social activity[18] that always takes a specific historical form, for "hunger is hunger, but the hunger that is satisfied by cooked meat eaten with knife and fork is different from the hunger that devours raw meat with the help of hands, nails and teeth."[19] Nevertheless, we do not find in his published work any analysis of domestic labor, the family, and the gender relations specific to capitalism, except for scattered reflections to the effect that the first division of labor was in the sexual act, that slavery is latent in the family, and so forth.[20] In volume one of *Capital*, sexual work is never considered even in its paid form, as prostitutes are excluded, together with criminals and vagabonds, even from sphere of the 'paupers,'[21] clearly associated with that 'lumpenproletariat' that Marx dismissed in *The Eighteenth Brumaire* as forever incapable of transforming its social condition.[22] Domestic work is dealt with in two footnotes, one registering its disappearance from the homes of the overworked female factory hands during the Industrial Revolution, and the other noting that the crisis caused by the American Civil War brought the female textile workers in England back to their domestic duties.[23] Procreation is generally treated as a natural function,[24] rather than a form of labor that in capitalism is subsumed to the reproduction of the workforce and therefore subject to a specific state regulation. Even when presenting his 'relative surplus population' theory,[25] Marx barely mentions the interest of capital and the state in women's reproductive capacity, attributing the determination of a surplus population to the requirements of technological innovation,[26] although arguing that the exploitation of the workers' children set a premium on their production.[27]

Because of these omissions many feminists have accused Marx of reductionism and viewed the integration of feminism and Marxism as a process of subordination.[28] The authors I have quoted, however, have demonstrated that we can work with Marx's categories,[29] but we must reconstruct them and change their architectural order, so that the center of gravity is not exclusively wage labor and commodity production but the production and reproduction of labor power, especially that part of it that is carried out by women in the home. For in doing so, we make visible a new terrain of accumulation and struggle, as well as the full extent of capital's dependence on unpaid labor and the full length of the working day.[30] Indeed, by expanding Marx's theory of productive work to include reproductive labor in its different dimensions, we can not only craft a theory of gender relations in capitalism but gain a new understanding of the class struggle and the means by which capitalism reproduces itself through the creation of different labor regimes and different forms of uneven development and underdevelopment.

Placing the reproduction of labor power at the center of capitalist production unearths a world of social relations that remains invisible in Marx but is essential to exposing the mechanisms that regulate the exploitation of labor. It discloses that the unpaid labor that capital extracts from the working class is far greater than Marx ever imagined, extending to both the domestic work that women have been expected to perform and the exploitation of the colonies and peripheries of the capitalist world. There is a continuity, in fact, between the devaluation of the reproduction of labor power that takes place in the home and the devaluation of the labor employed in the many plantations that capitalism has constructed in the regions it has colonized, as well as in the heartlands of industrialization. In both cases, not only have the forms of work and coercion involved been naturalized, but both have become part of a global assembly line designed to cut the cost of reproducing the waged workers. On this line, the unpaid domestic labor ascribed to women as their natural destiny joins with and relays the work of millions of campesinas, subsistence farmers, and informal laborers, growing and producing for a pittance the commodities that waged workers consume or providing at the lowest cost the services their reproduction requires. Hence the hierarchies of labor that so much racist and sexist ideology has tried to justify, but which only demonstrate that the capitalist class has maintained its power through a system of indirect rule, effectively dividing the working class, with the wage used to delegate to the male workers' power over the unwaged, starting with the control and supervision of women's bodies and labor. This means that the wage is not only the terrain of confrontation between labor and capital—the terrain on which the working class negotiates the quantity and constitution of socially necessary work—but is also an instrument for the creation of unequal power relations and hierarchies between workers, and that workers' cooperation in the labor process is by no means sufficient to unify the working class. Consequently, the class struggle is a far more complicated process than Marx assumed. As feminists have discovered, it must often begin in the family, since in order to fight capitalism women have had to fight with their husbands and fathers, in the same way that people of color have had to fight against white workers and the particular type of class composition that capitalism imposes through the wage relation. Last, recognizing that domestic work is labor that produces the workforce enables us to understand gender identities as work functions and gender relations as relations of production, a move that liberates women from the guilt we have suffered whenever we have wanted to refuse domestic work and amplifies the significance of the feminist principle that 'the personal is the political.'

Why did Marx overlook that very part of reproductive work that is most essential to the production of labor power? Elsewhere,[31] I have suggested that the conditions of the working class in England in his time may provide an explanation, since when Marx was writing *Capital*, very little housework was performed in the working-class family (as Marx himself recognized), for women were employed side by side with men in the factories from dawn to sunset. Housework, as a branch of capitalist production, was below Marx's historical and political horizon. Only in the second part of the nineteenth century, after two decades of working-class revolts in which the specter of communism haunted Europe, did the capitalist class begin to invest in the reproduction of labor power, in conjunction with a shift in the form of accumulation, from light (textile-based) to heavy (coal- and steel-based) industry, requiring a more intensive labor discipline and a less emaciated workforce. As I wrote in a recent essay, "In Marxian terms, we can say that the development of reproductive work and the consequent emergence of the full-time proletarian housewife were in part the products of the transition from 'absolute' to 'relative surplus' value extraction as a mode of exploitation of labor."[32] They were the product of a shift from a system of exploitation based on the absolute lengthening of the working day to one in which the reduction of the workday would be compensated by a technological revolution intensifying the rate of exploitation. But a further factor was certainly the capitalists' fear that the superexploitation to which workers were subjected, due to the absolute extension of the workday and the destruction of their commons, was leading to the extinction of the working class and influencing women's refusal of housework and childcare—a frequent theme in the official reports that the English government ordered starting in the 1840s to assess the factory worker's conditions and state of health.[33] It was at this junction that a labor reform increasing capital's investment (of funds and work) in the reproduction of the workforce was introduced, promoting a series of Factory Acts that first reduced and then eliminated women's factory employment, and substantially increased (by 40 percent by the end of the century) the male wage.[34] In this sense, the birth of the full-time proletarian housewife—a phenomenon that Fordism accelerated—can be read as an attempt to restore to the male waged workers, in the form of a vast pool of women's unpaid labor, the commons that they had lost with the advent of capitalism.

These reforms marked "the passage to the modern state" as planner of the construction of the working-class family and the reproduction of the workforce.[35] But what most stood out when Marx was writing *Capital* was certainly that workers could not reproduce themselves. This can partly explain why housework is almost nonexistent in his work. It is likely, however, that Marx also ignored domestic labor because it represented the very type of work that he believed modern industry would and should replace, and he failed to see that the coexistence of different labor regimes would remain an essential component of capitalist production and work discipline.

I suggest that Marx ignored domestic labor because it lacked the characteristics that he considered essential to the capitalist organization of work, which he identified with large-scale industrialization—in his view the highest model of production. Being home-based, organized in a noncollective, noncooperative manner, and performed at a low level of technological development, even in the twentieth century at the peak of domesticity, housework has continued to be classified by Marxists as a vestigial remnant of precapitalist forms of production. As Dolores Hayden has pointed out in *The Grand Domestic Revolution*,[36] even when they called for socialized domestic work, socialist thinkers did not believe it could ever be meaningful work[37] and, like August Bebel, envisioned a time when housework would be reduced to a minimum.[38] It took a women's revolt against housework in the 1960s and 1970s to prove that domestic work is "socially necessary labor"[39] in the capitalist sense, that even though it is not organized on an industrial basis, it is extremely productive, and that to a large extent it is work that cannot be mechanized; for reproducing the individuals in which labor power subsists requires a variety of emotional as well as physical services that are interactive in nature and therefore very labor intensive. This realization has further destabilized Marx's theoretical and political framework, forcing us to rethink one of the main tenets of Marx's theory of revolution, that is, the assumption that with the development of capitalism all forms of work will be industrialized and, most important, that capitalism and modern industry are preconditions for the liberation of humanity from exploitation.

## Machinery, Modern Industry, and Reproduction

Marx presumed that capitalism and modern industry must set the stage for the advent of communism, because he believed that without a leap in the productivity of work that industrialization provides humanity would be condemned to an endless conflict motivated by scarcity, destitution, and the competition for the necessities of life.[40] He also viewed modern industry as the embodiment of a higher rationality, making its way into the world through sordid motives but teaching human beings attitudes apt to develop our capacities to the fullest, as well as liberating us from work. For Marx, modern industry is not only the means to reduce 'socially necessary labor,' but is also the very model of work, teaching workers uniformity, regularity, and the principles of technological development, thereby enabling us to engage interchangeably in different kinds of labor,[41] something (he reminds us) the detailed worker of manufacture and even the artisan tied to the métier could never achieve.

Capitalism, in this context, is the rough hand that brings large-scale industry into existence, clearing the way for the concentration of the means of production and cooperation in the work process, developments Marx considered essential for the expansion of the productive forces and an increase in the productivity of work. Capitalism is also for him the whip that schools human beings in the requirements of self-government, like the necessity to produce beyond subsistence and the capacity for social cooperation on a large scale.[42] Class struggle plays an important role in this process. Workers' resistance to exploitation forces the capitalist class to revolutionize production in such a way as to further economize labor in a sort of mutual conditioning, continually reducing the role of work in the production of wealth and replacing with machines the tasks that human beings have historically tried to escape. Marx believed that once this process was completed, once modern industry reduced socially necessary labor to a minimum, an era would begin in which we would finally be the masters of our existence and our natural environment, and we would not only be able to satisfy our needs but would be free to dedicate our time to higher pursuits.

How this rupture would occur he did not explain, except through a set of metaphoric images suggesting that once fully developed the forces of production would break the shell enveloping them triggering a social revolution. Again, he did not clarify how we would recognize when the forces of production should be mature enough for revolution, only suggesting that the turning point would come with the worldwide extension of capitalist relations, when the homogenization and universalization of the forces of production and the correspondent capacities in the proletariat would reach a global dimension.[43]

Nevertheless, his vision of a world in which human beings can use machines to free themselves from want and toil and free time becomes the measure of wealth has exercised an immense attraction. André Gorz's image of a postindustrial workless society where people dedicate themselves to their self-development owes much to it.[44] Witness also the fascination among Italian Autonomist Marxists with the "Fragment on Machines" in the *Grundrisse*, the site in which this vision is most boldly presented. Antonio Negri in particular, in *Marx beyond Marx*, has singled it out as the most revolutionary aspect of Marx's theory. Indeed, the pages of "Notebooks VI and VII," where Marx describes a world in which the law of value has ceased to function, science and technology having eliminated living labor from the production process and the workers only acting as the machines' supervisors, are breathtaking in their anticipatory power.[45] Yet, as feminists in particular, we are today in a good position to see how illusory are the powers that an automated system of production can place at our disposal. We can see that "the allegedly highly productive industrial system" that Marx so much admired, "has been in reality a parasite on the earth, the likes of which have never been seen in the history of humanity,"[46] and is now consuming it at a velocity that casts a long shadow on the future. Ahead of his time in recognizing the interplay of humanity and nature, as Saileh noted,[47] Marx intuited this process, observing that the industrialization of agriculture depletes the soil as much as it depletes the worker.[48] But he obviously believed that this trend could be reversed, that once taken over by the workers the means of production could be redirected to serve positive objectives, that they could be used to expand the social and natural wealth rather than deplete it, and that the demise of capitalism was so imminent as to limit the damage a profit-bound industrialization process inflicted on the earth.

On all these counts he was deeply mistaken. Machines are not produced by machines in a sort of immaculate conception. Taking the computer as an example, even this most common machine is an ecological disaster, requiring tons of soil and water and an immense amount of human labor for its production. Multiplied by the order of billions, we must conclude that, like sheep in sixteenth-century England, machines today are 'eating the earth' and at such a fast pace that even if a revolution were to take place in the near future, the work required to make this planet habitable again would be astounding.[49] Machines moreover require a material and cultural infrastructure that affects not only our nature commons—lands, woods, waters, mountains, seas, rivers, and coastlines—but also our psyche and social relations, molding subjectivities, creating new needs and habits, and producing dependencies that also place a mortgage on the future. This partly explains why, a century and a half after the publication of *Capital*, Vol. 1, capitalism gives no sign of dissolving, though the objective conditions that Marx envisioned as necessary for social revolution would seem more than mature. What we witness, instead, is a regime of permanent primitive accumulation reminiscent of the sixteenth-century enclosures, this time organized by the International Monetary Fund and the World Bank, with a cohort of mining and agribusiness companies that in Africa, Asia, and Latin America are privatizing communal lands and expropriating small-scale producers to acquire the lithium, coltan, and diamonds modern industry requires.[50] We must also stress that none of the means of production that capitalism has developed can be unproblematically taken over and applied to a different use. In the same way—as we will see later—that we cannot take over the state, we cannot take over capitalist industry, science, and technology, as the exploitative objectives for which they have been created shape their constitution and mode of operation.

That modern industry and technology cannot simply be appropriated and reprogrammed for different purposes is best demonstrated by the growth of the nuclear and chemical industries, which have poisoned the planet and provided the capitalist class with an immense arsenal of weapons now threatening us with annihilation or, at the very least, with the mutual destruction of the contending classes. As Otto Ullrich has put it, "The most outstanding achievement of scientized technology has undoubtedly been the increase in the destructive power of the war machine."[51] Similarly, the capitalist rational treatment of agriculture that Marx contrasted to presumably the irrational method of cultivation of the small producer[52] has destroyed the abundance, diversity, and value of food and much of it will have to be discarded in a society where production is for human beings rather than being humanity's goal.

There is another consideration that makes us question Marx's concept of the function of technology in the formation of a communist society, especially when examined from a feminist viewpoint. A machine-based communism relies on an organization of work that excludes the most basic activities human beings perform on this planet. As I have mentioned, the reproductive work that Marx's analysis bypasses is, to a large extent, work that cannot be mechanized. In other words, Marx's vision of a society in which necessary labor can be drastically reduced through automation clashes with the fact that the largest amount of work on earth is of a highly relational nature and hardly subject to mechanization. Ideally in a post-capitalist society we would mechanize several household chores, and we would certainly rely on new forms of communication for company, learning, and information, once we controlled what technology is produced, for what purposes, and under what conditions. But how can we mechanize washing, cuddling, consoling, dressing, and feeding a child, providing sexual services, or assisting those who are ill or the elderly and not self-sufficient? What machine could incorporate the skills and affects needed for these tasks? Attempts have been made with the creation of nursebots[53] and interactive lovebots, and it is possible that in the future we may see the production of mechanical mothers. But even assuming that we could afford such devices, we must wonder at what emotional cost we would introduce them in our homes in replacement of living labor. But if reproductive work can only in part be mechanized, then the Marxian scheme that makes the expansion of material wealth dependent on automation and the reduction of necessary labor implodes; for domestic work, and especially the care of children, constitutes most of the work on this planet. The very concept of socially necessary labor loses much of its cogency. How is socially necessary labor to be defined if the largest and most indispensable sector of work on the planet is not recognized as an essential part of it? And by what criteria and principles will the organization of care work, sexual work, and procreation be governed if these activities are not considered part of social necessary labor?

The increasing skepticism about the possibility of substantially reducing domestic work through mechanization is one of the reasons why there is now among feminists a renewed interest and experimentation with more collective forms of reproduction and the creation of reproductive commons,[54] redistributing work among a larger number of subjects than the nuclear family provides. Exemplary here is the Grand Domestic Revolution, an ongoing living research project inspired by Dolores Hayden's work, initiated by feminist artists, designers, and activists in Utrecht (Holland) to explore how the domestic sphere, as well as the neighborhoods and the cities, can be transformed and 'new forms of living and working in common' can be constructed. Meanwhile, under the pressure of the economic crisis, struggles in defense of our natural commons (lands, waters, forests) and the creation of commoning activities (e.g., collective shopping and cooking, urban gardening) are multiplying. It is also significant that "colonization and tech transfer notwithstanding, the bulk of the world's daily needs continue to be supplied by Third World women food growers outside the cash nexus" and with very limited technological inputs, often farming on unused public land.[55] At a time of genocidal austerity programs, the work of these female farmers is the difference between life and death for millions.[56] Yet this is the very type of subsistence-oriented work that Marx believed should be eliminated, as he considered the rationalization of agriculture—that is, its organization on a large scale and on a scientific basis—"one of the great merits of the capitalist mode of production" and argued that this was possible only through the expropriation of the direct producer.[57]

### On the Myth of the Progressiveness of Capitalism

While a critique of Marx's theory concerning the power of industrialization to free humanity from toil and want is in order, there are other reasons his belief in the necessity and progressiveness of capitalism must be rejected. First, this theory underestimates the knowledge and wealth produced by noncapitalist societies and the extent to which capitalism has built its power through their appropriation—a key consideration if we are not to be mesmerized by the capitalist advancement of knowledge and paralyzed in our will to exit from it. Indeed, it is politically important for us to recall that the societies capitalism destroyed achieved high levels of knowledge and technology thousands of years before the advent of mechanization, learning to navigate the seas across vast expanses of water, discovering by night watches the main astral constellations, inventing the crops that have sustained human life on the planet.[58] Witness the fantastic diversity of seeds and plants that the Native American populations were able to develop, reaching a mastery in agricultural technology so far unsurpassed, with more than two hundred varieties of corn and potatoes invented just in Mesoamerica—a stark contrast to the destruction of diversity we witness at the hands of the scientifically organized capitalist agriculture of our time.[59]

Capitalism did not invent social cooperation or large-scale intercourse, as Marx called trade and cultural exchanges. On the contrary, the advent of capitalism destroyed societies that had been tied by communal property relations and cooperative forms of work, as well as large trade networks. Highly cooperative work systems were the norm prior to colonization from the Indian Ocean to the Andes. We can recall the *ayllu* system in Bolivia and Peru and the communal land systems of Africa that have survived into the twenty-first century, all counterpoints to Marx's view concerning the "isolation of rural life."[60] In Europe, as well, capitalism destroyed a society of commons materially grounded not only in the collective use of land and collective work relations but in the daily struggle against feudal power, which created new cooperative forms of life, such as those experimented with by the heretic movements (Cathars, Waldensians) that I analyzed in *Caliban and the Witch*.[61] Not accidentally, capitalism could only prevail through a maximum of violence and destruction, including the extermination of thousands of women through two centuries of witch hunts, which broke a resistance that by the sixteenth century had taken the form of peasant wars. Far from being a carrier of progress, the development of capitalism was the counterrevolution, as it subverted the rise of new forms of communalism produced in the struggle, as well as those existing on the feudal manors on the basis of the shared use of the commons. Add that much more than the development of large-scale industry is needed to create the revolutionary combination and association of free producers that Marx envisioned at the very end of *Capital*, Vol. 1.[62] Capital and large-scale industry may boost the "concentration of the means of production" and the cooperation in the work process that results from the division of labor,[63] but the cooperation required for a revolutionary process is qualitatively different from the technical factor that Marx describes as being (together with science and technology) the "fundamental form of the capitalist mode of production."[64] It is even questionable whether we can speak of cooperation with regard to work relations that are not controlled by the workers themselves and therefore produce no independent decision-making, except at the moment of resistance when the capitalist organization of the work process is subverted. We also cannot ignore that the cooperation that Marx admired as the mark of the capitalist organization of work has historically become possible precisely on the basis of the destruction of workers' skills and cooperation in their struggle.[65]

Second, to assume that capitalist development has been inevitable, not to mention necessary or desirable, at any time in history, past or present, is to place ourselves on the other side of the struggles of people who have resisted it. But can we say that the heretics, the Anabaptists, the Diggers, the maroons, and all the rebel subjects who resisted the enclosures of their commons or fought to construct an egalitarian social order, writing, like Thomas Müntzer, *omnia sunt communia* (all property should be held in common) on their banners, were on the wrong side of history, viewed from the perspective of human liberation? This is not an idle question. For the extension of capitalist relations is not a thing of the past but an ongoing process, still requiring blood and fire, and still generating an immense resistance which undoubtedly is putting a brake to the capitalist subsumption of every form of production on earth and the extension of waged labor.

Third, to posit capitalism as necessary and progressive is to underestimate a fact on which I have insisted throughout this chapter: capitalist development is not, or is not primarily, the development of human capacities and above all the capacity for social cooperation, as Marx anticipated. It is also the development of unequal power relations, hierarchies, and divisions, which, in turn, generate ideologies, interests, and subjectivities that constitute a destructive social force. Not accidentally, in the face of the most concerted neoliberal drive to privatize the remaining communal and public resources, it has been not the most industrialized but the most cohesive communities that have been able to resist and, in some cases, reverse the privatization tide. As the struggles of indigenous people—the struggle of the Quechua and Aymara against the privatization of water in Bolivia[66] and the struggles of the U'wa people in Colombia against the destruction of their lands by oil drilling, among other examples—have demonstrated, it is not where capitalist development is the highest but where communal bonds are the strongest that capitalist expansion is put on hold and even forced to recede. Indeed, as the prospect of a world revolution fueled by capitalist development recedes, the reconstitution of communities devastated by racist and sexist policies and multiple rounds of enclosure appears not just an objective condition but as a precondition of social change.

## From Communism to the Commons: A Feminist Perspective

Opposing the divisions that capitalism has created on the basis of race, gender, and age, reuniting what it has separated in our lives and reconstituting a collective interest must then be a political priority for feminists and other social justice movements today. This is what is ultimately at stake in the politics of the commons, which, at its best, presupposes a sharing of wealth, collective decision-making, and a revolution in our relationship with ourselves and others. The social cooperation and knowledge building that Marx attributed to industrial work can be constructed only through commoning activities—urban gardening, time banking, open sourcing—that are self-organized and require, as well as produce, community. In this sense, insofar as it aims to reproduce our lives in ways that strengthen mutual bonds and set limits to capital accumulation,[67] the politics of the commons, in part, translates Marx's idea of communism as the abolition of the present state of things. It could also be argued that with the development of online commons—the rise of the free software and free culture movements—we are now approximating that universalization of human capacities that Marx anticipated as a result of the development of productive forces. But the politics of the commons is a radical departure from what communism has signified in the Marxist tradition and in much of Marx's work, starting with *The Communist Manifesto*. There are several crucial differences between the politics of the commons and communism that stand out, especially when we consider these political forms from a feminist and ecological viewpoint.

Commons, as discussed by feminist writers like Vandana Shiva, Maria Mies, and Ariel Salleh and practiced by grassroots women's organizations, do not depend for their realization on the development of the productive forces or the mechanization of production, or any global extension of capitalist relations—the preconditions for Marx's communist project. On the contrary, they contend with the threats posed to them by capitalist development and revalorize locale-specific knowledges and technologies.[68] They do not assume that there is a necessary connection between scientific/technological and moral/intellectual development, which is an underlying premise of Marx's conception of social wealth. They also place at the center of their political project the restructuring of reproduction as the crucial terrain for the transformation of social relations, thus subverting the value structure of capitalist organization of work. In particular, they attempt to break down the isolation that has characterized domestic work in capitalism, not in view of its reorganization on an industrial scale but in view of creating more cooperative forms of care work.

Commons are declined in the plural, in the spirit promoted by the Zapatistas, with the slogan "One No, Many Yeses," which recognizes the existence of diverse historical and cultural trajectories and the multiplicity of social outcomes that are compatible with the abolition of exploitation. For while it is recognized that the circulation of ideas and technological know-how can be a positive historical force, the prospect of a universalization of knowledges, institutions, and forms of behavior is increasingly opposed not only as a colonial legacy but as a project achievable only through the destruction of local lives and cultures. Above all, commons do not depend for their existence on a supporting state. Though in radical circles there is still a lingering desire for the state as a transitional form, presumably required to eradicate entrenched capitalist interests and administer those elements of the commonwealth that demand large-scale planning (water, electricity, transport services, etc.), the state form is today in crisis, and not only in feminist and other radical circles. Indeed, the popularity of the politics of the commons is directly related to the crisis of the state form, which the failure of realized socialism and the internationalization of capital has made dramatically evident. As John Holloway has powerfully put it in *Change the World without Taking Power*, to imagine that we can use the state to bring forth a more just world is to attribute an autonomous existence to it, abstract from its network of social relations, which inextricably tie it to capital accumulation and compel it to reproduce social conflict and mechanisms of exclusion. It is also to ignore the fact "that capitalist social relations have never been limited by state frontiers" but are globally constituted.[69] Moreover, with a world proletariat divided by gender and racial hierarchies, the 'dictatorship of the proletariat' concretized in a state form would risk becoming the dictatorship of the white/male sector of the working class. For those with more social power might very well steer the revolutionary process toward objectives that maintain the privileges they have acquired.

After decades of betrayed expectations and electoral ballots, there is now a profound desire, especially among younger people in every country, to reclaim the power to transform our lives, to reclaim the knowledge and responsibility that in a proletarian state we would alienate to an overarching institution that in representing us would replace us. This would be a disastrous turn. For rather than creating a new world, we would forfeit that process of self-transformation without which no new society is possible and reconstitute the very conditions that today make us passive even in front of the most egregious cases of institutional injustice. It is one of the attractions of the commons as the "embryonic form of a new society" that it stands for a power that comes from the ground, rather than from the state and relies on cooperation and collective forms of decision-making rather than coercion.[70] In this sense, the spirit of the commons resonates with Audre Lorde's insight that "the master's tools will never dismantle the master's house,"[71] and I believe that if Marx lived today he would agree on this point. For though he did not much dwell on the ravages produced by the capitalist organization of sexism and racism and gave scarce attention to the transformation in the subjectivity of the proletariat, he nevertheless understood that we need a revolution to liberate ourselves not only from external constraints but from the internalization of capitalist ideology and relations, from, as he put it, "all the muck of ages," so that we become "fitted to found society anew."[72]

## Notes

1    Karl Marx and Frederick Engels, *The German Ideology*, Part 1, ed. C.J. Arthur (New York: International Publishers, 1970), 56–57.
2    Heidi I. Hartmann, "The Unhappy Marriage of Marxism and Feminism: Towards a More Progressive Union," *Capital and Class* 3, no. 2 (Summer 1979): 1–33.
3    This argument is based on readings of Marx's "Ethnological Notebooks," notes he collected in the last years of his life in preparation for a major work on the topic. His comments here show that Lewis Henry Morgan's *Ancient Society*, "and especially its detailed account of the Iroquois, for the first time

gave Marx insights into the concrete possibilities of a free society as it had actually existed in history" and of a revolutionary path not dependent on the development of capitalist relations. Rosemont argues that Morgan was on Marx's mind when in correspondence with Russian revolutionaries he considered the possibility of a revolutionary process in Russia moving directly to communal forms of ownership on the basis of the Russian peasant commune, rather than through its dissolution. See Franklin Rosemont, "Karl Marx and the Iroquois." July 7, 2009, accessed June 2, 2018, http://libcom.org/library/karl-rnarx-iroquois-franklin-rosemant. On this subject, see also Kevin B. Anderson, "Marx's Late Writings on Non-Western and Precapitalist Societies and Gender," *Rethinking Marxism* 14, no. 4 (Winter 2002): 84–96; Teodor Shanin, *Late Marx and the Russian Road: Marx and the "Peripheries of Capitalism"* (New York: Monthly Review Press, 1983), 29–31.

4     Antonio Negri, for instance, has claimed that the *Grundrisse* should be seen as the culmination of Marx's thought and that the importance of *Capital* has been overestimated, for it is in the *Grundrisse* that Marx developed his major concepts and the most radical definition of communism. See Antonio Negri, *Marx beyond Marx: Lessons on the Grundrisse*, ed. Jim Fleming, trans. Harry Cleaver, Michael Ryan, and Maurizio Viano (Brooklyn: Autonomedia, 1991), 5–4, 8–9, 11–18. By contrast, George Caffentzis argues that *Capital* has a more integrative concept of capitalism and that in this later work Marx discarded some of the main theses in the *Grundrisse*, like the thesis that capitalism, through the automation of production, can go beyond the law of value. See Caffentzis, "From the *Grundrisse* to *Capital* and Beyond: Then and Now," *Workplace: A Journal for Academic Labor* no. 15 (September 2008): 59–74, accessed June 2, 2018, http://ices.library.ubc.ca/index.php/workplace/article/view/182216.

5     Ariel Salleh, *Ecofeminism as Politics: Nature, Marx and the Postmodern* (London: Zed Books, 1997), 71; Bertell Ollman, *Dialectical Investigations* (New York: Routledge, 1993).

6     Stevi Jackson, "Why a Materialist Feminism Is (Still) Possible," *Women's Studies International Forum* 24, no. 3–4 (May 2001): 284.

7     Negri, *Marx beyond Marx*.

8     As Frantz Fanon wrote: "This is why Marxist analysis should always be slightly stretched every time we have to do with the colonial problem. Everything up to and including the very nature of precapitalist society, so well explained by Marx, must here be thought out again"; Fanon, *The Wretched of the Earth* (New York: Grove, 1986), 40.

9     Roderick Thurton, "Marxism in the Caribbean," in *Two Lectures by Roderick Thurton: A Second Memorial Pamphlet* (New York: George Caffentzis and Silvia Federici, 2000).

10    See, for instance, Joel Kovel, "On Marx and Ecology," *Capitalism, Nature, Socialism* 22, no. 1 (September 2011): 11–14. Kovel argues that Marx remained prisoner of a scientist and productivistic viewpoint postulating "a passive nature worked over by an active Man," and encouraging the "all-out development of the productive forces" (13, 15). There is, however, a broad debate on

the subject to which I can only cursorily refer. See, for instance, John Bellamy Foster, "Marx and the Environment," *Monthly Review* 47, no. 3 (July–August 1995): 108–23.

11   Roman Rosdoldsky, The Making of Marx's "Capital" (London: Pluto Press, 1977).

12   Negri, *Marx beyond Marx*.

13   Mariarosa Dalla Costa, "Women and the Subversion of the Community," in *The Power of Women and the Subversion of the Community*, eds. Selma James and Mariarosa Dalla Costa (Bristol: Falling Wall Press, 1975).

14   Selma James, *Sex, Race and Class* (Bristol: Falling Wall Press, 1975).

15   Leopoldina Fortunati, *The Arcane of Reproduction: Housework, Prostitution, Labor and Capital*, ed. Jim Fleming, trans. Hillary Creek (Brooklyn: Autonomedia, 1995).

16   Maria Mies, *Patriarchy and Accumulation on a World Scale* (London: Zed Books, 1986).

17   Salleh, *Ecofeminism as Politics*.

18   Karl Marx, *Capital: A Critique of Political Economy*, Vol. 1, ed. Frederick Engels, trans. Ben Fowkes (London: Penguin, 1990), 274. As he writes, "the value of labour-power is determined, as in the case of every other commodity, by the labour-time necessary for the production, and consequently, also the reproduction of this specific article. In so far as it has value, it represents no more than a definite quantity of the average social labor objectified in it. Labour-power exists only as a capacity of the living individual. Its production consequently presupposes his existence. Given the existence of the individual, the production of labour-power consists in his reproduction of himself or his maintenance."

19   Karl Marx, *A Contribution to the Critique of Political Economy*, ed. Maurice Dobb (New York: International Publishers, 1970), 197.

20   Marx and Engels, *The German Ideology*, 51–52.

21   Marx, *Capital*, Vol. 1, 797.

22   Karl Marx, *The Eighteenth Brumaire of Louis Napoleon* (New York: International Publishers, 1963).

23   This occurs in a footnote, in "Machinery and Large-Scale Industry," commenting on the growing substitution of female for male workers, resulting from the introduction of machinery in the factory, "throwing every member of the family onto the labor market." He writes: "Since certain family functions, such as nursing and suckling children, cannot be entirely suppressed, the mothers who have been confiscated by capital must try substitutes of some sort. Domestic work, such as sowing and mending, must be replaced by the purchase of ready-made articles. Hence the diminished expenditure of labour in the house is accompanied by an increased expenditure of money outside. The cost of production of the working-class family therefore increases"; Marx, *Capital*, Vol. 1., 518n. Referring to this passage Leopoldina Fortunati has noted that "Marx managed to see housework only when capital destroyed it, and saw it through reading government reports which had realized the

problems posed by the usurpation of housework far earlier"; Fortunati, *The Arcane of Reproduction*, 169.

24    Marx writes, for instance, that "the natural increase of the workers does not satisfy the requirements of the accumulation of capital"; Marx, *Capital*, Vol. 1, 794.

25    *Capital*, Vol. 1. 794–97.

26    *Capital*, Vol. 1, 782.

27    *Capital*, Vol. 1, 795. Marx does not clarify, however, who determines this increased production—an apt question given that in *Capital*, Vol. 1, his descriptions of maternal relations in England's industrial districts indicates a widespread refusal of mothering such as to preoccupy the contemporary policymakers and employers; *Capital*, Vol. 1, 521, 521n, 522.

28    Hartmann, "The Unhappy Marriage," 1.

29    An exception is Maria Mies, who has repeatedly stated that within Marxism it is impossible to think gender relations; Mies, *Patriarchy and Accumulation on a World Scale*.

30    Federici, *Revolution at Point Zero: Housework, Reproduction, and Feminist Struggle* (Oakland: PM Press, 2012), 38.

31    Federici, *Revolution at Point Zero*, 94–95. For an analysis and critique of Marx's conceptualization of the reproduction of labor-power, see also Federici, "Capital and Gender," in *Reading 'Capital' Today*, eds. Ingo Schmidt and Carlo Fanelli (London, Pluto Press, 2017), 79–96.

32    Marx, *Capital*, Vol. 1, Chapter 16, Part V.

33    *Capital*, Vol. 1, 348, 591, 599, 630. The last three page numbers cited here discuss the effect of women's factory employment on their discipline and reproductive work. As Marx put it, "Aside from the daily more threatening advance of the working-class movement, the limiting of factory labor was dictated by the same necessity as forced the manuring of English fields with guano. The same blind desire for profit that in one case exhausted the soil had in the other case seized hold of the vital force of the nation at its roots."

34    It is no coincidence that by 1870 we simultaneously have in England both a new Marriage Act and the Education Act (which introduced the right to universal primary education), both signifying a new level of investment in the reproduction of the workforce. Starting in the same period, hand in hand with the hike in the family wage, we have a change in the eating habits of people in Britain, and the means of food distribution, with the appearance of the first neighborhood food shops. In the same period the sewing machine begins to enter the proletarian home. See Eric J. Hobsbawm, *Industry and Empire: The Making of Modern English Society, Vol. 2, 1750 to the Present Day* (New York: Random House, 1968), 135–36, 141.

35    Fortunati, *The Arcane of Reproduction*, 173.

36    Dolores Hayden, *The Grand Domestic Revolution: A History of Feminist Designs for American Homes, Neighborhoods, and Cities* (Cambridge, MA: MIT Press, 1985 [1981]).

37    Hayden, *The Grand Domestic Revolution*, 6.

38    August Bebel, *Women under Socialism* (New York: Schocken Books, 1971).

39  "Socially necessary labour-time is the labour-time required to produce any use value under the conditions of production normal for a given society and with the average degree of skill and intensity of labour prevalent in that society"; Marx, *Capital*, Vol. 1, 129.

40  Marx and Engels, *The German Ideology*, 56.

41  Marx, *Capital*, Vol. 1, 618.

42  *Capital*, Vol. 1, 775.

43  Marx and Engels, *The German Ideology*, 55–56; Karl Marx and Frederick Engels, *The Communist Manifesto*, trans. Samuel More (New York: Penguin, 1967).

44  André Gorz, *A Farewell to the Working Class* (London: Pluto, 1982); Gorz, *Paths to Paradise: On the Liberation from Work* (London: Pluto, 1985); on this subject, see also Edward Granter, *Critical Social Theory and the End of Work* (Burlington, VT: Ashgate, 2009), 121. Granter points out that Gorz's idea of a society in which free time is a measure of wealth is a Marxian idea, and in fact Gorz makes explicit reference to Marx with quotes from the *Grundrisse*.

45  Negri, *Marx beyond Marx*.

46  Otto Ullrich, "Technology," in *The Development Dictionary: A Guide to Knowledge as Power*, ed. Wolfgang Sachs (London: Zed Books, 1993), 281.

47  Salleh, *Ecofeminism as Politics*, 70.

48  As he wrote in *Capital*, Vol. 1, at the end of the chapter on "Machinery and Large-Scale Industry": "all progress in capitalist agriculture is a progress in the art, not only of robbing the worker, but of robbing the soil; all progress in increasing the fertility of the soil for a given time is a progress towards ruining the more long-lasting sources of that fertility. The more a country proceeds from large-scale industry as the background of its development, as in the case of the United States, the more rapid is this process of destruction. Capitalist production, therefore, only develops the techniques and the degree of combination of the social process of production by simultaneously undermining the original sources of all wealth—the soil and the worker"; Marx, *Capital*, Vol. 1, 638.

49  Think, for example, of the work necessary to monitor and neutralize the damaging effects of the nuclear waste piles accumulated across the globe.

50  See Federici, "War, Globalization and Reproduction," in *Revolution at Point Zero*, 76–84; Federici, "Women, Land Struggles, and the Reconstruction of the Commons," *Working USA* 14, no. 1 (March 2011); Federici, "Witch-Hunting, Globalization, and Feminist Solidarity in Africa Today," *Journal of International Women's Studies* 10, no. 1 (October 2008): 29–35, reprinted in Federici, *Witches, Witch-Hunting, and Women* (Oakland: PM Press, 2018), 60–86.

51  Ullrich, "Technology!," 227.

52  Karl Marx, *Capital: A Critique of Political Economy*, Vol. 3, ed. Frederick Engels, trans. Ben Fowkes (London: Penguin, 1991), 948–49.

53  Nancy Folbre, "Nursebots to the Rescue? Immigration, Automation, and Care," *Globalizations* 3, no. 3 (September 2006): 356.

54 On this subject, see Federici, "Feminism and the Politics of the Commons in an Era of Primitive Accumulation," in *Revolution at Point Zero*, 138–48.

55 Salleh, *Ecofeminism as Politics*, 79; Federici, "Feminism and the Politics of the Commons," 138–48.

56 According to the United Nations Population Fund, in 2001, "some 200 million city dwellers" were growing food "providing about 1 billion people with at least part of their food supply"; United Nations Population Fund, *State of the World Population 2001: Footprints and Milestones: Population and Environmental Change* (New York: United Nations, 2001). A Worldwatch Institute report, "Farming the Cities Feeding an Urban Future," June 16, 2011, accessed June 4, 2018, http://www.worldwatch.org/node/8448 confirms the importance of subsistence farming, noting in a press release: "Currently an estimated 800 million people worldwide are engaged in urban agriculture, producing 15–20 percent." It should be noted that these figures do not include subsistence farming in the rural areas; Worldwatch Institute, "State of the World 2011: Innovations that Nourish the Planet," accessed June 2, 2018, http://www.worldwatch.org/sow11.

57 Marx, *Capital*, Vol. 3, 754–55.

58 Clifford D. Conner, *A People's History of Science: Miners, Midwives, and "Low Mechanicks"* (New York: Nation Books, 2005).

59 Jack Weatherford, *Indian Givers: How the Indians of the Americas Transformed the World* (New York: Fawcett Books, 1988).

60 On this translation, see Hal Draper, *The Adventures of the Communist Manifesto* (Berkeley: Center for Socialist History, 1994).

61 Federici, *Caliban and the Witch: Women, the Body and Primitive Accumulation* (Brooklyn: Autonomedia, 2004).

62 Marx, *Capital*, Vol. 1, 930n.

63 *Capital*, Vol. 1, 927.

64 *Capital*, Vol. 1, 454.

65 On this subject, see Marx, *Capital*, Vol. 1, 563–68. In "Machinery and Large-Scale Industry," section 5, "The Struggle between Worker and Machine," Marx writes: "The instrument of labor strikes down the worker." Not only do the capitalists use machines to free themselves from dependence on labor, but machinery is "the most powerful method for suppressing strikes. . . . It would be possible to write a whole history of the inventions made since 1830 for the sole purpose of providing capital with weapons against working-class revolt"; *Capital*, Vol. 1, 562–63.

66 Raquel Guitérrez Aguilar, *Los ritmos del Pachakuti: levantamiento y movilización en Bolivia (2000–2005)* (Mexico: Sisifo Ediciones, 2009).

67 Massimo De Angelis, *The Beginning of History: Value Struggles and Global Capital* (London: Pluto Press, 2007).

68 Maria Mies and Vandana Shiva, *Ecofeminism* (London: Zed Books, 1993); *The Ecologist, Whose Common Future? Reclaiming the Commons* (London: Earthscan, 1993).

69 John Holloway, *Change the World without Taking Power: The Meaning of Revolution Today* (London: Pluto Press, 2002) 14, 95.

70   John Holloway, *Crack Capitalism* (London: Pluto Press, 2010), 29.
71   Audre Lorde, "The Master's Tools Will Never Dismantle the Master's House," in *This Bridge Called My Back: Writings by Radical Women of Color*, eds. Cherríe Moraga and Gloria Anzaldúa (New York: Kitchen Table, 1983), 98–101.
72   Marx and Engels, *The German Ideology*, 95.

# From Crisis to Commons: Reproductive Work, Affective Labor and Technology, and the Transformation of Everyday Life

## Introduction

Everyday life is the primary terrain of social change, and within it we find a critique of institutional and political orthodoxy that has a long history. As early as *The German Ideology* (1847), Marx contrasted the study of the material conditions of our existence to the speculations of the neo-Hegelians. A century later, the French sociologist Henry Lefebvre and the Situationists appealed to 'everyday life' as an antidote to the bureaucratic French Marxism of the time. Challenging the left's concentration on factory struggles as the engine of social change, Lefebvre argued that social theory must address the life of the "whole worker"[1] and set out to investigate how "everydayness" is constituted and why the philosophers have constantly devalued it. In this process he inspired and anticipated a new generation of radicals, starting with the Situationists, as his discussion of "consumerism" and technological alienation and his critique of work in capitalist society set the stage for much of the literature of the New Left.

It was with the rise of the feminist movement, however, that the critique of 'everyday life' became a key to that comprehensive understanding of society that Lefebvre was seeking in his work. By rebelling against women's confinement to reproductive work and the hierarchies constructed through the sexual division of labor, the women's movement gave a material basis to the critique of everyday life and uncovered the 'deep structure,' the 'arche,' underlining and binding the multiplicity of daily acts and events that Lefebvre had sought for but never truly grasped.[2] From a feminist viewpoint it became possible to recognize that 'everyday life' is not a generic complex of events, attitudes, and experiences searching for an order. It is a structured reality, organized around a specific process of production, the production of human beings, which, as Marx and Engels pointed out, is "the first historical act" and "a fundamental condition of all history."[3] A theoretical and practical revolution has followed from this discovery that has transformed our concept of work, politics, 'femininity,' and the methodology of the social sciences, enabling us to transcend the traditional psychological viewpoint that individualizes our experiences and separates the mental from the social.

At the core of the feminist revolution there has been the recognition that we cannot look at social life from the viewpoint of an abstract, universal, sexless social subject, because the racial and sexual hierarchies that characterize the social division of labor in capitalism, and especially the divide between the waged and the unwaged, produce not only unequal power relations but qualitatively different experiences and perspectives on the world. Second, while all experiences are subject to societal construction, it is of special significance that in capitalist society the reproduction of daily life has been subsumed to the reproduction of the labor force and it has been constructed as unpaid labor and 'women's work.'[4] In the absence of a wage, domestic work has been so naturalized that it has been difficult for women to struggle against it without experiencing an enormous sense of guilt and becoming vulnerable to abuse. For if it is natural for women to be mothers and housewives, then those who refuse these roles are not treated as workers on strike but as 'bad women.' Third, if domestic work is subsumed to the needs of the labor market, then familial, sexual, and gender relations are 'relations of production,' and we should not be surprised by the contradictions that permeate them and our inability to make them fulfill our desires. This realization has been a liberating experience for women, and we can say that it has given the everyday "access to history and political life."[5] It has revealed that not only is the personal political,[6] but the private/public divide is a ruse mystifying women's unpaid work as a 'labor of love.'[7]

It is important to stress that the feminist critique of everyday life has been not only theoretical but practical and political, triggering a democratization process that has left no aspect of our life unchanged. Thanks to it, for the first time battering and rape in the family, traditionally condoned as conditions of housework, have been seen as crimes against women. The right of husbands to control their wives' bodies and to demand their sexual services against their will has been denied. In several countries, the feminist movement has led to the legalization of divorce and the right to abortion. More broadly, women have transformed their everyday inter-action with the world, asserting a new power with regard to language, knowledge, relations with men, and the expression of their desire. Even the sexual act has been placed on a more egalitarian basis, as many women have begun to refuse the 'fast sex' typical of marital life, advocating their right to sexual experimentation and to a sexual intercourse more con-forming to the configuration of the pleasure points in their bodies. Most important, the feminist movement has established that women will no longer accept a subordinate social position and a relation to the state and capital mediated by men.

This in itself has produced a social revolution, forcing significant institutional changes, such as the censoring of many practices and policies that discriminate on a gender basis. Thus, from the viewpoint of Lefebvre's problematic,[8] we could say that the feminist movement 'has rehabilitated' and revalorized everyday life, making a searing critique of some of the most important institutions by which it has been structured. But to the extent that the movement could not turn its critique of the family and what I call the 'the patriarchy of the wage' into a critique of other forms of exploitation, and equated 'liberation' with 'equal rights' and access to wage labor, it could not escape co-optation by governments and the United Nations, which, by the mid-1970s, were ready to embrace edited forms of feminism as key elements in the restructuring of the world economy.

As I have written elsewhere,[9] three considerations plausibly moti-vated the decision of the United Nations to intervene in the field of feminist politics and appoint itself as the agency in charge of de-patriarchalizing its international power structure. First, the realization that the relation-ship between women, capital, and the state could no longer be organized through the mediation of the male/waged workers, as the women's lib-eration movement expressed a massive refusal of it and a demand for autonomy from men that could no longer be repressed. Second, there was the need to domesticate a movement that had a great subversive poten-tial, being fiercely autonomous (until that point), committed to a radical transformation of everyday life, and suspicious of political represen-tation. Taming the movement was especially urgent at a time when, in response to the intractable 'labor crisis' of the mid-1970s, a global capital-ist counteroffensive was underway, aiming to reestablish the command of the capitalist class over work discipline and dismantle the organizational forms responsible for workers' resistance to exploitation. It is in this context that we must place the launching of the Decade of Women and the first International Conference in Mexico City in 1975, which marked the beginning of the institutionalization of the feminist movement and the integration of women into the globalizing world economy.

As we know, in the space of a decade, women entered the waged workforce in large numbers, but with that the feminist revolution of everyday life came to an end. Reproduction was abandoned as a terrain of feminist struggle, and soon the feminist movement itself was demobilized and could not resist the dismantling of the welfare programs that had been an essential part of the social contract between labor and capital since World War II. Even more problematic is that fighting for equal opportunity and waged work the feminist movement contributed to relegitimizing the flagging work ethic and countering the refusal of work that had been so prominent in workplaces across the industrial world in the 1960s and 1970s. The lesson we have learned in this process is that we cannot change our everyday life without changing its immediate institutions and the political and economic system by which they are structured. Otherwise, our struggles to transform our 'everydayness' can be easily digested and become a launching pad for a rationalization of relations more difficult to challenge. This is the situation that we are currently experiencing in the U.S., which confronts us with an immense 'crisis of reproduction' and recurrent revolts, opening the possibility of the creation of more cooperative forms of social reproduction in response. This, however, has yet to occur. In what follows I discuss the conditions for the emergence of a society of commons. First, however, I look at the current reproduction crisis, with particular reference to the situation in the United States, which is the one I am most familiar with and that best exhibits the developments I have mentioned.

## Everyday Life as Permanent Crisis

While some feminists have read the changes that have taken place in the lives of American women since the 1970s as an instance of progress, in many respects both women and men are today in a more difficult economic and social position than they were at the time when the feminist movement took off. Even the evidence of more egalitarian relations is spotty. The feminization of the workforce has increased women's autonomy from men. Also, as Nancy MacLean has pointed out, the fight for entrance into male dominated jobs has contributed to "our own era's heightened consciousness concerning the social construction and instability of the categories of gender, race and class."[10]

Women, however, have entered the waged workforce at the very moment when waged work was being stripped of the benefits and guarantees that it had previously provided, making it impossible to negotiate the sort of changes in the organization of work and the workweek that could enable them to reconcile work outside the home with the care of families and communities. Few jobs provide childcare or a schedule compatible with homemaking, even when it is shared. As for the commercialization of domestic work, that is its organization as a purchasable service, this much hailed development has proven to have serious limitations, starting with the high cost and low quality of the services provided. We know, for instance, that the fast food that many workers rely upon is one of the leading causes of obesity that now affects many children. An option for those who have a steady income is hired domestic labor, but the present conditions of paid domestic work and the fact that those employed are mostly immigrant women who seek this employment because of the harsh economic conditions in their countries of origin rule this out as a desirable solution.[11]

Added to this is the fact that the cuts in education, health care, and hospital care have brought back to the home a significant quantity of housework, particularly with regard to the care of children, the elderly, and those with illnesses or disabilities. Thus, the economic independence that entrance into waged work had promised has proven to be an illusion, at least for the majority of women, so much so that even among those who were career bound, there has recently been a return to the home and revalorization of domesticity.[12] Tired of struggling in a workplace that no longer tries to care for the workers' reproduction, still assuming they have wives at home, many women, in middle-class families at least, have presumably 'thrown in the towel' and dedicated themselves to providing their families with a 'high-quality' reproduction: baking bread, growing vegetables, shopping for nutritious food, schooling children at home, and so forth. As Emily Matchar points out in *Homeward Bound* (2013), the newly reclaimed domesticity is also shaped by ecological concerns and the desire to know where food comes from, leading to the refusal of convenience food and industrially produced goods in general. Many women opting for it are also affected by the DIY (do it yourself) movements and are not as secluded as their mothers might have been when centering their lives in the home, even becoming bloggers to spread and acquire information. But these are individual solutions that do not address the problems that the majority of women face and only deepen the social distances among them. They are a manifestation of the rise of a new individualism pursuing the 'good life,' but not through a social struggle for the 'common good.'

Because of the double load to which many women are condemned, the long hours of work, the low wages they earn, and the cuts of essential reproductive services, for most women everyday life has become a permanent crisis. In the United States, proletarian women on average work about fifty hours a week, thirty-five or more outside the home and about three hours a day in the home. If we add the (expanding) transport time and the time spent preparing to go to work, we see that little time is left for relaxation or other activities. Furthermore, much of the work that women do is emotional/affective labor—pleasing, exciting, comforting, and reassuring others—a task that, especially when performed for the market, is very draining and over time leads to a profound sense of depersonalization and an incapacity to know what one really desires.[13] Compounded by the economic downturn and the precarization of life, this too explains why women are twice as likely to suffer from clinical depression and anxiety as men. The figures are staggering. Women form the majority of the fifteen million adults in the United States affected by depression. Some forty million women suffer daily from anxiety; one in five will suffer from depression at some point in her life.[14] Other countries exhibit similar statistics, and the numbers are on the rise. In the United States, indicators also show a decline in happiness for women over the last decade and, most significantly, a decline in life expectancy that is especially pronounced for working-class women, who between 1990 and 2008 have lost five years of life expectancy compared with their mothers' generation.[15]

The crisis of everyday life is not limited to women. Both overwork and insecurity with respect to employment and the possibility to plan for the future are now pervasive problems affecting all social groups and ages. There is also a breakdown in social solidarity and family relations. In the absence of a steady wage, families are falling apart at the very time when the forms of organization that as late as the 1960s characterized working-class communities are also disintegrating, unable to resist the impact of economic restructuring, gentrification, and forced mobility. Clearly the neoliberal restructuring of the world economy is mostly responsible for this situation. But as Leopoldina Fortunati points out in her introduction to *Telecomunicando in Europa*—a study of the impact of communicative technology on the reproduction of everyday life in Europe—we are also witnessing the consequence of the inability of the various social subjects, who structure everyday life to mediate their interests and find forms of organization that enable them to resist the devastating consequences of globalization.[16] Men's refusal to accept women's autonomy, for instance, as reflected in the increasing male violence against women, has contributed to weakening social bonds. Under these circumstances, everyday life, which is the primary terrain of mediation among people, has been allowed to shipwreck; it has become a terrain from which many are fleeing, unable to sustain interpersonal relations that appear too laborious and difficult to handle.[17] This means that care work, either by family members or friends, is not attended to, with consequences that are especially severe in the case of children and the elderly. Witness the new trend that is developing in Europe, which is to send elderly relatives, especially when affected by Alzheimer's, to be cared for abroad.[18] Interpersonal, face-to-face communication, a key component of our reproduction, is also declining, both among adults and between adults and children, diminished in quantity and content and reduced to a purely instrumental use, as the internet, Facebook and Twitter gradually replace it.

In brief, one of the most prominent facts concerning everyday life at present is a 'crisis of reproduction' in the sense of a drastic decline in the resources devoted to it, a decline as well of the work of caring for other people, beginning with family members, and a further devaluation of everyday life to which the new communication technologies contribute, although they are not its primary cause. In this case too statistics are telling. As we have seen, life expectancy is diminishing and so is the quality of life, as daily experience is characterized by a profound sense of alienation, anxiety, and fear. Mental disorders are rampant, for many fear that dispossession and homelessness may be just around the corner and experience a destabilizing lack of projectuality. What is most worrisome is that now these pathologies affect even children, plausibly caused by the collapse of the care work that family and school once provided. To what extent these mental disorders are real or are constructed—by doctors and pharmaceutical companies with the tacit assent of parents and teachers—in order to medicalize the unhappiness of a generation of children who, both at home and at school, are denied time, space, and creative activities, is difficult to tell. What is certain is that never have so many children and such young children been diagnosed with so many mental illnesses. By 2007, the number of mentally ill children in the U.S. had risen to thirty-five times the number in 1990. One in five, including toddlers, according to the Center for Disease Control, may suffer a mental disorder.[19] These include depression, hyperactivity, and attention deficit disorders. And for all of them the 'cure' is a variety of psychoactive drugs that the schools and families liberally administer, so that by the time they are ten years old some children take up to seven pills a day, even though the negative effects on their mental development are well known.

The reality is that in today's society children are the great losers. In a world where monetary accumulation is all, and all our time must be 'productively' engaged, satisfying children's needs is a low priority and must be reduced to a minimum. This, at least, is the message that comes from the capitalist class, for whom children today are essentially a consumer market. There is almost a desire to erase childhood itself as a nonproductive state, for instance by teaching toddlers—as some economists recommend—how to manage money and become wise consumers and submitting them to 'attitude tests' as early as age four, to presumably give them a good start in the race for economic competition. The erasure of childhood is also proceeding apace in working-class families, as parents are more and more absent from home and face severe economic crises that are a constant source of despair and rage. Adults, whether parents or teachers, have neither time nor energy and resources to dedicate to children. As Fortunati asserts in *Telecomunicando in Europa*, they may teach them to speak but not to communicate. And judging from the spread of child abuse, they clearly see them as a disturbance. It is a worrisome sign of the intense crisis of parent-child relations we are now experiencing in the United States that between 2001 and 2011 more than 20,000 children—75 percent of them under the age of four—were killed by their families, this being four times the number of troops killed in Iraq and Afghanistan in the same years.[20] No wonder, then, that even the massacres of children by gunmen entering the schools—a recent development that dramatically captures the devaluation of children's lives and disintegration of social relations—is evoking such tepid response and no real attempt to put an end to it.

## "Riprendiamoci la vita"—"Let's Retake Our Own Lives"[21]

How to stem this flight from the terrain of daily relations and reproduction? How to reconstitute the social fabrics of our lives and transform the home and the neighborhood into places of resistance and political reconstruction? These, today, are some of the most important questions on humanity's agenda. They are certainly the motivating force behind the growing interest—practical and philosophical—in the production of 'commons'; that is, the creation of social relations and spaces built on solidarity, the communal sharing of wealth, and cooperative work and decision-making.[22]

This project—often inspired by the struggles of indigenous peoples and now shared by a variety of movements (feminist, anarchist, green, Marxist)—responds to a variety of needs. First, there is the need to survive in a context in which the state and market provide less and less of the means of our reproduction. In Latin America, as Raúl Zibechi has documented in his *Territories in Resistance*, in the 1980 and 1990s, women in particular pooled their resources to support their families in the face of harsh austerity measures that left their communities demonetized or dependent on the remittances of those who have migrated. In Lima, women created thousands of committees—shopping and cooking committees, urban garden committees, glass of milk (for children) committees, etc.—that provided different forms of assistance that for many made a difference between life and death.[23] Similar forms of organization have developed in Chile, where, after the Pinochet coup of 1973, in the face of devastating impoverishment and political repression, the popular kitchen "never stopped."[24] In Argentina as well, elements of a 'collectivization' or socialization of reproduction appeared in the crisis of 2002, when women brought their cooking pots to the *piquetes*.[25] In Colombia, in the early 1990s, proletarian women constituted themselves as *madres comunitarias* to care for children living in the streets. Begun as a voluntary initiative, after a prolonged struggle the madres comunitarias project is currently undergoing a formalization process whereby, by 2014, about seventy thousand madres will receive a small salary from the country's welfare department.[26] But their work is still performed on the basis of communal solidarity, with the salary gained barely enabling them to survive and provide for the care of the children.

Neither in the United States nor in Europe have we seen the kind of collectivization of reproductive work mentioned above, yet more communal and self-managed forms of reproductive work are beginning to appear across the 'developed' world. Both in the United States and Europe, urban gardens and community-supported agriculture are now well established practices in many towns, providing not only vegetables for the pot but various forms of instruction, especially for children, who may attend classes on how to plant and preserve food and how grow things.[27] Time banks, once a radical project, are currently spreading in mainstream America, as a means of acquiring services without monetary exchanges and above all acquiring new support networks and friendships.[28]

All such initiatives may appear small things in the face of the enormous disasters—social and ecological—that we are facing. But in a context of growing impoverishment and the militarization of everyday life, leading to paralysis, withdrawal, and distrust of neighbors, these signs of a will to cooperate are encouraging. They are sign of a growing realization that to face the crisis alone is a path to defeat, for in a social system committed to the devaluation of our lives the only possibility of economic and psychological survival resides in our capacity to transform everyday practices into a terrain of collective struggle.

There is a further reason why it is crucial that we create new forms of social bonding and cooperation in the reproduction of our everyday life. Domestic work, including care work and affective work, is extremely isolating, being performed in a way that separates us from each other, individualizes our problems, and hides our needs and suffering. It is also extremely laborious, requiring many, often simultaneous, activities that cannot be mechanized, performed mostly by women as unpaid labor, often in addition to a full-time waged job. Technology—communication technology in particular—undoubtedly plays a role in the organization of domestic work and is now an essential part of our daily life. But, as Fortunati argues, it has primarily served to replace, rather than to enhance, interpersonal communication, allowing each family member to escape the communication crisis by taking refuge in the machine.[29] Similarly, the attempts by companies in Japan and the United States to robotize our reproduction—with the introduction of nursebots and lovebots customized to satisfy our desires[30]—are more signs of a growing solitude and loss of supportive relations than alternatives to it, and it is doubtful that in the future they will enter many homes. This is why the efforts that women above all are making to deprivatize our everyday lives and create cooperative forms of reproduction are so important. Not only do they pave the way to a world where care for others can become a creative task rather than a burden, they also break down the isolation that characterizes the process of our reproduction, creating those solidarity bonds without which our life is an affective desert and we have no social power.

In this context, commons are both objectives and conditions of our everyday life and struggles. In an embryonic form, they represent the social relations we aim to achieve, as well as the means for their construction. They are not a separate struggle but a perspective we bring to every struggle and every social movement in which we participate. As a member of a Zapatista community put it: "Resistance is not merely refusing to support a bad government, or not paying taxes or electric bills. Resistance is constructing everything that we need to maintain the life of our people."[31]

## Notes

1    Henri Lefebvre, *The Critique of Everyday Life*, Vol. 1, trans. John Moore (London: Verso, 1991 [1947]), 87–88.

2    As Henri Lefebvre wrote, "daily life, like language, contains manifest forms and deep structures that are implicit in its operations, yet concealed in and through them"; *The Critique of Everyday Life*, Vol. 3, trans. Gregory Elliott (London: Verso, 2005[1981]), 2.

3    Karl Marx and Frederick Engels, *The German Ideology*, Part 1, ed. C.J. Arthur (New York: International Publishers, 1970), 48–49.

4    The first feminist document to analyze domestic work as producing labor power was Mariarosa Dalla Costa, "Women and the Subversion of the Community," in *The Power of Women and the Subversion of the Community*, ed. Selma James and Mariarosa Dalla Costa (Bristol: Falling Wall Press, 1975).

5    Lefebvre, *The Critique of Everyday Life*, Vol. 2, trans. John Moore (London: Verso, 2002 [1961]), 41.

6    On the origin of this slogan, see Carol Hanisch, "The Personal Is Political: The Women's Liberation Classic with a New Explanatory Introduction," (2006 [1969]), accessed May 31, 2018, http://carolhanisch.org/CHwritings/PIP.html.

7    On this subject, see Federici, "Wages against Housework," in *Revolution at Point Zero: Housework, Reproduction and Feminist Struggle* (Oakland: PM Press, 2012), 15–22.

8    Lefebvre, *The Critique of Everyday Life*, Vol. 1, 87.

9    Federici, "Andare a Pechino: come le nazioni unite hanno colonizzato il movimento femminista," in *Il punto zero della rivoluzione: lavoro domestico, riproduzione e lotta femminista* (Verona: Ombre Corte, 2014).

10   Nancy MacLean, "The Hidden History of Affirmative Action: Working Women's Struggles in the 1970s and the Gender of Class," *Feminist Studies* 25, no. 1 (Spring 1999): 68.

11   On the "globalization of care," see Barbara Ehrenreich and Arlie Russell Hochschild, *Global Woman: Nannies, Maids and Sex Workers in the New Economy* (New York: Henry Holt, 2002).

12  Emily Matchar, *Homeward Bound: Why Women Are Embracing the New Domesticity* (New York: Simon & Schuster, 2013).

13  Arlie Russell Hochschild, *The Managed Heart: Commercialization of Human Feeling* (Berkeley: University of California Press, 1983).

14  Mayo Clinic staff, "Depression in Women: Understanding the Gender Gap," *Mayo Clinic*, accessed May 29, 2018, www.mayoclinic.org/diseases/in-depth/depression/art-20047725; Pam Fessler, "Panel Charged with Eliminating Child Abuse," *National Public Radio*, February 25, 2014, accessed May 29, 2018, www.npr.org/2014/02/25/282359501/panel-charged-with-eliminating-child-abuse-deaths.

15  See S. Jay Olshansky et al. "Differences in Life Expectancy Due to Race and Educational Differences Are Widening, and Many May Not Catch Up," *Health Affairs* 31, no. 8 (August 2012): 1803–13. Also, the March 2013 issue of *Health Affairs* reported that life expectancy in the United States has lost ground in the past decade compared to other countries, so the United States now ranks at the bottom of twenty-one industrialized nations for life expectancy. The drop was especially notable for non-educated white women, who on average could expect to live five years less than their mothers; David A. Kindig and Erika R. Cheng, "Even as Mortality Fell in Most US Counties, Female Mortality Nonetheless Rose in 42.8 Percent of Counties from 1992 to 2006," *Health Affairs* 32, no. 3 (March 2013): 451–58. Suicide rates among women, especially middle-aged ones, have sharply increased in recent years. However, men are still leading in the number of suicides. Quoting figures issued by the Center for Disease Control, see Tara Parker-Pope, "Suicide Rates Rise Sharply in U.S." *New York Times*, May 2, 2013, accessed May 29, 2018, https://www.nytimes.com/2013/05/03/health/suicide-rate-rises-sharply-in-us.html?mtrref=www.google.ca.

16  Leopoldina Fortunati, ed., *Telecomunicando in Europa* (Milan: Franco Angeli, 1998).

17  Fortunati, *Telecomunicando in Europa*, 27.

18  Heike Haarhoff reports that about seven thousand elderly Germans have been "delocalized" and now live in nursing homes in the Czech Republic, Greece, Hungary, Spain, and Thailand; "Les Allemands exportent aussi leurs grands-parents," *Le Monde Diplomatique*, June 2013, accessed May 29, 2018, https://www.monde-diplomatique.fr/2013/06/HAARHOFF/49160.

19  Misty Williams, "CDC: Mental Disorders Rising in Children," *Atlanta Journal-Constitution*, May 16, 2013, accessed May 29, 2018, https://www.myajc.com/news/cdc-mental-disorders-rising-children/MxRBjZ8EcqQDPt88oPt3VP/.

20  Michael Petit, "America Can Fix Problem of Child Abuse Fatalities," *BBC News*, October 17, 2011, accessed May 29, 2018, http://www.bbc.com/news/av/15345278/michael-petit-america-can-fix-problem-of-child-abuse-fatalities; see also Fessler, "Panel Charged with Eliminating Child Abuse." The United States leads the developed world in child abuse deaths, according to this organization. More than twenty thousand American children have died over the past decade in their own homes because of the actions of family members, with about 75 percent being under four years of age and nearly half

being under one. The U.S. child maltreatment death rate is three times higher than Canada's and eleven times that of Italy.

21    "Riprendiamoci la vita" was the slogan chanted by feminists in Italy in the 1970s in many demonstrations, giving voice a struggle that exceeded any specific demand, aspiring instead to free women's lives from the hold of the state.

22    George Caffentzis and Silvia Federici, "Commons against and beyond Capitalism," *Upping the Anti* 15 (September 2013): 83–99.

23    Raúl Zibechi, *Territories in Resistance: A Cartography of Latin American Social Movements* (Oakland: AK Press, 2012), 236–37.

24    Jo Fisher, "Chile: Democracy in the Country and Democracy in the Home," in *Out of the Shadows: Women, Resistance and Politics in South America* (London: Latin America Bureau, 1993), 177–200.

25    Isabel Rauber, "Mujeres piqueteras: el caso de Argentina," in *Economie mondialisée et identités de genre*, ed. Fenneke Reysoo (Geneve: IUED, 2002), 115–16.

26    "Madres comunitarias: del voluntariado a la formalidad," *Unimedios, Universidad National de Colombia*, October 4, 2013, accessed May 29, 2018, http://agenciadenoticias.unal.edu.co/detalle/article/madres-comunitarias-del-voluntariado-a-la-formalidad.html.

27    Community-supported agriculture (CSA) is the name of a number of initiatives that have grown in recent years in the Unites States, whereby 'consumers' connect directly with the producers, in this case the farmers, paying them in advance for the coming crops and sharing their risks; Federici, "Feminism and the Politics of the Commons in an Era of Primitive Accumulation," in *Revolution at Point Zero*, 141–42.

28    "Diane Sawyer's Hometown in Kentucky Saves Money by Helping Each Other Out," *ABC News*, January 15, 2014, accessed May 29, 2018, https://www.youtube.com/watch?v=Zb_uu3v48Rk. In this news segment on the growing practice of time banking in the United States, the reporter stated that there were time-banking efforts going on in forty-two states.

29    Fortunati warns against assuming that communicative technologies are by themselves responsible for the communication crisis that we are witnessing. Rejecting this type of 'technological determinism,' which ignores that the 'consumers' are active political subjects, she argues that communicative technologies intervene in a social reality already "structurally organized in an alienated way"; Fortunati, *Telecomunicando in Europa*, 38. That is, the crisis of family relations is the ground enabling technologies to break into and dominate our daily life; Fortunati, 34–48.

30    Nancy Folbre, "Nursebots to the Rescue? Immigration, Automation, and Care," *Globalizations* 3, no. 3 (September 2006): 349–60.

31    EZLN, *Autonomous Resistance—First Grade Textbook*, trans. El Kilombo (2014), 70, accessed May 29, 2018, www.schoolsforchiapas.org/library/autonomous-resistance-grade-textbook; for the course "Freedom According to the Zapatistas."

# Re-enchanting the World:
# Technology, the Body, and the
# Construction of the Commons

Almost a century has passed since Max Weber argued in "Science as a Vocation" that "the fate of our times is characterized, above all, by the disenchantment of the world," a phenomenon he attributed to the intellectualization and rationalization produced by the modern forms of social organization.[1] By 'disenchantment' Weber referred to the vanishing of the religious and the sacred from the world. But we can interpret his warning in a more political sense, as referring to the emergence of a world in which our capacity to recognize the existence of a logic other than that of capitalist development is every day more in question. This 'blockage' has many sources that prevent the misery we experience in everyday life from turning into transformative action. The global restructuring of production has dismantled working-class communities and deepened the divisions that capitalism has planted in the body of the world proletariat. But what prevents our suffering from becoming productive of alternatives to capitalism is also the seduction that technology exerts on us, as it appears to give us powers without which it seems impossible to live. It is the purpose of this article to challenge this myth. This is not to engage in a sterile attack against technology, yearning for an impossible return to a primitivist paradise, but to acknowledge the cost of the technological innovations by which we are mesmerized and, above all, to remind us of the knowledges and powers that we have lost with their production and acquisition. It is to the discovery of reasons and logics other than those of capitalist development that I refer when I speak of 're-enchanting the world,' a practice that I believe is central to most anti-systemic movements and a precondition for resistance to exploitation. If all we know and crave is what capitalism has produced, then any hope of qualitative change is doomed. Societies not prepared to scale down their use of industrial technology must face ecological catastrophes, competition for diminishing resources, and a growing sense of despair about the future of the earth and the meaning of our presence on it. In this context, struggles aiming to re-ruralize the world—e.g., through land reclamation, the liberation of rivers from dams, resistance to deforestation, and, central to all, the revalorization of reproductive work—are crucial to our survival. These are the condition not only of our physical survival but of a 're-enchantment' of the earth, for they reconnect what capitalism has divided: our relation with nature, with others, and with our bodies, enabling us not only to escape the gravitational pull of capitalism but to regain a sense of wholeness in our lives.

## Technology, the Body, and Autonomy

Starting from these premises, I argue that the seduction that technology exerts on us is the effect of the impoverishment—economic, ecological, cultural—that five centuries of capitalist development have produced in our lives, even—or above all—in the countries in which it has climaxed. This impoverishment has many sides. Far from creating the material conditions for the transition to communism, as Marx imagined, capitalism has produced scarcity on a global scale. It has devalued the activities by which our bodies and minds are reconstituted after being consumed in the work process and has overworked the earth to the point that it is increasingly incapable of sustaining our life. As Marx put it with reference to the development of agriculture:

> All progress in capitalist agriculture is a progress in the art not only of robbing the worker, but of robbing the soil; all progress in increasing the fertility of the soil for a given time is a progress towards ruining the more long-term sources of that fertility. The more a country proceeds from large-scale industry as a background of its development, as in the case of the United States, the more rapid is this process of destruction. Capitalist production, therefore, only develops the techniques and the degree of combination of the social process of production by simultaneously undermining the original source of all wealth—the soil and the workers.[2]

This destruction is not more obvious, because the global reach of capitalist development has placed most of its social and material consequences out of sight, so that it becomes difficult for us to assess the full cost of any new forms of production. As the German sociologist Otto Ullrich wrote, only modern technology's capacity to transfer its costs over considerable times and spaces and our consequent inability to see the suffering caused by our daily usage of technological devices allow the myth that technology generates prosperity to persist.[3] In reality, the capitalist application of science and technology to production has proven so costly in terms of its effects on human lives and our ecological systems that if it were generalized it would destroy the earth. As it has often been argued, its generalization would only be possible if another planet were available for more plunder and pollution.[4]

There is, however, another form of impoverishment, less visible yet equally devastating, that the Marxist tradition has largely ignored. This is the loss produced by the long history of capitalist assault on our autonomous powers. I refer here to that complex of needs, desires, and capacities that millions of years of evolutionary development in close relation with nature have sedimented in us, which constitute one of the main sources of our resistance to exploitation. I refer to our need for the sun, the wind, the sky, the need for touching, smelling, sleeping, making love, and being in the open air, instead of being surrounded by closed walls (keeping children enclosed within four walls is still one of the main challenges that teachers encounter in many parts of the world). Insistence on the discursive construction of the body has made us lose sight of this reality. Yet this accumulated structure of needs and desires that has been the precondition of our social reproduction has been a powerful limit to the exploitation of labor, which is why, from the earliest phase of its development, capitalism had to wage a war against our body, making it a signifier for all that is limited, material, and opposed to reason.[5]

Foucault's intuition concerning the ontological primacy of resistance[6] and our capacity to produce liberating practices can be explained on these grounds. That is, it can be explained on the basis of a constitutive interaction between our bodies and an 'outside'—call it the cosmos, the world of nature—that has been immensely productive of capacities and collective visions and imagination, though obviously mediated through social/cultural interaction. All the cultures of the South Asian region— Vandana Shiva has reminded us—have originated from societies living in close contact with the forests.[7] Also the most important scientific discoveries have originated in precapitalist societies, in which people's lives were profoundly shaped at all levels by a daily interaction with nature. Four thousand years ago Babylonians and Maya sky watchers discovered and mapped the main constellations and the cyclical motions of heavenly bodies.[8] Polynesian sailors could navigate the high seas on the darkest nights, finding their way to the shore by reading the ocean swells—so attuned were their bodies to changes in the undulations and surges of the waves.[9] Preconquest Native American populations produced the crops that now feed the world, with a mastery unsurpassed by any agricultural innovations introduced over the last five hundred years, generating an abundance and diversity that no agricultural revolution has matched.[10] I have turned to this history, so little known or reflected upon, to underline the great impoverishment that we have undergone in the course of capitalist development, for which no technological device has compensated. Indeed, parallel to the history of capitalist technological innovation we could write a history of the disaccumulation of our precapitalist knowledges and capacities, which is the premise on which capitalism has built the exploitation of our labor. The capacity to read the elements, to discover the medical properties of plants and flowers, to gain sustenance from the earth, to live in woods and forests, to be guided by the stars and winds on the roads and the seas was and remains a source of 'autonomy' that had to be destroyed. The development of capitalist industrial technology has been built on that loss and has amplified it.

Not only has capitalism appropriated the workers' knowledges and capacities in the process of production, so that, in Marx's words, "the instrument of labor appears as a means of enslaving, exploiting and impoverishing the worker,"[11] as I argued in *Caliban and the Witch*, the mechanization of the world was premised on and preceded by the mechanization of the human body, realized in Europe through the 'enclosures,' the persecution of vagabonds, and the sixteenth- and seventeenth-century witch hunts. It is important here to remember that technologies are not neutral devices but involve specific systems of relations, "particular social and physical infrastructures,"[12] as well as disciplinary and cognitive regimes capturing and incorporating the most creative aspects of living labor used in the production process. This remains true in the case of digital technologies. Nevertheless, it is difficult to disabuse ourselves of the assumption that the introduction of the computer has been a benefit to humanity, that it has reduced the amount of socially necessary labor and increased our social wealth and capacity for cooperation. Yet an account of what computerization has required casts a long shadow over any optimistic view of the information revolution and knowledge-based society. As Saral Sarkar reminds us, just to produce one computer requires on average fifteen to nineteen tons of materials and thirty-three thousand liters of pure water, obviously taken away from our common-wealth, plausibly the common lands and waters of communities in Africa or Central and South America.[13] Indeed, we can apply to computerization what Raphael Samuel has written about industrialization: "if one looks at [industrial] technology from the point of view of labor rather than that of capital, it is a cruel caricature to present machinery as dispensing with toil. . . . Apart from the demands which machinery itself imposed there was a huge army of labor engaged in supplying it with raw material."[14]

Computerization has also increased the military capacity of the capitalist class and its surveillance of our work and lives—all developments compared to which the benefits we can draw from the use of personal computers pale.[15] Most important, computerization has reduced neither the workweek, the promise of all techno-utopias since the 1950s, nor the burden of physical work. We now work more than ever. Japan, the mother-land of the computer, has led the world in the new phenomenon of 'death by work.' Meanwhile, in the United States a small army of workers—numbering in the thousands—dies every year of work accidents, while many more contract diseases that will shorten their lives.[16]

Not least, with computerization, the abstraction and regimentation of labor is reaching its completion and so is our alienation and desocialization. The level of stress digital labor is producing can be measured by the epidemic of mental illnesses—depression, panic, anxiety, attention deficit, dyslexia—now typical of the most technologically advanced countries like the U.S.—epidemics that can also be read as forms of passive resistance, as refusals to comply, to become machine-like and make capital's plans our own.[17]

In brief, computerization has added to the general state of misery, bringing to fulfillment Julian de La Mettrie's idea of the 'man-machine.' Behind the illusion of interconnectivity, it has produced a new type of isolation and new forms of distancing and separation. Thanks to the computer millions of us now work in situations where every move we make is monitored, registered, and possibly punished; social relations have broken down, as we spend weeks in front of our screens, forfeiting the pleasure of physical contact and face-to-face conversations; communication has become more superficial as the attraction of immediate response replaces pondered letters with superficial exchanges. We are also becoming aware that the fast rhythms to which computers habituate us generate a growing impatience in our daily interactions with other people, as these cannot match the velocity of the machine.

In this context, we must reject the axiom common in analyses of the Occupy movement that digital technologies (Twitter, Facebook) are conveyor belts of global revolution, the triggers of the 'Arab Spring' and the movement of the squares. Undoubtedly, Twitter can bring thousands to the streets, but only if they are already mobilized. And it cannot dictate how we come together, whether in the serial manner or the communal, creative way we have experienced in the squares, fruit of a desire for the other, for body-to-body communication, and for a shared process of reproduction. As the experience of the Occupy movement in the United States has demonstrated, the internet can be a facilitator, but transformative activity is not triggered by the information passed online; it is by camping in the same space, solving problems together, cooking together, organizing a cleaning team, or confronting the police, all revelatory experiences for thousands of young people raised in front of computer screens. Not accidentally, one of the most cherished experiences in the Occupy movement was the 'mic check'—a device invented because the police banned the use of loudspeakers in Zuccotti Park, but which soon became a symbol of independence from the state and the machine and a signifier of a collective desire, a collective voice and practice. "Mic check!" people said for months in meetings, even when not needed, rejoicing in this affirmation of collective power.

All these considerations fly in the face of arguments that attribute to the new digital technologies an expansion of our autonomy and assume that those who work at the highest levels of technological development are in the best position to promote revolutionary change. In reality, the regions less technologically advanced from a capitalist viewpoint are today those in which political struggle is most intense and most confident in the possibility of changing the world. An example are the autonomous spaces built by peasant and indigenous communities in South America, which, despite centuries of colonization, have maintained communal forms of reproduction.

Today the material foundations of this world are under attack as never before, being the target of an incessant process of enclosure conducted by mining, agribusiness, and biofuel companies. That even reputedly 'progressive' Latin American states have been unable to overcome the logic of extractivism is a sign of the depth of the problem. The present assault on lands and waters is compounded by an equally pernicious attempt by the World Bank and a plethora of NGOs to bring all subsistence activities under the control of monetary relations through the politics of rural credit and microfinance, which has turned multitudes of self-subsistent traders, farmers, and food and care providers, mostly women, into debtors. But despite this attack, this world, which some have called 'rurban,' to stress its simultaneous reliance on town and country, refuses to wither away. Witness the multiplication of land squatting movements, water wars, and the persistence of solidarity practices like the *tequio*,[18] even among immigrants abroad. Contrary to what the World Bank would tell us, the 'farmer'—rural or urban—is a social category not yet destined for the dustbin of history. Some, like the late Zimbabwean sociologist Sam Moyo, have spoken of a process of 're-peasantization,' arguing that the drive against land privatization and for land reappropriation sweeping from Asia to Africa is possibly the most decisive, certainly the fiercest, struggle on earth.[19]

From the mountains of Chiapas to the plains of Bangladesh many of these struggles have been led by women, a key presence in all squatters' and land reclamation movements. Faced with a renewed drive toward land privatization and the rise in food prices, women have also expanded their subsistence farming, appropriating for this purpose any available public land, in the process transforming the urban landscape of many towns. As I have written elsewhere, regaining or expanding land for subsistence farming has been one of the main battles for women in Bangladesh, leading to the formation of the Landless Women's Association, which has been carrying on land occupations since 1992.[20] In India, as well, women have been in the forefront of land reclamations, as they have in the movement opposing the construction of dams. They have also formed the National Alliance for Women's Food Rights, a national movement made up of thirty-five women's groups that has campaigned in defense of the mustard seed economy, which has been under threat since the attempt by a U.S. corporation to patent it. Similar struggles are also taking place in Africa and South America and increasingly in industrialized countries, with the growth of urban farming and solidarity economies in which women have a prominent part.

## Other Reasons

What we are witnessing, then, is a 'transvaluation' of political and cultural values. Whereas a Marxian road to revolution would have the factory workers lead the process, we are beginning to recognize that the new paradigms may come from those who in fields, kitchens, and fishing villages across the planet struggle to disentangle their reproduction from the hold of corporate power and preserve our common wealth. In the industrialized countries, as well, as Chris Carlsson has documented in his *Nowtopia*, more people are seeking alternatives to a life regulated by work and the market, both because in a regime of precarity work can no longer be a source of identity formation and because of their need to be more creative. Along the same lines, workers' struggles today follow a different pattern than the traditional strike, reflecting a search for new models of protest and new relations between human beings and between human beings and nature. We see the same phenomenon in the growth of commoning practices like time banks, urban gardens, and community accountability structures. We see it also in the preference for *androgynous* models of gender identity, the rise of the transsexual and intersex movements and the queer rejection of gender, with its implied rejection of the sexual division of labor. We must also mention the global diffusion of the passion for tattoos and the art of body decoration that is creating new and imagined communities across sex, race, and class boundaries. All these phenomena point not only to a breakdown of disciplinary mechanisms but to a profound desire for a remolding of our humanity in ways different from, in fact the opposite to, those that centuries of capitalist industrial discipline have tried to impose on us.

As this volume well documents, women's struggles over reproductive work play a crucial role in the construction of this 'alternative.' As I have written elsewhere, there is something unique about this work—whether it is subsistence farming, education, or childrearing—that makes it particularly apt to generate more cooperative social relations. Producing human beings or crops for our tables is in fact a qualitatively different experience than producing cars, as it requires a constant interaction with natural process whose modalities and timing we do not control. As such, reproductive work potentially generates a deeper understanding of the natural constraints within which we operate on this planet, which is essential to the re-enchantment of the world that I propose. By contrast, the attempt to force reproductive work into the parameters of an industrialized organization of work has had especially pernicious effects. Witness the consequences of the industrialization of childbirth that has turned this potentially magical event into an alienating and frightening experience.[21]

In different ways, through these new social movements, we glimpse the emergence of another rationality not only opposed to social and economic injustice but reconnecting us with nature and reinventing what it means to be a human being. This new culture is only on the horizon, for the hold of the capitalist logic on our subjectivity remains very strong. The violence that men in every country and of all classes display against women is a measure of how far we must travel before we can speak of commons. I am also concerned that some feminists cooperate with the capitalist devaluation of reproduction. Witness their fear of admitting that women can play a special role in the reorganization of reproductive work and the widespread tendency to conceive of reproductive activities as necessarily forms of drudgery. This, I believe, is a serious mistake. For reproductive work, insofar as it is the material basis of our life and the first terrain on which we can practice our capacity for self-government, is the 'ground zero of revolution.'

## Notes

1 Max Weber, "Science as a Vocation" [1918-1919], in *For Max Weber: Essays in Sociology*, eds. H.H. Gerth and C. Wright Mills (New York: Oxford University Press, 1946), 155.

2 Karl Marx, *Capital: A Critique of Political Economy*, Vol.1, ed. Frederick Engels, trans. Ben Fowkes (London: Penguin, 1990), 638.

3 Otto Ullrich, "Technology," in *The Development Dictionary*, ed. Wolfgang Sachs (London: Zed Books, 1992), 283.

4 Mathis Wackernagel and William Rees, *Our Ecological Footprint: Reducing Human Impact on the Earth* (Gabriola Island, BC: New Society Press, 1996).

5 See Federici, *Caliban and the Witch: Women, the Body and Primitive Accumulation* (Brooklyn: Autonomedia 2004), especially Chapter 3.

6 Referred to in Michael Hardt and Antonio Negri, *Commonwealth* (Cambridge, MA: Harvard University Press, 2009), 31.

7 Vandana Shiva, *Staying Alive: Women, Ecology and Development* (London: Zed Books, 1989).

8 Clifford D. Conner, *A People's History of Science: Miners, Midwives, and Low Mechanicks* (New York: Nation Books, 2005), 63–64.

9 Conner, *A People's History of Science*, 190–92, also reports that it was from Native sailors that European navigators gained the knowledge about winds and currents that enabled them to cross the Atlantic Ocean.

10   Jack Weatherford, *Indian Givers: How the Indians of the Americas Transformed the World* (New York: Fawcett Books, 1988).

11   Marx, Capital, Vol. 1, 638.

12   Ullrich, "Technology," 285.

13   Saral Sarkar, *Eco-Socialism or Eco-Capitalism? A Critical Analysis of Humanity's Fundamental Choices* (London: Zed Books, 1999), 126–27; see also Tricia Shapiro, *Mountain Justice: Homegrown Resistance to Mountaintop Removal for the Future of Us All* (Oakland: AK Press, 2010).

14   Raphael Samuel. "Mechanization and Hand Labour in Industrializing Britain," in *The Industrial Revolution and Work in Nineteenth-Century Europe*, ed. Lenard R. Berlanstein. London: Routledge, 1992, 26–40.

15   Jerry Mander, *In the Absence of the Sacred: The Failure of Technology and the Survival of the Indian Nations* (San Francisco: Sierra Club Books, 1991).

16   According to JoAnn Wypijewski, 40,019 workers died on the job between 2001 and 2009. More than 5,000 died on the job in 2007, with an average of 15 corpses a day, and more than 10,000 were maimed or hurt. She calculates that "because of under-reporting, the number of injured workers every year is likely closer to 12 million than to the official 4 million"; "Death at Work in America," *Counterpunch*, April 29, 2009, accessed June 2, 2018, https://www.counterpunch.org/2009/04/29/death-at-work-in-america/.

17   Franco "Bifo" Berardi, *Precarious Rhapsody* (London: Minor Compositions, 2009).

18   *Tequio* is a form of collective work, dating back from precolonial Mesoamerica, in which members of a community join their forces and resources for a community project, like a school, a well, or a road.

19   Sam Moyo and Paris Yeros, eds., *Reclaiming the Land: The Resurgence of Rural Movements in Africa, Asia and Latin America* (London: Zed Books, 2005).

20   Federici, *Revolution at Point Zero: Housework, Reproduction, and Feminist Struggle* (Oakland: PM Press, 2012).

21   Robbie Pfeufer Kahn, "Women and Time in Childbirth and Lactation," in *Taking Our Time: Feminist Perspectives on Temporality*, eds. Frieda Johles Forman and Caoran Sowron (New York: Pergamon Press, 1989), 20–36.

# Bibliography

Abdullah, Hussaina J., and Hamza Ibrahim. "Women and Land in Northern Nigeria: The Need for Independent Ownership Rights." In Wanyeki, *Women and the Land in Northern Nigeria*, 133–75.

Achebe, Chinua. *Things Fall Apart*. London: Heinemann, 1958.

Adoko, Judy. "Land Rights: Where We Are and Where We Need to Go." *Mokoro*, September 2005. Accessed May 31, 2018. http://mokoro.co.uk/land-rights-article/land-rights-where-we-are-and-where-we-need-to-go/.

Alden Wily, Liz. "Reconstructing the African Commons." *Africa Today* 48, no. 1 (Spring 2001): 77–99. Accessed May 31, 2018. https://muse.jhu.edu/article/3084.

Allen, Paula Gunn. "Who Is Your Mother? Red Roots of White Feminism." In *Multicultural Literacy: Opening the American Mind*, edited by Rick Simonson and Scott Walker. Saint Paul, MN: Graywolf Press, 1988.

Altvater, Elmar, Kurt Hubner, Jochen Lorentzen, and Raúl Rojas. *The Poverty of Nations: A Guide to the Debt Crisis from Argentina to Zaire*. London: Zed Books, 1991 [1987].

Amoore, Louise, ed. *The Global Resistance Reader*. New York: Routledge, 2005.

Anderson, Kevin B. "Marx's Late Writings on Non-Western and Precapitalist Societies and Gender." *Rethinking Marxism* 14, no. 4 (Winter 2002): 84–96.

Anderson, Nels. *On Hobos and Homelessness*. Chicago: University of Chicago Press, 1998.

Andreas, Carol. *When Women Rebel: The Rise of Popular Feminism in Peru*. Westport, CT: Lawrence Hill, 1985.

Angell, Marcia. "The Epidemics of Mental Illness: Why?" *New Yorker*, June 23, 2011. Accessed May 31, 2018 http://www.nybooks.com/articles/2011/06/23/epidemic-mental-illness-why/.

Anton, Anatole. "Public Goods as Commonstock: Notes on the Receding Commons." In *Not for Sale: In Defense of Public Goods*, edited by Anatole Anton, Milton Fisk, and Nancy Holmstrom, 3–40. Boulder, CO: Westview Press, 2000.

Bajaj, Vikas. "Microlenders, Honored with Novel, Are Struggling." *New York Times*, January 5, 2011. Accessed May 31, 2018. http://www2.econ.iastate.edu/classes/econ353/tesfatsion/MicrolendersStruggling.NYT2011.pdf.

Barrera, Claire, and Merideth Butner. *When Language Runs Dry: A Zine for People with Chronic Pain and Their Allies*. Portland, OR: Microcosm Publishing, 2008.

Barrow E.G.C. "Customary Tree Tenure in Pastoral Land." In Juma and Ojwang, *In Land We Trust*, 259–78.

Bateman, Milford. *Why Doesn't Microfinance Work? The Destructive Rise of Local Neoliberalism*. London: Zed Books, 2010.

Bebel, August. *Woman under Socialism*. New York: Schocken Books, 1971.

Beito, David T. *From Mutual Aid to the Welfare State: Fraternal Societies and Social Services, 1890–1967*. Chapel Hill: University of North Carolina Press, 2000.

Berardi, Franco "Bifo." *Precarious Rhapsody*. London: Minor Compositions, 2009.

Bikaako, Winnie, and John Ssenkumba. "Gender, Land and Rights: Contemporary Contestations in Law, Policy and Practice in Uganda." In Wanyeki, *Women and the Land in Northern Nigeria*, 232–77.

Boal, Iain, Janferie Stone, Michael Watts, and Cal Winslow. *West of Eden: Communes and Utopia in Northern California*. Oakland: PM Press, 2012.

Bollier, David. *Silent Theft: The Private Plunder of Our Common Wealth*. London: Routledge, 2002.

Bollier, David, and Silke Helfrich. *The Wealth of the Commons: A World beyond Market and State*. Amherst, MA: Levellers Press, 2012.

Bollier, David, and Burns H. Weston. *Green Governance: Ecological Survival, Human Rights and the Law of the Commons*, Cambridge: Cambridge University Press, 2013.

Bonate Liazzat. "Women's Land Rights in Mozambique: Cultural, Legal and Social Contexts." In Wanyeki, *Women and Land in Africa*, 96–131.

Bonefeld, Werner, Richard Gunn, John Holloway, and Kosmas Psychopedis, eds. *Open Marxism, Vol. 3: Emancipating Marx*. London: Pluto Press, 1995.

Brandon, William. *New Worlds for Old: Reports from the New World and Their Effect on the Development of Social Thought in Europe, 1500–1800*. Athens: Ohio University Press, 1986.

Buck, Susan J. *The Global Commons: An Introduction*. Washington, DC: Island Press, 1998.

Burcet, Josep, Leopoldina Fortunati, and Anna Maria Manganelli Rattazzi. "Le tele-comunicazioni e il loro uso sociale nelle aree geografiche europee." In Fortunati, *Telecomunicando in Europa*, 249–59.

Burke, Peter. *Popular Culture in Early Modern Europe*. New York: New York University Press, 1978.

Butterfield, Fox. "Aspiring Party Leaders at the Forefront of Revolt." *New York Times*, May 25, 1989. Accessed May 20, 2018. https://www.nytimes.com/1989/05/25/world/aspiring-party-leaders-at-forefront-of-revolt.html.

———. "Crackdown in Beijing; An Army with Its Own Grievances." *New York Times*. Accessed May 20, 2018. https://www.nytimes.com/1989/06/06/world/crackdown-in-beijing-an-army-with-its-own-grievances.html.

Caffentzis, George. "African American Commons." Unpublished manuscript, 2015.

————. "Divisions in the Commons? Ecuador's FLOK Society versus the Zapatistas' Escuelita." Paper presented at the Creative Alternatives to Capitalism Conference, CUNY Graduate Center, New York, May 24, 2014.

————. "From the *Grundrisse* to *Capital* and Beyond: Then and Now." *Workplace: A Journal for Academic Labor* no. 15 (September 2008): 59–74. Accessed June 2, 2018. http://ices.library.ubc.ca/index.php/workplace/article/view/182216.

————. "The Fundamental Implications of the Debt Crisis for Social Reproduction in Africa." In *Paying the Price: Women and the Politics of International Economic Strategy*, edited by Mariarosa Dalla Costa and Giovanna F. Dalla Costa, 15–41. London: Zed Books, 1995.

————. "The Future of the Commons: Neoliberalism's 'Plan B' or the Original Disaccumulation of Capital?" *New Formations* no. 69 (Summer 2010): 23–41.

————. "Globalization, the Crisis of Neoliberalism and the Question of the Commons." Paper presented to the First Conference of the Global Justice Center, San Miguel d'Allende, Mexico, July 2004.

————. In *Letters of Blood and Fire: Work, Machines, and Crisis*. Oakland: PM Press, 2013.

————. "The Making of the Knowledge Commons: From Lobsters to Universities." *St. Anthony's International Review* 8, no. 1 (2012): 25–42. Accessed May 31, 2018. https://tinyurl.com/ya5omsce.

————. *No Blood for Oil! Essays on Energy, Class Struggle and War, 1998–2016*. Brooklyn: Autonomedia, 2017.

————. "Notes on the Financial Crisis: From Meltdown to Deep Freeze." In Team Colors Collective, eds., *Uses of a Whirlwind*, 273–82.

————. "Three Temporal Dimensions of Class Struggle." Paper presented at ISA annual meeting, San Diego, CA, March 2006.

————. "Two Cases in the History of Debt Resistance: Catiline and El Barzón." Occupy University Fall Series on Debt, Elizabeth Foundation of the Arts, New York, October 17, 2012.

————. "University Struggles at the End of the Edu-Deal." *Mute: Culture and Politics after the Net* 2, no. 16 (June 2010): 110–17.

————. "Workers against Debt Slavery and Torture: An Ancient Tale with a Modern Moral." *UE News*, July 2007. Accessed May 31, 2018. http://mpineio.vrahokipos.net/wp-content/uploads/2010/09/workers-against-debt-slavery-and-torture-an-ancient-tale-with-a-modern-moral.pdf.

Caffentzis, George, and Silvia Federici. "Commons against and beyond Capitalism." *Upping the Anti* 15 (September 2013): 83–99.

————. "Notes on Edu-factory and Cognitive Capitalism." In *Toward a Global Autonomous University: Cognitive Labor, the Production of Knowledge, and Exodus from the Education Factory*, edited by the Edu-factory Collective, 119–24. Brooklyn: Autonomedia, 2009.

————. "Notes on Edu-factory and Cognitive Capitalism," *eipcp*, May 2007. Accessed July 12, 2018. http://eipcp.net/transversal/0809/caffentzisfederici/en.

Carlsson, Chris. *Nowtopia: How Pirate Programmers, Outlaw Bicyclists, and Vacant-Lot Gardeners Are Inventing the Future Today!*. Oakland: AK Press, 2008.

Chancosa, Blanca. "Saramanta Warmikuna (Hijas del Maíz) un espacio de aliadas naturales." In Colectivo Miradas Críticas, *La vida en el centro y el crudo bajo tierra*, 51–53.

Chant, Sylvia, ed. *The International Handbook of Gender and Poverty: Concepts, Research, Policy.* London: Edward Elgar Publishing, 2010.

Chávez, Daniel. "El Barzón: Performing Resistance in Contemporary Mexico." *Arizona Journal of Hispanic Cultural Studies* 2 (1998): 87–112.

Cheru, Fantu. "The Silent Revolution and the Weapons of the Weak: Transformation and Innovation from Below." In Amoore, *The Global Resistance Reader*, 74–85.

Cleaver, Harry. Introduction to *Marx beyond Marx: Lessons on the Grundrisse*, by Antonio Negri, xix–xxvii. New York: Autonomedia, 1991.

———. "Notes on the Origins of the Debt Crisis." In *Midnight Notes* no. 10 (Fall 1990).

Coba Mejía, Lisset. "Agua y aceite: la sostenibilidad de la vida en crisis en la Amazonía," *Flor del Guanto* no. 5 (January 2016).

Cochrane, Kira. "Why Do So Many Women Have Depression?" *Guardian*, April 29, 2010. Accessed May 31, 2018. www.theguardian.com/society/2010/apr/29/women-depression-allison-pearson.

Colectivo Miradas Críticas del Territorio Desde el Feminismo. *La vida en el centro y el crudo bajo tierra: El Yasuní en clave feminista.* Quito: Colectivo Miradas Críticas del Territorio Desde el Feminismo, 2014.

Collinson Helen, ed. *Green Guerrilla: Environmental Conflicts and Initiatives in Latin America and the Caribbean: A Reader.* London: Latin American Bureau, 1996.

*Committee for Academic Freedom in Africa Newsletter* (1991–2003). *libcom.org*. Accessed June 24, 2018. http://libcom.org/tags/committee-academic-freedom-africa.

*The Commoner* no. 2 (September 2001). Accessed June 2, 2018. http://www.commoner.org.uk/?p=5.

"Common Land." *Naturenet.* Accessed May 23, 2018. http://naturenet.net/law/commonland.html.

"Commons Sense: Why It Still Pays to Study Medieval English Landholding and Sahelian Nomadism." *Economist*, July 31, 2008. Accessed May 31, 2018. http://www.economist.com/financePrinterFriendly.cfm?story_id=11848182.

Conner, Clifford D. *A People's History of Science: Miners, Midwives, and "Low Mechanicks."* New York: Nation Books, 2005.

"Conversatorio con Ivonne Ramos." In Colectivo Miradas Críticas, *La vida en el centro y el crudo bajo tierra*, 82–85.

Cotula, Lorenzo, Camilla Toulmin, and Ced Hesse. *Land Tenure and Administration in Africa: Lessons of Experiences and Emerging Issues.* London: International Institute for Environment and Development, 2004.

Creischer, Alice, Max Jorge Hinderer, and Andreas Siekmann, eds., *The Potosí Principle: Colonial Image Production in the Global Economy.* Cologne: Verlag der Buchhandlung Walther König, 2010.

Cronon, William. *Changes in the Land: Indians, Colonists, and the Ecology of New England.* New York: Hill and Wang, 2011.

Cross, Gary S. *Time and Money: The Making of a Consumer Culture.* New York: Routledge, 1993.

Crossette, Barbara. "U.N. Report Raises Questions About Small Loans to the Poor." *New York Times*, September 3, 1998, A8.

Dalla Costa, Mariarosa. "Capitalism and Reproduction." In Bonefeld et al., *Open Marxism, Vol. 3: Emancipating Marx*, 7–16.

———. "Women and the Subversion of the Community." In *The Power of Women and the Subversion of the Community*, edited by Mariarosa Dalla Costa and Selma James, 21–56. Bristol: Falling Wall Press, 1975.

Dalla Costa, Mariarosa, and Monica Chilese. *Our Mother Ocean: Enclosure, Commons, and the Global Fishermen's Movement*. Brooklyn: Common Notions, 2015.

Dalla Costa, Mariarosa, and Giovanna Franca Dalla Costa, eds. *Women, Development and Labor Reproduction: Struggles and Movements*. Trenton: NJ: Africa World Press, 1995.

Davis, Mike. *Planet of Slums*. New York: Verso, 2006.

Davoudi, Simin, and Dominic Stead. "Urban-Rural Interrelationship in Land Administration—Urban Perspective." *Built Environment* 28, no. 4 (January 2002): 269–77.

De Angelis, Massimo. *The Beginning of History: Value Struggles and Global Capital*. London: Pluto Press, 2007.

———. "The Commons and Social Justice." Unpublished manuscript, 2009.

———. *Omnia Sunt Communia: On the Commons and the Transformation to Postcapitalism*. London: Zed Books, 2017.

Deere, Carmen Diana, and Magdelena León de Leal. *Empowering Women: Land and Property Rights in Latin America*. Pittsburgh: University of Pittsburgh Press, 2001.

DePastino, Todd. *Citizen Hobo: How a Century of Homelessness Shaped America*. Chicago: University of Chicago Press, 2003.

"Diane Sawyer's Hometown in Kentucky Saves Money by Helping Each Other Out." *ABC News*, January 15, 2014. Accessed May 29, 2018. https://www.youtube.com/watch?v=Zb_uu3v48Rk.

Dias, Elizabeth. "First Blood Diamonds, Now Blood Computers?" *Time*, July 24, 2009. Accessed May 31, 2018. http://content.time.com/time/world/article/0,8599,1912594,00.html.

Diduk, Susan. "The Civility of Incivility: Grassroots Political Activism, Female Farmers, and the Cameroonian State." *African Studies Review* 47, no. 2 (September 2004): 27–54.

Dinham, Barbara, and Colin Hines. *Agribusiness in Africa: A Study of the Impact of Big Business on Africa's Food and Agricultural Production*. Trenton, NJ: Africa World Press, 1984.

Dowling, Emma. "The Big Society, Part 2: Social Value, Measure and the Public Services Act." *New Left Project*, July 30, 2012. Accessed May 31, 2018. https://tinyurl.com/yamy6evv.

Draper, Hal. *The Adventures of the Communist Manifesto*. Berkeley: Center for Socialist History, 1998.

"East Portland Neighbors: Mapping our Local Commons." *On the Commons*, June 13, 2012. Accessed June 2, 2018. http://www.onthecommons.org/work/east-portland-neighbors-mapping-our-local-commons#sthash.fDWTwYac.dpbs.

Eckersley, Robyn. "Socialism and Ecocentrism: Towards a New Synthesis." In *The Greening of Marxism*, edited by Ted Benton, 272–97. New York: Guildford Publications, 1996.

*The Ecologist. Whose Common Future? Reclaiming the Commons*. London: Earthscan, 1993.

Ehrenreich, Barbara, and Arlie Russell Hochschild. *Global Woman: Nannies, Maids and Sex Workers in the New Economy*. New York: Henry Holt, 2002.

"Elinor Ostrom, Defender of the Commons, Died on June 12th, Aged 78." *Economist*, June 30, 2012. Accessed May 31, 2018. http://www.economist.com/node/21557717.

Elyachar, Julia. "Empowerment Money: The World Bank, Non-Governmental Organizations and the Value of Culture in Egypt." *Public Culture* 14, no. 3 (Fall 2002): 493–513.

Emergency Exit Collective. "The Great Eight Masters and the Six Billion Commoners." Bristol, May Day, 2008.

Engels, Frederick. "The Housing Question" (1887). Accessed June 2, 2018. https://www.marxists.org/archive/marx/works/1872/housing-question/.

———. "The Mark." In *Socialism: Utopian and Scientific*. New York: International Publishers, 1935.

———. *Socialism: Utopian and Scientific* (1880). Accessed June 4, 2018 https://www.marxists.org/archive/marx/works/1880/soc-utop/index.htm.

Esman, Milton J. *Landlessness and Near Landlessness in Developing Countries*. Ithaca: Cornell University Press, 1978.

Esteva, Gustavo. "Enclosing the Encloser: Autonomous Experiences from the Grassroots beyond Development, Globalization and Postmodernity." Paper presented at the Anomie of the Earth conference, University of North Carolina, Chapel Hill, May 3–5, 2012.

EZLN. *Autonomous Resistance—First Grade Textbook*. Translated by El Kilombo. (2014), 70. Accessed May 29, 2018. www.schoolsforchiapas.org/library/autonomous-resistance-grade-textbook; for the course "Freedom According to the Zapatistas."

———. *Zapatistas! Documents of the New Mexican Revolution*. Brooklyn: Autonomedia, 1994. http://lanic.utexas.edu/project/Zapatistas.

*Fala Guerreira* no 3. "Especial Mães de Maio 10 anos," March 22, 2016. Accessed June 23, 2018. https://issuu.com/falaguerreira/docs/03_revistafala_guerreira.

Fanon, Frantz. *The Wretched of the Earth*. New York: Grove, 1986.

Fatton, Robert, Jr. "Gender, Class, and State in Africa." In *Women and the State in Africa*, edited by Jane L. Parpart and Kathleen A. Staudt, 47–66. Boulder, CO: Lynne Rienner Publishers, 1989.

Federici, Silvia. "Andare a Pechino: come le nazioni unite hanno colonizzato il movimento femminista." In Federici, *Il punto zero della rivoluzione: lavoro domestico, riproduzione e lotta femminista*. Verona: Ombre Corte, 2014.

———. *Caliban and the Witch: Women, the Body and Primitive Accumulation*. Brooklyn: Autonomedia, 2004.

———. "*Capital* and Gender." In *Reading 'Capital' Today*, edited by Ingo Schmidt and Carlo Fanelli, 79–96. London, Pluto Press, 2017.

———. "Commoning against Debt." *Tidal* no. 4 (2013).

——. "Commoning the City." *Journal of Design Strategies* 9, no. 1 (Fall 2017): 33–37; published by the Parsons School for Design, New York State.

——. "The Debt Crisis, Africa and the New Enclosures." In *Midnight Notes* no. 10 (Fall 1990).

——. "Feminism and the Politics of the Commons in an Era of Primitive Accumulation." In Federici, *Revolution at Point Zero*, 2012, 138–48.

——. "Feminism and the Politics of the Commons in an Era of Primitive Accumulation." In Team Colors Collective, eds., *Uses of a Whirlwind*.

——. "On Affective Labor." In *Cognitive Capitalism, Education and Digital Labor*, edited by Michael A. Peters and Eergin Blut, 57–74. New York: Peter Lang, 2011.

——. *Revolution at Point Zero: Housework, Reproduction, and Feminist Struggle.* Oakland: PM Press, 2012.

——. War, Globalization and Reproduction." In Federici, *Revolution at Point Zero*, 76–84.

——. *Witches, Witch-Hunting, and Women.* Oakland: PM Press, 2018.

——. "Witch-Hunting, Globalization and Feminist Solidarity in Africa Today." *Journal of International Women's Studies* 10, no. 1 (October 2008): 29–35; joint special issue with WAGADU.

——. "Women, Globalization, and the International Women's Movement." *Canadian Journal of Development Studies* 22, no. 4 (January 2001): 1025–36.

——. "Women, Land Struggles and Globalization: An International Perspective." *Journal of Asian and African Studies* 39, no. 1–2 (April 2004): 47–62.

——. "Women, Land Struggles, and the Reconstruction of the Commons." *WorkingUSA* 14, no. 1 (March 2011): 41–56.

——. "Women's Liberation and the Struggle for Democratization." Paper presented at the Second Congress on Critical Political Analysis, on the theme of "Democracy," University of the Basque Country, November 19–20.

Federici, Silvia, George Caffentzis, and Ousseina Alidou. *A Thousand Flowers: Social Struggles against Structural Adjustment in African Universities.* Trenton, NJ: Africa World Press, 2000.

Fernandez, Margarita. "Cultivating Community, Food, and Empowerment: Urban Gardens in New York City." Unpublished manuscript, 2003.

Fessler, Pam. "Panel Charged with Eliminating Child Abuse." *National Public Radio*, February 25, 2014. Accessed May 29, 2018. http://www.npr.org/2014/02/25/282359501/panel-charged-with-eliminating-child-abuse-deaths.

Fisher, Jo. *Out of the Shadows: Women, Resistance and Politics in South America.* London: Latin America Bureau, 1993.

Folbre, Nancy. "Nursebots to the Rescue? Immigration, Automation, and Care." *Globalizations* 3, no. 3 (September 2006): 349–60.

Food and Water Watch. "Nestlé's Move to Bottle Community Water." *Food and Water Watch Fact Sheet*, July 2009. Accessed May 31, 2018. https://www.foodandwaterwatch.org/sites/default/files/nestle_bottle_community_water_fs_july_2009_1.pdf.

Fortunati, Leopoldina. *The Arcane of Reproduction: Housework, Prostitution, Labor and Capital.* Brooklyn: Autonomedia, 1995; translated from the Italian *Arcano della riproduzione*. Venezia: Marsilio Editori, 1981.

————, ed. *Telecomunicando in Europa*. Milan: Franco Angeli, 1998.

Foster, John Bellamy. "Marx and the Environment." *Monthly Review* 47, no. 3 (July–August 1995): 108–23.

Fox, Jeff. "Mapping the Commons: The Social Context of Spatial Information Technologies." *The Common Property Resource Digest* no. 45 (May 1998): 1–4.

Freeman, Donald B. "Survival Strategy or Business Training Ground? The Significance of Urban Agriculture for the Advancement of Women in African Cities." *African Studies Review* 36, no. 3 (December 1993): 1–22.

Fried, Albert, and Ronald Sanders, eds. *Socialist Thought: A Documentary History*. Garden City, NY: Doubleday Anchor Books, 1964.

Fullerton Joireman, Sandra. "Applying Property Rights Theory to Africa: The Consequences of Formalizing Informal Land Rights." Paper presented at the International Society for New Institutional Economics conference, Boulder, CO, September 21–24, 2006.

Galeano, Eduardo. *The Book of Embraces*. New York: W.W. Norton, 1991.

Galindo, María. "La pobreza, un gran negocio." *Mujer Pública* no. 7 (December 2012).

Gally, Rosemary E., and Ursula Funk. "Structural Adjustment and Gender in Guinea-Bissau." In Thomas-Emeagwali, *Women Pay the Price*, 13–30.

Gargallo, Francesca. *Feminismos desde Abya Yala*. Buenos Aires: America Libre, 2013.

Gibbon Peter, Kjell J. Havnevik, and Kenneth Hermele. *A Blighted Harvest: The World Bank and African Agriculture in the 1980s*. Trenton, NJ: Africa World Press, 1993.

Gitlin, Todd. *Occupy Nation: The Roots, the Spirit, and the Promise of Occupy Wall Street*. New York: HarperCollins, 2012.

Gladwin, Christina H., ed. *Structural Adjustment and African Women Farmers*. Gainesville: University of Florida Press, 1991.

Gorz, André. *A Farewell to the Working Class*. London: Pluto Press, 1982.

————. *Paths to Paradise: On the Liberation from Work*. London: Pluto Press, 1985.

Graeber, David. *Debt: The First Five Thousand Years*. Brooklyn: Melville House Publishing, 2011.

————. *Fragments of an Anarchist Anthropology*. Chicago: Prickly Paradigm Press, 1993.

————. "The Greek Debt Crisis in an Almost Unimaginably Long-Term Historical Perspective." In Vradis and Dalakoglou, *Revolt and Crisis in Greece*, 229–48.

Granter, Edward. *Critical Social Theory and the End of Work*. Burlington, VT: Ashgate, 2009.

Gray, Leslie, and Michael Kevane. "Diminished Access, Diverted Exclusion: Women and Land Tenure in Sub-Saharan Africa." *African Studies Review* 42, no. 2 (September 1999): 15–39.

Griswold, Deirdre. "Racism, Schooling Gap Cuts Years from Life." *Workers' World*, September 27, 2012. Accessed June 2, 2018. https://www.workers.org/2012/09/27/racism-schooling-gap-cut-years-from-life/.

Gualinga, Patricia. "La voz y la lucha de las mujeres han tratado de ser minimizada." In Colectivo Miradas Críticas, *La vida en el centro y el crudo bajo tierra*, 48–50.

Gutiérrez Aguilar, Raquel. "Políticas en femenino: transformaciones y subversiones no centradas en el estado." *Contrapunto* no. 7 (December 2015): 123–39.

———. *Los ritmos del Pachakuti: levantamiento y movilizacion en Bolivia (2000–2005)*. Miguel Hidalgo, Mexico: Sisifo Ediciones, 2009.

Haarhoff, Heike. "Les Allemands exportent aussi leurs grands-parents." *Le Monde Diplomatique*, June 2013, 14–15 Accessed May 29, 2018. https://www.monde-diplomatique.fr/2013/06/HAARHOFF/49160.

Hakansson, Thomas. *Bridewealth, Women and Land: Social Change Among the Gusii of Kenya*. Uppsala Studies in Cultural Anthropology 10. Stockholm: Almquist and Wiksell International, 1988.

———. "Landless Gusii Women: A Result of Customary Land Law and Modern Marriage Pattern." Working Papers in African Studies. African Studies Programme, Department of Cultural Anthropology, University of Uppsala, 1988.

Hanisch, Carol. "The Personal Is Political: The Women's Liberation Classic with a New Explanatory Introduction," (2006 [1969]). Accessed May 31, 2018 http://carolhanisch.org/CHwritings/PIP.html.

Hanson, Stephanie. "Backgrounder: African Agriculture." In *New York Times*, May 28, 2008. Accessed June 21, 2018. https://archive.nytimes.com/www.nytimes.com/cfr/world/slot2_20080528.html?pagewanted=print.

Hardt, Michael, and Alvaro Reyes. "'New Ways of Doing': The Construction of Another World in Latin America: An Interview with Raúl Zibechi." *South Atlantic Quarterly* 111, no. 1 (January 2012): 165–91.

Hardt, Michael, and Antonio Negri. *Commonwealth*. Cambridge, MA: Harvard University Press, 2009.

———. *Empire*. Cambridge, MA: Harvard University Press, 2000.

———. *Multitude: War and Democracy in the Age of Empire*. New York: Penguin Press, 2004.

Hartmann, Heidi. "The Unhappy Marriage of Marxism and Feminism: Towards a More Progressive Union." *Capital and Class* 3, no. 2 (Summer 1979): 1–33.

Hartsock, Nancy. "The Feminist Standpoint: Developing the Ground for a Specifically Feminist Historical Materialism." In *Discovering Reality: Feminist Perspectives on Epistemology, Metaphysics, Methodology, and Philosophy of Science*, edited by Sandra Harding and Merrill B. Hintikka, 283–310. Dordrecht: D. Reidel, 1983.

———. "Feminist Theory and Revolutionary Strategy." In *Capitalist Patriarchy and the Case for Socialist Feminism*, edited by Zillah R. Eisenstein, 56–77. New York: Monthly Review Press, 1979.

Harvey, David. *The New Imperialism*. Oxford: Oxford University Press, 2003.

———. *Rebel Cities: From the Right to the City to the Urban Revolution*. London: Verso, 2012.

Hayden, Dolores. *The Grand Domestic Revolution: A History of Feminist Designs for American Homes, Neighborhoods, and Cities*. Cambridge, MA: MIT Press, 1985 [1981].

———. *Redesigning the American Dream: The Future of Housing, Work, and Family Life*. New York: W.W. Norton, 1986.

Hess, Charlotte. "Mapping the New Commons." Unpublished paper, 2008.

Hobsbawm, Eric. J. *Industry and Empire: The Making of Modern English Society: Vol. 2, 1750 to the Present Day*. New York: Random House, 1968.

Hochschild, Arlie Russell. *The Commercialization of Intimate Life: Notes from Home and Work*. Berkeley: University of California Press, 2003.

———. *The Managed Heart: Commercialization of Human Feeling*. Berkeley: University of California Press, 1983.

———. *The Outsourced Self: Intimate Life in Market Times*. New York: Metropolitan Books, 2012.

Hochschild, Arlie Russell, and Anne Machung. *The Second Shift: Working Families and the Revolution at Home*. London: Penguin, 2012.

Holloway, John. *Change the World without Taking Power: The Meaning of Revolution Today*. London: Pluto Press, 2002.

———. *Crack Capitalism*. London: Pluto Press, 2010.

———. "From Scream of Refusal to Scream of Power: The Centrality of Work." In Werner Bonefeld et al., *Open Marxism, Vol. 3: Emancipating Marx*, 155–81.

Hostetler, Sharon et al. '*Extractivism': A Heavy Price to Pay*. Washington, DC: Witness for Peace, 1995.

Hunt. D. "Power and Participation in the Design of Institutions Governing Rural Land Rights." Research Report no. 1. Federico Caffè Centre, 2005.

Ignatius, Adi. "China's Restructuring Is Enriching Peasants but Not City Dwellers." *Wall Street Journal*, October 10, 1988.

Inter-American Development Bank. "Database: Latin Macro Watch." Accessed July 12, 2018. https://www.iadb.org/en/databases/latin-macro-watch/latin-macro-watch-country-profiles%2C18579.html.

"International—Western Firms Dump Toxic Waste in Africa." *An Phoblacht*, October 19, 2006. Accessed May 20, 2018. https://www.anphoblacht.com/contents/15909.

Isla, Ana. "Conservation as Enclosure: Sustainable Development and Biopiracy in Costa Rica: An Ecofeminist Perspective." Unpublished manuscript, 2006.

———. "Enclosure and Microenterprise as Sustainable Development: The Case of the Canada–Costa Rica Debt-for-Nature Investment." *Canadian Journal of Development Studies* 22, no. 4 (January 2001): 935–43.

———. "Who Pays for the Kyoto Protocol?" In *Eco-Sufficiency and Global Justice*, edited by Ariel Salleh. London: Pluto, 2009.

Jackson, Stevi. "Why a Materialist Feminism Is (Still) Possible." *Women's Studies International Forum* 24, no. 3–4 (May 2001): 283–93.

James, Selma. *Sex, Race and Class*. Bristol: Falling Wall Press, 1975.

Jilani, Seema. "America's Child Abuse Epidemic." *Guardian*, October 24, 2011. Accessed May 31, 2018. https://www.theguardian.com/commentisfree/cifamerica/2011/oct/24/america-child-abuse-epidemic.

Juma Calestous, and J.B. Ojwang, eds. *In Land We Trust: Environment, Private Property and Constitutional Change*. London: Zed Books, 1996.

Kahn, Robbie Pfeufer. "Women and Time in Childbirth and Lactation." In *Taking Our Time: Feminist Perspectives on Temporality*, edited by Frieda Johles Forman and Caoran Sowron. Oxford: Pergamon Press, 1989, 20–36.

Karim, Lamia. *Microfinance and Its Discontents: Women in Debt in Bangladesh*. Minneapolis: University of Minnesota Press, 2011.

Kazan, Olga. "A Shocking Decline in American Life Expectancy." *Atlantic.* December 21, 2017. Accessed June 21, 2018. https://www.theatlantic.com/health/archive/2017/12/life-expectancy/548981/.

Kim, Jim Yong, Joyce V. Millen, Alec Irwin, and John Gershman, eds. *Dying for Growth: Global Inequality and the Health of the Poor.* Monroe, ME: Common Courage Press, 2000.

Kimani, Mary, "Women Struggle to Secure Land Rights: Hard Fight for Access and Decision-Making Power." *Africa Renewal* 22, no. 1 (April 2008): 10–13. Accessed May 31, 2018. http://www.un.org/en/africarenewal/vol22no1/221-women-struggle-to-secure-land-rights.html.

Kindig, David A., and Erika R. Cheng. "Even as Mortality Fell in Most US Counties, Female Mortality Nonetheless Rose in 42.8 Percent of Counties from 1992 to 2006." *Health Affairs* 32, no. 3 (March 2013): 451–58.

Kingsnorth, Paul. *One No, Many Yeses: A Journey to the Heart of the Global Resistance Movement.* London: Free Press, 2003.

Kiros, Fasil G., ed. *Challenging Rural Poverty: Experiences in Institution-Building and Popular Participation for Rural Development in Eastern Africa.* Trenton, NJ: Africa World Press, 1985.

Klein, Hilary. *Compañeras: Zapatista Women's Stories.* New York: Seven Stories Press, 2015.

Kovel, Joel. *The Enemy of Nature: The End of Capitalism or the End of the World?* 2nd ed. London: Zed Books, 2007.

———. "On Marx and Ecology." *Capitalism Nature Socialism* 22, no. 1 (September 2011): 4–17.

Kristof, Nicholas D. "Beijing Journal; Second Thoughts: Laissez Faire or Plain Unfair?" *New York Times*, April 6, 1989. Accessed May 20, 2018. https://www.nytimes.com/1989/04/06/world/beijing-journal-second-thoughts-laissez-faire-or-plain-unfair.html.

———. "Chinese Face Epochal Wait for Housing." *New York Times*, March 1, 1989. Accessed May 20, 2018. https://www.nytimes.com/1989/03/01/world/chinese-face-epochal-wait-for-housing.html.

———. "Socialism Grabs a Stick: Bankruptcy in China." *New York Times*, March 7, 1989. Accessed May 20, 2018. https://www.nytimes.com/1989/03/07/business/socialism-grabs-a-stick-bankruptcy-in-china.html.

La Mettrie, Julien Offray de. *Machine Man and Other Writings.* Cambridge: Cambridge University Press, 1996.

Laesthaeghe, Ron J. "Production and Reproduction in Sub-Saharan Africa: An Overview of Organizing Principles." In *Reproduction and Social Organization in Sub-Saharan Africa*, edited by Ron J. Laesthaeghe, 13–59. Berkeley: University of California Press, 1989.

Lazzarato, Maurizio. *The Making of the Indebted Man: An Essay on the Neoliberal Condition.* Semiotext(e) Intervention Series, no. 13. Cambridge, MA: MIT Press, 2012.

Lefebvre, Henri. *The Critique of Everyday Life*, Vol. 1. Translated by John Moore. London: Verso, 1991 [1947].

———. *The Critique of Everyday Life*, Vol. 2. Translated by John Moore. London: Verso, 2002 [1961].

———. *The Critique of Everyday Life*, Vol. 3. Translated by Gregory Elliott. London: Verso, 2005 [1981].

———. *Everyday Life in the Modern World*. Translated by Sacha Rabinovitch. New York: Harper & Row, 1971 [1968].

Linebaugh, Peter. "Enclosures from the Bottom Up." In Bollier and Helfrich, *The Wealth of the Commons*, 114–24.

———. *The Incomplete, True, Authentic, and Wonderful History of May Day*. Oakland: PM Press, 2016.

———. *The Magna Carta Manifesto: Liberties and Commons for All*. Berkeley: University of California Press, 2008.

Linsalata, Lucia. *Cuando manda la asamblea: lo comunitario popular en Bolivia*. Mexico City: SOCEE, 2015.

Longo, Roxana. *El protagonismo de las mujeres en los movimientos sociales: innovaciones y desafíos*. Buenos Aires: America Libre, 2012.

Lorde, Audre. "The Master's Tools Will Never Dismantle the Master's House." In *This Bridge Called My Back: Writings by Radical Women of Color*, edited by Cherríe Moraga and Gloria Anzaldúa, 98–101. New York: Kitchen Table, 1983.

Maathai, Wangari. *Unbowed: One Woman's Story*. London: Arrow Books, 2008.

MacLean, Nancy. "The Hidden History of Affirmative Action: Working Women's Struggles in the 1970s and the Gender of Class." *Feminist Studies* 25, no. 1 (Spring 1999): 43–78.

"Madres comunitarias: del voluntariado a la formalidad." *Unimedios, Universidad National de Colombia*, October 4, 2013. Accessed May 29, 2018. http://agenciadenoticias.unal.edu.co/detalle/article/madres-comunitarias-del-voluntariado-a-la-formalidad.html.

Mander, Jerry. *In the Absence of the Sacred: The Failure of Technology and the Survival of the Indian Nations*. San Francisco: Sierra Club Books, 1991.

Manji, Ambreena. *The Politics of Land Reform in Africa: From Communal Tenure to Free Markets*. London: Zed Books, 2006.

Marazzi, Christian. *The Violence of Financial Capitalism*. Semiotext(e) Intervention Series no. 2. Cambridge, MA: MIT Press, 2010.

Martin, Randy. *Financialization of Daily Life*. Philadelphia: Temple University Press, 2002.

Martínez, Esperanza. "La actividad petrolera exacerba el machismo." In Colectivo Miradas Críticas, *La vida en el centro y el crudo bajo tierra*, 42–45.

Marx, Karl. *Capital: A Critique of Political Economy*. Edited by Frederick Engels, translated by Ben Fowkes. 3 vols. London: Penguin, 1990–1993.

———. *A Contribution to the Critique of Political Economy*. Edited by Maurice Dobb, translated by S.W. Ryanzanskaya. New York: International Publishers, 1970.

———. *Economic and Philosophical Manuscripts of 1844*. Translated by Martin Milligan. Moscow: Foreign Languages Publishing House, 1961.

———. *The Eighteenth Brumaire of Louis Napoleon*. New York: International Publishers, 1963.

———. *Grundrisse: Foundations of the Critique of Political Economy*. Translated by Martin Nicolaus. London: Penguin, 1973.

———. *Pre-Capitalist Economic Formations*. New York: International Publishers, 1964.

Marx, Karl, and Friedrich Engels. *The Communist Manifesto*. Translated by Samuel More. New York: Penguin, 1967 [1848].

———. *The German Ideology*, Part 1. Edited by C.J. Arthur. New York: International Publishers, 1970.

Marx-Aveling, Eleanor, and Edward Aveling. *The Woman Question*. Edited by Joachim Müller and Edith Schotte. Leipzig: Verlag fur die Frau, 1986 [1886].

Matchar, Emily. *Homeward Bound: Why Women Are Embracing the New Domesticity*. New York: Simon & Schuster, 2013.

Mayo Clinic staff. "Depression in Women: Understanding the Gender Gap." *Mayo Clinic*. Accessed May 29, 2018. www.mayoclinic.org/diseases/in-depth/depression/art-20047725.

McIntyre, Kathleen. *The Worst: A Compilation Zine on Grief and Loss*. Portland, OR: Microcosm Publishing, 2008.

Mendiola García, Sandra C. "Vendors, Mothers, and Revolutionaries: Street Vendors and Union Activism in 1970s Puebla, Mexico." *Oral History Forum*. Special Issue on Oral History and the Working Class (2013): 1–26. Accessed May 25, 2018. http://www.oralhistoryforum.ca/index.php/ohf/article/view/463/542.

Midnight Notes Collective. *Midnight Oil: Work, Energy, War, 1973–1992*. *Midnight Notes* no. 11 (1992). Brooklyn: Autonomedia, 1992.

———. *The New Enclosures*. *Midnight Notes* no. 10 (1990). Accessed June 13, 2018. https://libcom.org/files/mn10-new-enclosures.pdf.

Midnight Notes Collective and Friends. *Promissory Notes: From Crisis to Commons* (2009). Accessed May 31, 2018. http://www.midnightnotes.org/Promissory%20Notes.pdf.

Mies, Maria. *Patriarchy and Accumulation on a World Scale*. London: Zed Books, 1986.

Mies, Maria, and Veronika Bennholdt-Thomsen. "Defending, Reclaiming, and Reinventing the Commons." In *The Subsistence Perspective: Beyond the Globalized Economy*.

———. *The Subsistence Perspective: Beyond the Globalized Economy*. London: Zed Books, 1999.

Mies, Maria, and Vandana Shiva. *Ecofeminism*. London: Zed Books, 1993.

Mikwell, Gwendolyn. *Cocoa and Chaos in Ghana*. New York: Paragon House, 1989.

Millán, Márgara. *Des-ordenando el género/¿Des-centrando la nación? El Zapatismo de las mujeres indígenas y sus consecuencias*. Mexico City: Ediciones del Lirio, 2014.

Milton, John. *Means to Remove Hirelings* (1659). Accessed June 2, 2018. https://archive.org/details/miltonsconsideroomiltgoog.

———. *Paradise Lost* (1667). Accessed May 31, 2018. http://triggs.djvu.org/djvu-editions.com/MILTON/LOST/Download.pdf.

Mitchell, John Hanson. *Trespassing: An Inquiry into the Private Ownership of Land*. Reading, MA: Perseus Books, 1998.

Morgan, Henry Lewis. *Ancient Society*. Cambridge, MA: Harvard University Press, 1964 [1877].

Moyo, Sam. "Land in the Political Economy of African Development: Alternative Strategies for Reform." *Africa Development* 32, no. 4 (2007): 1–34. Accessed May 31, 2018. https://www.ajol.info/index.php/ad/article/viewFile/57319/45700.

Moyo, Sam, and Paris Yeros, eds. *Reclaiming the Land: The Resurgence of Rural Movements in Africa, Asia and Latin America.* London: Zed Books, 2005.

Mukangara, Fenella, and Bertha Koda. *Beyond Inequalities. Women in Tanzania.* Harare: Southern Africa Research and Documentation Centre, 1997.

Muro, Asseny. "Women Commodity Producers and Proletariats: The Case of African Women." In *Challenging Rural Poverty. Experiences in Institution-Building and Popular Participation for Rural Development in Eastern Africa,* edited by Fassil G. Kiros, 61–79. Trenton, NJ: Africa World Press, 1985.

Mwangi, Esther. "Subdividing the Commons: The Politics of Property Rights Transformation in Kenya Maasailand." CAPRI Working Paper no. 46 (January 2006). Accessed May 31, 2018 https://core.ac.uk/download/pdf/6242675.pdf.

National Institutes of Health. "Large-Scale HIV Vaccine Trial to Launch in South Africa," May 18, 2016. Accessed May 20, 2018. https://www.nih.gov/news-events/news-releases/large-scale-hiv-vaccine-trial-launch-south-africa.

Navarro, Mina. *Luchas por lo común: antagonismo social contra el despojo capitalista de los bienes naturales en Mexico.* Puebla: Bajo Tierra Ediciones, 2015.

Negri, Antonio. *Marx beyond Marx: Lessons on the Grundrisse.* Edited by Jim Fleming. Translated by Harry Cleaver, Michael Ryan, and Maurizio Viano. Brooklyn: Autonomedia, 1991.

Netting, Robert McC. *Balancing on an Alp: Ecological Change and Continuity in a Swiss Mountain Village.* Cambridge: Cambridge University Press, 1981.

"Nigeria Survey." *Economist,* May 3, 1986.

"Nobel Prize Winner in Glasgow Poverty Battle." *Reuters,* March 12, 2012. Accessed June 2, 2018. https://www.reuters.com/article/britain-bangladesh-microcredit/bangladesh-nobel-winner-in-glasgow-poverty-battle-idUSL4E8EC6GM20120312.

Nordhoff, Charles. *The Communistic Societies of the United States.* New York: Dover Publications, 1966.

Ogembo Justus M. *Contemporary Witch-Hunting in Gusii, Southwestern Kenya.* Lewiston, NY: Edwin Mellen Press, 2006.

Ogolla Bondi D., and John Mugabe. "Land Tenure Systems and Natural Resource Management." In Juma and Ojwang, *In Land We Trust,* 85–116.

Olivera, Oscar, with Tom Lewis. *Cochabamba! Water War in Bolivia.* Cambridge, MA: South End Press, 2004.

Ollman, Bertell. *Dialectical Investigations.* New York: Routledge, 1993.

Olshansky, S. Jay, Toni Antonucci, Lisa Berkman, Robert H. Binstock, Axel Boersch-Supan, John T. Cacioppo, Bruce A. Carnes, et al. "Differences in Life Expectancy Due to Race and Educational Differences Are Widening, and Many May Not Catch Up." *Health Affairs* 31, no. 8 (June 2012): 1803–13.

Ostrom, Elinor. *Governing the Commons: The Evolution of Institutions for Collective Action.* Cambridge: Cambridge University Press, 1990.

Palmer, Robin. "Gendered Land Rights: Process, Struggle, or Lost C(l)ause?" *Mokoro,* November 28, 2002. Accessed June 2, 2018. http://mokoro.co.uk/land-rights-article/gendered-land-rights-process-struggle-or-lost-clause/.

Paltrow, Lynn M., and Jeanne Flavin. "Arrests of and Forced Interventions on Pregnant Women in the United States, 1973–2005: Implications for Women's Legal Status and Public Health." *Journal of Health Politics, Policy and Law* 38, no. 2 (April 2013): 299–343.

———. "New Study Shows Anti-Choice Policies Leading to Widespread Arrests of and Forced Interventions on Pregnant Women," *Rewire News*, January 14, 2013. Accessed June 2, 2018. https://rewire.news/article/2013/01/14/new-study-reveals-impact-post-roe-v-wade-anti-abortion-measures-on-women/.

Parker-Pope, Tara. "Suicide Rates Rise Sharply in U.S." *New York Times*, May 13, 2013. Accessed May 29, 2018. https://www.nytimes.com/2013/05/03/health/suicide-rate-rises-sharply-in-us.html?mtrref=www.google.ca.

Parpart Jane L., and Kathleen A. Staudt. *Women and the State in Africa*. Boulder, CO: Lynne Rienner Publishers, 1989.

Pearce, Fred. *The Land Grabbers: The New Fight over Who Owns the Earth*. Boston: Beacon Press, 2012.

Petit, Michael. "America Can Fix Problem of Child Abuse Fatalities." *BBC News*, October 17, 2011. Accessed May 29, 2018. http://www.bbc.com/news/av/15345278/michael-petit-america-can-fix-problem-of-child-abuse-fatalities.

Podlashuc, Leo. "Saving Women: Saving the Commons." In Salleh, *Eco-Sufficiency and Global Justice*, 374–96.

Polgreen, Lydia, and Vikas Bajaj. "India Microcredit Sector Faces Collapse from Defaults." *New York Times*, November 17, 2010. Accessed June 2, 2018. https://www.nytimes.com/2010/11/18/world/asia/18micro.html.

———. "Microcredit Pioneer Ousted Head of Bangladeshi Bank Says." *New York Times*, March 2, 2011. Accessed June 2, 2018. https://www.nytimes.com/2011/03/03/world/asia/03yunus.html.

Polanyi, Karl. *The Great Transformation: The Political and Economic Origins of Our Time*. Boston: Beacon Press, 1957 [1944].

Porter, Raewyn Isabel. "Questioning De Soto: The Case of Uganda." *Philippine Journal of Development* 28, no. 2 (2001): 205–33. Accessed June 2, 2018. https://dirp4.pids.gov.ph/ris/pjd/pidspjd01-2desoto.pdf.

Potts, Monica. "What's Killing Poor White Women?" *American Prospect*, September 3, 2014. Accessed June 2, 2018. http://prospect.org/article/whats-killing-poor-white-women.

Quiroga Díaz, Natalia, and Verónica Gago. "Los comunes en femenino: cuerpo y poder ante la expropiación de las economías para la vida," *Economía y Sociedad* 19, no. 45 (June 2014): 1–18.

Rauber, Isabel. "Mujeres piqueteras: el caso de Argentina." In *Economie mondialisée et identités de genre*, edited by Fenneke Reysoo, 107–23. Cahiers Genre et Développement no. 3. Genève: IUED, 2002.

Rawick, George. *From Sundown to Sunup: The Making of the Black Community*, Westport, CT: Greenwood, 1972.

Reitman, Ben. *Sister of the Road: The Autobiography of Boxcar Bertha*. Oakland: AK Press, 2002 [1937].

Rosdolsky, Roman. *The Making of Marx's "Capital."* London: Pluto Press, 1977.

Rosemont, Franklin. "Karl Marx and the Iroquois." *libcom.org*, July 7, 2009. Accessed June 2, 2018, https://libcom.org/library/karl-marx-iroquois-franklin-rosemont.

"Saint under Siege: A Microfinance Pioneer Is Under Attack in His Homeland." *Economist*, January 6, 2011. Accessed June 4, 2018). https://www.economist.com/node/17857429.

Sale, Kirkpatrick. *The Conquest of Paradise: Christopher Columbus and the Columbian Legacy*. New York: Knopf, 1990.

Salleh, Ariel. *Ecofeminism as Politics: Nature, Marx and the Postmodern*. London: Zed Books, 1997.

———, ed. *Eco-Sufficiency and Global Justice: Women Write Political Ecology*. New York, London: Macmillan Palgrave, 2009.

Samperio, Ana Cristina. *Se nos reventó el Barzón: radiografía del movimiento barzonista*. Mexico, DF: Edivision, 1996.

Samuel, Raphael. "Mechanization and Hand Labour in Industrializing Britain." In *The Industrial Revolution and Work in Nineteenth-Century Europe*, edited by Lenard R. Berlanstein, 26–40. London: Routledge, 1992.

Sarkar, Saral. *Eco-Socialism or Eco-Capitalism? A Critical Analysis of Humanity's Fundamental Choices*. London: Zed Books, 1999.

Schreiber, Laurie. "Catch Shares or Share-Croppers?" *Fishermen's Voice* 14, no. 12 (December 2009). Accessed June 2, 2018. http://www.fishermensvoice.com/archives/1209index.html.

Shanin, Teodor. *Late Marx and the Russian Road: Marx and the "Peripheries" of Capitalism*. New York: Monthly Review Press, 1983.

Shapiro, Tricia. *Mountain Justice: Homegrown Resistance to Mountaintop Removal for the Future of Us All*. Oakland: AK Press, 2010.

Shiva, Vandana. *Earth Democracy: Justice, Sustainability, and Peace*. Cambridge, MA: South End Press, 2005.

———. *Ecology and the Politics of Survival: Conflicts over Natural Resources in India*. New Delhi: Sage Publications, 1991.

———. *Monocultures of the Mind: Perspectives on Biodiversity and Biotechnology and the Third World*. London: Zed Books, 1993.

———. *Staying Alive: Women, Ecology and Development*. London: Zed Books, 1989.

———. "The Suicide Economy of Corporate Globalisation." *countercurrents.org*, April 5, 2004. Accessed June 2, 2018. https://www.countercurrents.org/gloshiva050404.htm.

———. "Vandana Shiva Responds to the Grameen Bank." *Synthesis/Regeneration* 17 (Fall 1998). Accessed June 2, 2018. http://www.greens.org/s-r/17/17-15.html.

Sitrin, Marina A. *Everyday Revolutions: Horizontalism and Autonomy in Argentina*. London: Zed Books, 2012.

Snell, G.S. *Nandi Customary Law*. Nairobi: Kenya Literature Bureau, 1986 [1954].

Snyder, Margaret C., and Mary Tadesse. *African Women and Development: A History*. London: Zed Books, 1995.

SOF (Sempreviva Organização Feminista). *En lucha contra la mercantilización de la vida: la presencia de la Marcha Mundial de las Mujeres en la Cumbre de los Pueblos*. São Paulo, 2012.

Stavrides, Stavros. *Common Space: The City as Commons*. London: Zed Books, 2016.

Strike Debt! and Occupy Wall Street. *The Debt Resisters' Operations Manual*. Oakland: PM Press; Brooklyn: Common Notions, 2014. Earlier edition available at http://strikedebt.org/The-Debt-Resistors-Operations-Manual.pdf.

Team Colors Collective, eds. *Uses of a Whirlwind: Movement, Movements, and Contemporary Radical Currents in the United States*. Oakland: AK Press, 2010.

Thomas-Emeagwali, Gloria, ed. *Women Pay the Price: Structural Adjustment in Africa and the Caribbean*. Trenton, NJ: Africa World Press, 1995.

Thurton, Roderick. "Marxism in the Caribbean." In *Two Lectures by Roderick Thurton: A Second Memorial Pamphlet*. New York: George Caffentzis and Silvia Federici, 2000.

Toro Ibáñez, Graciela. *La Pobreza, un gran negocio: un análisis crítico sobre oeneges, microfinancieras y banca*. La Paz: Mujeres Creando, 2009.

Townsend, Janet G. "Pioneer Women and the Destruction of the Rain Forest." In *Green Guerrilla: Environmental Conflicts and Initiatives in Latin America and the Caribbean: A Reader*, edited by Helen Collinson, 108–14. London: Latin American Bureau, 1996.

Toyama, Kentaro. "Lies, Hype and Profit: The Truth About Microfinance." *Atlantic*, January 28, 2011. Accessed June 2, 2018. https://www.theatlantic.com/business/archive/2011/01/lies-hype-and-profit-the-truth-about-microfinance/70405/.

TPTG (The Children of the Gallery). "Burdened with Debt: 'Debt Crisis' and Class Struggle in Greece." In Vradis and Dalakoglou, *Revolt and Crisis in Greece*, 245–78.

Trainor, Bernard E. "Crackdown in Beijing; Civil War for Army." *New York Times*, June 6, 1989. Accessed May 20, 2018. https://www.nytimes.com/1989/06/06/world/crackdown-in-beijing-civil-war-for-army.html.

Trefon, Theodore. "The Political Economy of Sacrifice: *Kinois* and the State." *Review of African Political Economy* 29, no. 93–94 (2002): 481–98.

Tripp, Aili Mari. "Women's Movements, Customary Law, and Land Rights in Africa: The Case of Uganda." *African Studies Quarterly* 7, no. 4 (Spring 2004): 1–19. Accessed June 2, 2018. http://asq.africa.ufl.edu/files/Tripp-Vol-7-Issue-4.pdf.

*Turbulence: Ideas for Movement* no. 5 (December 5, 2009). Accessed June 2, 2018. http://www.turbulence.org.uk.

Turner, Terisa E. and M.O. Oshare. "Women's Uprising against the Nigerian Oil Industry." In *Arise Ye Mighty People! Gender, Class and Race in Popular Struggles*, edited by Terisa E. Turner and Brian J. Ferguson. Trenton, NJ: Africa World Press, 1994.

Tzul Tzul, Gladys, "Gobierno comunal indigena y estado guatemalteco. *Departamento Ecuménico de Investigaciones*, April 25, 2018. Accessed June 2, 2018. http://www.deicr.org/+presentacion-de-libro-gladys-tzul+.

———. *Sistemas de gobierno communal indigena: mujeres y tramas de parentesco en Chuimeq'ena'*. Puebla: Sociedad Comunitaria de Estudios Estratégicos, 2016.

Ullrich, Otto. "Technology." In *The Development Dictionary: A Guide to Knowledge as Power*, edited by Wolfgang Sachs, 275–87. London: Zed Books, 1992.

United Nations Population Fund. *State of the World Population 2001: Footprints and Milestones: Population and Environmental Change*. New York: United Nations, 2001.

"U.S. Experts to Manage Ailing Liberian Economy." *New York Times*, March 5, 1987. Accessed May 20, 2018. https://www.nytimes.com/1987/03/05/business/us-experts-to-manage-ailing-liberia-economy.html.

Vaneigem, Raoul. *The Revolution of Everyday Life*. Translated by Donald Nicholson-Smith. Oakland: PM Press, 2012 [1967].

van Gelder, Sarah, and the staff of *Yes! Magazine*. *This Changes Everything: Occupy Wall Street and the 99% Movement*. Oakland: Berrett-Koehler Publishers, 2011.

von Werlhof, Claudia. "Globalization and the 'Permanent' Process of 'Primitive Accumulation': The Example of the MAI, the Multilateral Agreement on Investment." *Journal of World-Systems Research* 6, no. 3 (2000): 728–47. Accessed June 11, 2018. http://jwsr.pitt.edu/ojs/index.php/jwsr/article/view/199/211.

Vradis, Antonis, and Dimitri Dalakoglou, eds. *Revolt and Crisis in Greece: Between a Present Yet to Pass and a Future Still to Come*. Oakland: AK Press, 2011.

Wackernagel, Mathis, and William Rees. *Our Ecological Footprint: Reducing Human Impact on the Earth*. Gabriola Island, BC: New Society Publishers, 1996.

Wanyeki, L. Muthoni, ed. *Women and Land in Africa: Culture, Religion and Realizing Women's Rights*. London: Zed Books, 2003.

Weatherford, Jack. *Indian Givers: How the Indians of the Americas Transformed the World*. New York: Fawcett Books, 1988.

Weber, Max. "Science as a Vocation." In *For Max Weber: Essays in Sociology*, edited by H.H. Gerth and C. Wright Mills, 129–58. New York: Oxford University Press, 1946.

Weston, Burns H., and David Bollier. *Green Governance: Ecological Survival, Human Rights, and the Law of the Commons*. Cambridge: Cambridge University Press, 2013.

Whatley, Christopher A. *Scottish Society 1707–1830: Beyond Jacobitism, towards Industrialization*. Manchester: Manchester University Press, 2000.

Whitaker, Robert. *Anatomy of an Epidemic: Magic Bullets, Psychiatric Drugs, and the Astonishing Rise of Mental Illness in America*. New York: Broadway Books, 2010.

Wichterich, Christa. *The Globalized Woman: Reports from a Future of Inequality*. London: Zed Books, 2000.

Williams, Misty. "CSC: Mental Disorders Rising in Children." *Atlanta Journal-Constitution*, May 16, 2013. Accessed May 29, 2018. https://www.myajc.com/news/cdc-mental-disorders-rising-children/MxRBjZ8EcqQDPt88oPt3VP/.

Wilson, Peter Lamborn, and Bill Weinberg. *Avant Gardening: Ecological Struggle in the City and the World*. Brooklyn: Autonomedia, 1999.

Winstanley, Gerrard. *The True Levellers Standard Advanced: Or the State of Community Opened and Presented to the Sons of Men* (1649). Accessed June 2, 2018. https://www.marxists.org/reference/archive/winstanley/1649/levellers-standard.htm.

Wong, Kristina. "Rumsfeld Still Opposes Law of the Sea Treaty: Admirals See It as a Way to Settle Maritime Claims." *The Washington Times*, June 14, 2012. Accessed June 2, 2018. https://www.washingtontimes.com/news/2012/jun/14/rumsfeld-hits-law-of-sea-treaty/.

Woodward, Colin. *The Lobster Coast: Rebels, Rusticators, and the Struggle for a Forgotten Frontier*. New York: Penguin Books, 2004.

World Bank. "Bank Publications and Research Now Easier to Access, Reuse." *News and Broadcast*, April 10, 2012. Accessed May 23, 2018. https://tinyurl.com/7axc7j3.

———. *Sub-Saharan Africa: From Crisis to Sustainable Growth*. Washington, DC: World Bank, 1989.

World Hunger Education Service. "Africa Hunger Facts." *Hunger Notes*. Accessed June 2, 2018. https://www.worldhunger.org/africa-hunger-poverty-facts/.

Worldwatch Institute. "Farming the Cities, Feeding an Urban Future." June 16, 2011. Accessed June 4, 2018. http://www.worldwatch.org/node/8448.

———. "State of the World 2011: Press Release," January 2, 2011. Accessed May 23, 2018. http://www.worldwatch.org/sow11/press-release.

Wudunn, Sheryl. "Upheaval in China; Chinese Take Umbrage at Attack on Mao's Portrait." *New York Times*, May 25, 1989. Accessed May 20, 2018. https://www.nytimes.com/1989/05/24/world/upheaval-in-china-chinese-take-umbrage-at-attack-on-mao-portrait.html.

Wypijewski, JoAnn. "Death at Work in America." *Counterpunch*, April 29, 2009. Accessed June 2, 2018. https://www.counterpunch.org/2009/04/29/death-at-work-in-america/.

Xezwi, Bongani. "The Landless People Movement." Research Report no. 10. In *Center for Civil Society, RASSP Research Reports 2005* 1, 179–203.

Yoshida, Masao. "Land Tenure Reform Under the Economic Liberalization Regime: Observation from the Tanzanian Experience." *African Development* 30, no. 4 (2005): 139–49.

Zapatista National Liberation Army. *See* EZLN.

Zibechi, Raúl. *Brasil potencia: entre la integración regional y un nuevo imperialismo*. Malaga: Badre y Zambra, 2012.

———. *Descolonizar el pensamiento crítico y las práticas emancipatorias*. Bogotá: Edíciones Desde Abajo, 2015.

———. *Genealogía de la revuelta: Argentina: la sociedad en movimiento*. La Plata: Letra Libre, 2003.

———. *Territories in Resistance: A Cartography of Latin American Social Movements*. Oakland: AK Press, 2012.

Zinn, Howard. *A People's History of the United States*. New York: HarperCollins, 1999 [1980].

# About the authors

**Silvia Federici** is a feminist writer, teacher, and militant. In 1972, she was cofounder of the International Feminist Collective, which launched the Wages for Housework campaign. Along with Wages for Housework members Mariarosa Dalla Costa and Selma James and feminist authors such as Maria Mies and Vandana Shiva, Federici has been instrumental in developing the concept of 'reproduction' as a key to class relations of exploitation and domination in local and global contexts, as well as central to forms of autonomy and the commons.

In the 1990s, after a period of teaching and research in Nigeria, she was active in the anti-globalization movement and the U.S. anti–death penalty movement. She is one of the cofounders of the Committee for Academic Freedom in Africa, an organization dedicated to generating support for the struggles of students and teachers in Africa against the structural adjustment of African economies and education systems. From 1987 to 2005, she taught international studies, women's studies, and political philosophy courses at Hofstra University in Hempstead, NY.

Her decades of research and political organizing accompanies a long list of publications on philosophy and feminist theory, women's history, education, culture, international politics, and the worldwide struggle against capitalist globalization and for a feminist reconstruction of the commons. Federici's steadfast commitment to these issues resounds in her focus on autonomy and her emphasis on the power of what she calls self-reproducing movements as a challenge to capitalism through the construction of new social relations. Her most recent books are *Witches, Witch-Hunting, and Women* and *Re-enchanting the World*.

**Peter Linebaugh** is a historian and a member of the Midnight Notes Collective. He is the author of *The Magna Carta Manifesto: Liberties and Commons for All* (2008); *Stop, Thief! The Commons, Enclosures, and Resistance* (2014); and *The Incomplete, True, Authentic, and Wonderful History of May Day* (2016); and the coauthor of *The Many-Headed Hydra: Sailors, Slaves, Commoners and the Hidden History of the Revolutionary Atlantic* (2001).

# Index

"Passim" (literally "scattered") indicates intermittent discussion of a topic over a cluster of pages.

# ABOUT PM PRESS

PM Press was founded at the end of 2007 by a small collection of folks with decades of publishing, media, and organizing experience. PM Press co-conspirators have published and distributed hundreds of books, pamphlets, CDs, and DVDs. Members of PM have founded enduring book fairs, spearheaded victorious tenant organizing campaigns, and worked closely with bookstores, academic conferences, and even rock bands to deliver political and challenging ideas to all walks of life. We're old enough to know what we're doing and young enough to know what's at stake.

We seek to create radical and stimulating fiction and non-fiction books, pamphlets, T-shirts, visual and audio materials to entertain, educate, and inspire you. We aim to distribute these through every available channel with every available technology—whether that means you are seeing anarchist classics at our bookfair stalls, reading our latest vegan cookbook at the café, downloading geeky fiction e-books, or digging new music and timely videos from our website.

PM Press is always on the lookout for talented and skilled volunteers, artists, activists, and writers to work with. If you have a great idea for a project or can contribute in some way, please get in touch.

**PM Press**
**PO Box 23912**
**Oakland, CA 94623**
**www.pmpress.org**

**PM Press in Europe**
**europe@pmpress.org**
**www.pmpress.org.uk**

# FRIENDS OF PM PRESS

These are indisputably momentous times—the financial system is melting down globally and the Empire is stumbling. Now more than ever there is a vital need for radical ideas.

In the years since its founding—and on a mere shoestring— PM Press has risen to the formidable challenge of publishing and distributing knowledge and entertainment for the struggles ahead. With over 300 releases to date, we have published an impressive and stimulating array of literature, art, music, politics, and culture. Using every available medium, we've succeeded in connecting those hungry for ideas and information to those putting them into practice.

*Friends of PM* allows you to directly help impact, amplify, and revitalize the discourse and actions of radical writers, filmmakers, and artists. It provides us with a stable foundation from which we can build upon our early successes and provides a much-needed subsidy for the materials that can't necessarily pay their own way. You can help make that happen—and receive every new title automatically delivered to your door once a month—by joining as a Friend of PM Press. And, we'll throw in a free T-shirt when you sign up.

Here are your options:

- **$30 a month** Get all books and pamphlets plus 50% discount on all webstore purchases

- **$40 a month** Get all PM Press releases (including CDs and DVDs) plus 50% discount on all webstore purchases

- **$100 a month** Superstar—Everything plus PM merchandise, free downloads, and 50% discount on all webstore purchases

For those who can't afford $30 or more a month, we have **Sustainer Rates** at $15, $10 and $5. Sustainers get a free PM Press T-shirt and a 50% discount on all purchases from our website.

Your Visa or Mastercard will be billed once a month, until you tell us to stop. Or until our efforts succeed in bringing the revolution around. Or the financial meltdown of Capital makes plastic redundant. Whichever comes first.

# Revolution at Point Zero: Housework, Reproduction, and Feminist Struggle

## Silvia Federici

**ISBN: 978-1-60486-333-8**
**$15.95   208 pages**

Written between 1974 and 2012, *Revolution at Point Zero* collects forty years of research and theorizing on the nature of housework, social reproduction, and women's struggles on this terrain—to escape it, to better its conditions, to reconstruct it in ways that provide an alternative to capitalist relations.

Indeed, as Federici reveals, behind the capitalist organization of work and the contradictions inherent in "alienated labor" is an explosive ground zero for revolutionary practice upon which are decided the daily realities of our collective reproduction.

Beginning with Federici's organizational work in the Wages for Housework movement, the essays collected here unravel the power and politics of wide but related issues including the international restructuring of reproductive work and its effects on the sexual division of labor, the globalization of care work and sex work, the crisis of elder care, the development of affective labor, and the politics of the commons.

*"Finally we have a volume that collects the many essays that over a period of four decades Silvia Federici has written on the question of social reproduction and women's struggles on this terrain. While providing a powerful history of the changes in the organization of reproductive labor,* Revolution at Point Zero *documents the development of Federici's thought on some of the most important questions of our time: globalization, gender relations, the construction of new commons."*
—Mariarosa Dalla Costa, coauthor of *The Power of Women and the Subversion of the Community* and *Our Mother Ocean*

*"As the academy colonizes and tames women's studies, Silvia Federici speaks the experience of a generation of women for whom politics was raw, passionately lived, often in the shadow of an uncritical Marxism. She spells out the subtle violence of housework and sexual servicing, the futility of equating waged work with emancipation, and the ongoing invisibility of women's reproductive labors. Under neoliberal globalization women's exploitation intensifies—in land enclosures, in forced migration, in the crisis of elder care. With ecofeminist thinkers and activists, Federici argues that protecting the means of subsistence now becomes the key terrain of struggle, and she calls on women North and South to join hands in building new commons."*
—Ariel Salleh, author of *Ecofeminism as Politics: Nature, Marx, and the Postmodern*

# Witches, Witch-Hunting, and Women

Silvia Federici

**ISBN: 978-1-62963-568-2**
**$14.00    120 pages**

We are witnessing a new surge of interpersonal and institutional violence against women, including new witch hunts. This surge of violence has occurred alongside an expansion of capitalist social relations. In this new work that revisits some of the main themes of *Caliban and the Witch*, Silvia Federici examines the root causes of these developments and outlines the consequences for the women affected and their communities. She argues that, no less than the witch hunts in sixteenth- and seventeenth-century Europe and the "New World," this new war on women is a structural element of the new forms of capitalist accumulation. These processes are founded on the destruction of people's most basic means of reproduction. Like at the dawn of capitalism, what we discover behind today's violence against women are processes of enclosure, land dispossession, and the remolding of women's reproductive activities and subjectivity.

As well as an investigation into the causes of this new violence, the book is also a feminist call to arms. Federici's work provides new ways of understanding the methods in which women are resisting victimization and offers a powerful reminder that reconstructing the memory of the past is crucial for the struggles of the present.

*"It is good to think with Silvia Federici, whose clarity of analysis and passionate vision come through in essays that chronicle enclosure and dispossession, witch-hunting and other assaults against women, in the present, no less than the past. It is even better to act armed with her insights."*
—Eileen Boris, Hull Professor of Feminist Studies, University of California, Santa Barbara

*"Silvia Federici's new book offers a brilliant analysis and forceful denunciation of the violence directed towards women and their communities. Her focus moves between women criminalized as witches both at the dawn of capitalism and in contemporary globalization. Federici has updated the material from her well-known book* Caliban and the Witch *and brings a spotlight to the current resistance and alternatives being pursued by women and their communities through struggle."*
—Massimo De Angelis, professor of political economy, University of East London

# Stop, Thief!
# The Commons, Enclosures, and Resistance

Peter Linebaugh

**ISBN: 978-1-60486-747-3**
**$21.95  304 pages**

In this majestic tour de force, celebrated historian Peter Linebaugh takes aim at the thieves of land, the polluters of the seas, the ravagers of the forests, the despoilers of rivers, and the removers of mountaintops. Scarcely a society has existed on the face of the earth that has not had commoning at its heart. "Neither the state nor the market," say the planetary commoners. These essays kindle the embers of memory to ignite our future commons.

From Thomas Paine to the Luddites, from Karl Marx—who concluded his great study of capitalism with the enclosure of commons—to the practical dreamer William Morris—who made communism into a verb and advocated communizing industry and agriculture—to the 20th-century communist historian E.P. Thompson, Linebaugh brings to life the vital commonist tradition. He traces the red thread from the great revolt of commoners in 1381 to the enclosures of Ireland, and the American commons, where European immigrants who had been expelled from their commons met the immense commons of the native peoples and the underground African-American urban commons. Illuminating these struggles in this indispensable collection, Linebaugh reignites the ancient cry, "STOP, THIEF!"

*"There is not a more important historian living today. Period."*
—Robin D.G. Kelley, author of *Freedom Dreams: The Black Radical Imagination*

*"E.P. Thompson, you may rest now. Linebaugh restores the dignity of the despised luddites with a poetic grace worthy of the master... [A] commonist manifesto for the 21st century."*
—Mike Davis, author of *Planet of Slums*

*"Peter Linebaugh's great act of historical imagination... takes the cliché of 'globalization' and makes it live. The local and the global are once again shown to be inseparable—as they are, at present, for the machine-breakers of the new world crisis."*
—T.J. Clark, author of *Farewell to an Idea*

# The Incomplete, True, Authentic, and Wonderful History of May Day

Peter Linebaugh

**ISBN: 978-1-62963-107-3**
**$15.95   200 pages**

"May Day is about affirmation, the love of life, and the start of spring, so it has to be about the beginning of the end of the capitalist system of exploitation, oppression, war, and overall misery, toil, and moil." So writes celebrated historian Peter Linebaugh in an essential compendium of reflections on the reviled, glorious, and voltaic occasion of May 1st.

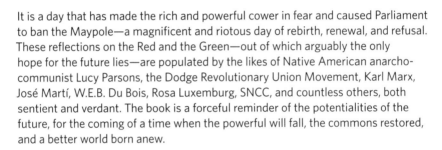

It is a day that has made the rich and powerful cower in fear and caused Parliament to ban the Maypole—a magnificent and riotous day of rebirth, renewal, and refusal. These reflections on the Red and the Green—out of which arguably the only hope for the future lies—are populated by the likes of Native American anarcho-communist Lucy Parsons, the Dodge Revolutionary Union Movement, Karl Marx, José Martí, W.E.B. Du Bois, Rosa Luxemburg, SNCC, and countless others, both sentient and verdant. The book is a forceful reminder of the potentialities of the future, for the coming of a time when the powerful will fall, the commons restored, and a better world born anew.

*"There is not a more important historian living today. Period."*
—Robin D.G. Kelley, author of *Freedom Dreams: The Black Radical Imagination*

*"E.P. Thompson, you may rest now. Linebaugh restores the dignity of the despised luddites with a poetic grace worthy of the master."*
—Mike Davis, author of *Planet of Slums*

*"Ideas can be beautiful too, and the ideas Peter Linebaugh provokes and maps in this history of liberty are dazzling reminders of what we have been and who we could be."*
—Rebecca Solnit, author of *Storming the Gates of Paradise*

# Birth Work as Care Work: Stories from Activist Birth Communities

Alana Apfel, with a foreword by Loretta
J. Ross, preface by Victoria Law, and
introduction by Silvia Federici

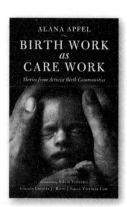

**ISBN: 978-1-62963-151-6**
**$14.95    128 pages**

*Birth Work as Care Work* presents a vibrant collection of
stories and insights from the front lines of birth activist
communities. The personal has once more become political, and birth workers,
supporters, and doulas now find themselves at the fore of collective struggles for
freedom and dignity.

The author, herself a scholar and birth justice organiser, provides a unique platform
to explore the political dynamics of birth work; drawing connections between birth,
reproductive labor, and the struggles of caregiving communities today. Articulating
a politics of care work in and through the reproductive process, the book brings
diverse voices into conversation to explore multiple possibilities and avenues for
change.

At a moment when agency over our childbirth experiences is increasingly
centralized in the hands of professional elites, *Birth Work as Care Work* presents
creative new ways to reimagine the trajectory of our reproductive processes. Most
importantly, the contributors present new ways of thinking about the entire life
cycle, providing a unique and creative entry point into the essence of all human
struggle—the struggle over the reproduction of life itself.

*"I love this book, all of it. The polished essays and the interviews with birth workers dare
to take on the deepest questions of human existence."*
—Carol Downer, cofounder of the Feminist Women's Heath Centers of California
and author of *A Woman's Book of Choices*

*"This volume provides theoretically rich, practical tools for birth and other care workers
to collectively and effectively fight capitalism and the many intersecting processes
of oppression that accompany it.* Birth Work as Care Work *forcefully and joyfully
reminds us that the personal is political, a lesson we need now more than ever."*
—Adrienne Pine, author of *Working Hard, Drinking Hard: On Violence and Survival in
Honduras*

# In, Against, and Beyond Capitalism: The San Francisco Lectures

John Holloway
with a Preface by Andrej Grubačić

**ISBN: 978-1-62963-109-7**
**$14.95    112 pages**

*In, Against, and Beyond Capitalism* is based on three recent lectures delivered by John Holloway at the California Institute of Integral Studies in San Francisco. The lectures focus on what anticapitalist revolution can mean today—after the historic failure of the idea that the conquest of state power was the key to radical change—and offer a brilliant and engaging introduction to the central themes of Holloway's work.

The lectures take as their central challenge the idea that "We Are the Crisis of Capital and Proud of It." This runs counter to many leftist assumptions that the capitalists are to blame for the crisis, or that crisis is simply the expression of the bankruptcy of the system. The only way to see crisis as the possible threshold to a better world is to understand the failure of capitalism as the face of the push of our creative force. This poses a theoretical challenge. The first lecture focuses on the meaning of "We," the second on the understanding of capital as a system of social cohesion that systematically frustrates our creative force, and the third on the proposal that we are the crisis of this system of cohesion.

"*His Marxism is premised on another form of logic, one that affirms movement, instability, and struggle. This is a movement of thought that affirms the richness of life, particularity (non-identity) and 'walking in the opposite direction'; walking, that is, away from exploitation, domination, and classification. Without contradictory thinking in, against, and beyond the capitalist society, capital once again becomes a reified object, a thing, and not a social relation that signifies transformation of a useful and creative activity (doing) into (abstract) labor. Only open dialectics, a right kind of thinking for the wrong kind of world, non-unitary thinking without guarantees, is able to assist us in our contradictory struggle for a world free of contradiction.*"
—Andrej Grubačić, from his Preface

"*Holloway's work is infectiously optimistic.*"
—Steven Poole, the *Guardian* (UK)

"*Holloway's thesis is indeed important and worthy of notice*"
—Richard J.F. Day, *Canadian Journal of Cultural Studies*

# Anthropocene or Capitalocene? Nature, History, and the Crisis of Capitalism

Edited by Jason W. Moore

ISBN: 978-1-62963-148-6
$21.95    304 pages

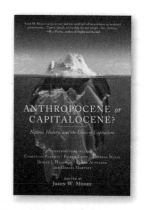

The Earth has reached a tipping point. Runaway climate change, the sixth great extinction of planetary life, the acidification of the oceans—all point toward an era of unprecedented turbulence in humanity's relationship within the web of life. But just what is that relationship, and how do we make sense of this extraordinary transition?

*Anthropocene or Capitalocene?* offers answers to these questions from a dynamic group of leading critical scholars. They challenge the theory and history offered by the most significant environmental concept of our times: the Anthropocene. But are we living in the Anthropocene, literally the "Age of Man"? Is a different response more compelling, and better suited to the strange—and often terrifying—times in which we live? The contributors to this book diagnose the problems of Anthropocene thinking and propose an alternative: the global crises of the twenty-first century are rooted in the Capitalocene; not the Age of Man but the Age of Capital.

*Anthropocene or Capitalocene?* offers a series of provocative essays on nature and power, humanity, and capitalism. Including both well-established voices and younger scholars, the book challenges the conventional practice of dividing historical change and contemporary reality into "Nature" and "Society," demonstrating the possibilities offered by a more nuanced and connective view of human environment-making, joined at every step with and within the biosphere. In distinct registers, the authors frame their discussions within a politics of hope that signal the possibilities for transcending capitalism, broadly understood as a "world-ecology" that joins nature, capital, and power as a historically evolving whole.

Contributors include Jason W. Moore, Eileen Crist, Donna J. Haraway, Justin McBrien, Elmar Altvater, Daniel Hartley, and Christian Parenti.

*"We had best start thinking in revolutionary terms about the forces turning the world upside down if we are to put brakes on the madness. A good place to begin is this book, whose remarkable authors bring together history and theory, politics and ecology, economy and culture, to force a deep look at the origins of global transformation."*
—Richard Walker, professor emeritus of geography, UC Berkeley, and author of *The Capitalist Imperative, The New Social Economy, The Conquest of Bread,* and *The Country in the City*